Mirza Haidar Dughlat
as depicted in Persian Sources

MIRZA HAIDAR DUGHLAT

Mirza Haidar Dughlat as depicted in Persian Sources

Original text, translated and introduced by

MANSURA HAIDAR

MANOHAR
2002

First published 2002

ISBN 81-7304-453-8

Published by
Ajay Kumar Jain for
Manohar Publishers & Distributors
4753/23 Ansari Road, Daryaganj
New Delhi 110 002

Printed at
Lordson Publishers Pvt. Ltd., New Delhi 110 002

Contents

Contents

Preface

Mirza Muhammad Haidar Dughlat remained to be one of the forgotten *khanzadas* of Mughalistan till the Kazakhs adopted him as their national historian-writer and decided to highlight his achievements and glorify his (already) immortal name. Needless to say that Mirza Haidar the illustrious, though a forsaken frier of the Kazakhs deserved this long overdue honour and exaltation, which the Kazakhs are determined to shower upon their compatriot. It was this enthusiastic search/research of Kazakh friends into Haidar Dughlat's innings that prompted me to compile the first set of information as supplied by some of the contemporary and later Indo-Persian sources primarily for my Kazakh friends. The extracts of texts from the sources are being presented here both in their original form and in their translated versions. Care has been taken to verify the translated texts and rectify them, if needed, by providing a fresh translation. Some of the works which had not yet been translated have been rendered into English. Such translations which did not need any corrections have been reproduced in this work

Mughal and the Kashmiri chroniclers have praised him equally for his amiability, righteous character, balanced personality (*hamwar*), trusting and uninjurious nature (*kam azar*) and above all for his humane attitude. Full of graces of life, he always preferred to buy peace (*afiyat talab*) at the highest price even at the cost of a personal loss. Although he was not born with a silver spoon in his mouth, he was certainly a 'golden man', well read and well versed in different forms of learning and art. The greatness, if any, was acquired by (and not thrust upon) him. Abul Fazl had bitterly criticized Haidar Dughlat though Babur, Arif Kandahari, Amin Ahmad Razi and several others have fully compensated for such a criticism by presenting Mirza Haidar as a useful talented individual who contributed fruitfully to the development of culture.

History (except for a few contemporary historians) had indeed ignored him as his fame merely seemed to rest on his magnum opus, the *Tarikh-i-Rashidi* though Haidar Dughlat was a celebrity in more ways than one—winning laurels as a warrior, a conqueror, an excellent administrator, a patron of fine arts and above all as a good human being. Despite all his extraordinary attainments and multifarious capabilities, he was outshone and overshadowed by his more eminent cousin Babur and his sons. He was a direct descendant of the Mongol rulers in the line of Chingiz Khan and should have, therefore, held a definite edge and superiority over the Timurids (the sucessors of Amir Qarachar Noyon) according to the then prevalent conventions. Yet his maternal relationship with the Timurids was never projected and he was often mentioned as a *mulazim* (servant), a follower or an ordinary noble of the Mughal rulers. Unlike Babur, who had enjoyed a royal lineage, regal pedigree and continuous support of a horde of close relatives, friends and nobles, Mirza Haidar Dughlat had none to fall back upon as he was the lone survivor of his family. From his early childhood, he suffered negation, pangs of deprivation due to the loss of his father, uncle and other close relatives. Forlorn and woe-begone, Haidar Dughlat had to suffer from a perpetual sense of insecurity and agony of adversities and struggles though he managed to play a praise-worthy role against all odds. His readily available services, unquestioning loyalties and selfless sacrifices to the Mughal dynasty failed to win for him even the minimal approbation and reward. He was exiled at the hands of his own near and dear ones. The behaviour of Rashid Khan (to whom Mirza had dedicated his work) and his brother Iskander was not so laudable but Mirza Haidar continued to feel grateful towards them. Even his wife and step son Mirza Aba Bakr did not spare the noble soul. The magnanimity of Mirza is very well proved in his attitude towards Daulat Chak who left Mirza Haidar's court in anger. His sense of propriety is confirmed further through his expressions of anguish over the murder committed by his lieutenant Mirak or over burning of buildings. His faith in human values was so deeply entrenched that he never suspected any foul play even when the acts of vandalism were clearly pointing towards mischief. His deep faith in his companion's words led to his isolation several times. Even when the deadly arrow had struck Mirza Haidar to death, no improper words escaped his dying lips. He is said to have uttered just two words: '*Qabahat Kardi*' ('What a villainy you committed').

In his book, his good values have been reflected as he often becomes judgemental. He was born and brought up in an age and a region which had preserved the imprints of the two most sensitizing creeds, namely, Buddhism and Sufism. The philosophy of love and brotherhood had dominated the region and pervaded over the life of people in the area. Mirza Haidar was a product of such an environment. He was a poet and composed his *diwan* also. One of his quartrain best depicts his attitude towards life:

عاشق شده را اسیر غم باید بود
محنت کش وادئی ستم بایدبود
یا از سر کوی یار باید برخاست
یا از سرکوی یارکم باید بود

one who falls in love ought to remain in the chains of sorrow;
an amorous person should endure the sufferings with perseverance,
(If, however that was not possible) either he should pack up and leave the lanes of the beloved or he should keep away and be seldom seen in those bylanes.

The dedication and sincerity with which he treated his patrons and kith and kin, is indeed rare.

I undertook this task merely to provide some additional material to my Kazakh friends and to assist them in the venture. I am grateful to the External Affairs Ministry, Government of India, and particularly to Mr Abhayankar, Mr Rajiv Dogra and Mr Geetesh Sharma for their kind assistance and encouragement in this endeavour.

I am also thankful to Mr Ramesh Jain who agreed to publish it at such a short notice.

MANSURA HAIDAR

Introduction

Mirza Muhammad Haidar Dughlat was a true representative of his age: he combined the chivalry and courage of a Mongol prince with an interest in the arts and love for the requirements of life. He was a humane, kind-hearted and highly civilized man.

One might say that he was a historian by choice, soldier by birth and profession, and a conqueror by virtue of his personal courage and gallantry. Like many other Mongol Khans whose names he tried to immortalize through his historical work,[1] he himself was forgotten, his achievements were effaced. He was neither born with a silver spoon in his mouth nor did he have the good fortune of having greatness thrust upon him. He achieved greatness through his own struggles and lost his life in one such endeavour. Mirza Muhammad Haidar Dughlat was a Mongol by birth who lived as a Mongol, wrote for the Mongols, and died while defending the interests of the Mongols. Amin Ahmad Razi says that Mirza Haidar was 'endowed with an excellent character and a rare talent for elegant composition in verse as well as in prose'. Further, that 'to the gifts of nature, Haidar Dughlat added those of bravery, extreme valour and all the qualities that constitute a great general'.[2]

His attributes were well-recognized and widely appreciated. Babur had valued his maternal cousin for his good qualities of mind and heart, and scribed him as a man of many parts: 'He has a hand deft in everything, penmanship and painting, and in making arrows and arrow barbs and string grips; moreover he is a born poet and in a petition written to me, even his style is not bad.'[3] It seems that Haidar Dughlat was also a fine musician.

Haidar Dughlat himself records that he became 'not only distinguished but a past master in the art of calligraphy, reading, composing verses, epistolary style (*insha*), painting and illuminating; excelled so much in such crafts as seal engraving, jeweller's and goldsmith's work, saddlery and armour making, also in the construction of arrows, spearheads and knives, gilding and many other things' that 'the masters of each could teach him no more'.[4]

Haidar Dughlat was born at Tashkent. The date of his birth has nowhere been specifically recorded, though he himself writes that at the age of sixteen he was orphaned and that he joined the service of Sultan Said Khan in AH 920/AD 1514, from which it is deduced that he was born in AD 1498. Nevertheless, Haidar Dughlat himself records that he 'entered the service of Said Khan when the latter was in Andijan and had just sustained a defeat at the hands of Souyunj Khwaja Khan'; Babur was at that time going to join Najm-i-Sani to fight against the Uzbegs, which places his birth even earlier. Muhibbul Hasan, however, determines that he was born *c.* 1499-1500.[5] Haidar Dughlat gives a 'detailed list' of his father's children.[6] Haidar's mother, Khubnigar Khanam, was the third daughter of Yunus Khan, the Mongol ruler of Moghulistan, and a sister of Babur's mother, Qutluq Nigar Khanam.[7]

The early life of Haidar Dughlat was full of sorrows, particularly the year 1508-9, when all his family were killed by Shaibani Khan. Not only was Haidar Dughlat's father put to death but Haidar himself escaped Shaibani only through the intervention and tacit support of Maulana Qazi who saved him from being drowned. Haidar Dughlat[8] gives a graphic account of the tragic events which followed. Different versions of his unhappy childhood have been given.

Shaibani Khan (or Shaibak) the Uzbeg conqueror, who had driven Babur from his homeland, was particularly hostile to the Mongols of the Central Asian region and had planned the murder of 30,000 Mongols (despite the fact that Shaibani Khan himself was of Mongol descent). He often commented that, 'given the opportunity, the Mongols would do to us exactly what we had done to them'. The only redeeming feature for Mirza Haidar was that one of his sisters, Habiba Sultan Khanish, was married by Shaibani Khan to his brilliant nephew, Ubaidullah Sultan, who, like his father Mahmud Sultan, proved to be a great saviour of the Mongols thereafter. Although Haidar Dughlat's mother was related to the Mongol rulers of Moghulistan, they did not have a royal background or a state of their own to fall back upon. Haidar's paternal uncle, Saiyid Muhammad Mirza, had been honoured by Sultan Said with the title 'Ulusbegi', which became a 'hereditary office' of his family. Sultan Said was particularly kind to Haidar and, soon after his return from the camp of Qasim Khan of Dasht-i Qipchaq, he conferred the (*musaharat*) of '*kurkani*' on him—Haidar Dughlat was married to Ahmad Khan's granddaughter, Muhibb Sultan Khanim. Nevertheless, such connections could not save Haidar from the Uzbeg onslaught in which even the two Sultans, Ahmad Khan and Mahmud Khan, the maternal uncles of Babur and Mirza Haidar, lost their lives.

Haidar Dughlat's father was the next target. Shaibani's invitation to Haidar Dughlat's father was accepted by him with a real fear that his own 'end was drawing near and on the tablet of his fate he recognised the hue of martyrdom'. Naturally, he 'was extremely anxious for his son Haidar's security'.

The fear was not without foundation. Almost all the sources confirm that racial chauvinism was acute among the Mongols, hence Haidar Dughlat's father was seen as a 'treacherous and intriguing man', convicted of a mischievous plot (for this reason) against Babur at Kabul. Later on, his intriguing nature was 'thought by Shaibani Beg to be dangerous even at a distance' which ultimately led him to order his murder.

This exposed Mirza Haidar Dughlat also to danger. The Uzbeg princes, Hamza and Mutlab, wanted him put to death. While fleeing from Shaibani Beg, Haidar Dughlat fell from his donkey at Langar Mir Ahmad and dislocated his left elbow. Not till his bone was set again after two months of torture, was he able to sleep at night. It was broken a second time and set once again at Pushang. When the Mirza left Qalai Zafar, such was the plight of his companions and their travails and tribulations that, in Haidar's own words: 'We only had two horses with us, and so limited was our baggage that I had nothing to lie on at night. Maulana Muhammad who was a sort of father to the party had nothing but one meagre shawl, such as is worn by the poorest men in Badakhshan, what the condition of the others was may be surmised.' On reaching Kabul, however, they were received by Shirum Taghai (maternal uncle of Haidar) and one of the pillars of the state.[9]

In this whirlpool of miseries and fog of adversity, Haidar Dughlat's only ray of hope were his benefactors who served as a lighthouse for him. Haidar Dughlat was greatly influenced by the four towering personalities of his times, one of whom was Hazrat Maulana Qazi to whom he owed his life. The Maulana, who was his Ustad, was 'a blessing in the land'.

Haidar Dughlat recounting the story of his own birth in his book, says that he was the answer to the supplications and continuous earnest prayers of his mother who had been 'disappointed' four times earlier and had, therefore, 'unbounded love' for the child. While Haidar was yet an infant, he was 'subjected to such severe haemorrhoids that the doctors gave up all hope of recovery'. His mother 'turned in every direction in search of help, till at length she went to Maulana Muhammad Kazi,[10] who was one of the most distinguished of the companions of His Holiness (Maulana Qazi). So much so that even at that time his family had many disciples.' Haidar Dughlat recounts how 'when Maulana looked on me with his Christ-like glance he became very thoughtful, and after he had gone out said, if I had known that the Mirza's son was in such a grave condition, I should not have come'. He ordered no remedy, except frugality, and then went on his way. 'One morning he sent the news of my recovery from His Heavenly Abode and the two miracles occurred: my recovery without any medicine and elimination of the disease completely . . . from that date', records Mirza Haidar, 'to the end of his life, the Maulana helped and instructed me, both publicly and privately.'

Another person who had a deep impact on Haidar Dughlat was Hafiz Miram, 'a pious and ascetic man . . . possessed of numerous talents' who could recite the Quran with special attention to the modulations of the voice and wrote the Naskh taliq and other styles of writing beautifully'. He was appointed Haidar's teacher, and instructed him in the Quran and in calligraphy.[11]

Haidar Dughlat had spent his formative years under the patronage of or in the company of Babur whose many traits he had imbibed. After the assassination of his father, Haidar Dughlat was taken to Bukhara, from there to Badakhshan and then to Kabul in Baubur's company. He remained in the service of Babur at Kabul for three or four years and is said to have participated in some of his campaigns. On reaching Kabul, Haidar Dughlat's adversity changed into prosperity. He writes: 'the moon of my ascendancy and the star of my good luck emerged from their eclipse, and my misfortune changed to prosperity. It may be imagined how I enjoyed so sudden a transition to comfort, ease and abundance from a state of poverty, misfortune, suffering and hardship which had rendered the soul weary of its confinement within the case of the body.' Haidar Dughlat found 'fatherly love' in his (Babur's) close embrace and was much consoled by [his] assurances. On his part, Babur did everything to make the Mirza comfortable, saying 'Your father and all other relatives were made to drink the wine of martyrdom but thank God, you have come back again in safety. Do not grieve too much at their loss for I will take their place.' Haidar confesses that 'with such promises and tenderness did he comfort me, that the bitterness of orphanage and the poison of banishment were driven from my mind'. He remained in the service of the Emperor till 1512 'in perfect happiness and freedom from care, and he was forever either by promises of kindness or by threats of severity encouraging me to study. If he ever noticed any little virtue or new acquisition, he would praise it in the highest terms, commend it to everybody.'[12]

Babur was unhappy at Mirza Haidar's departure to the barren wastes of Moghulistan or to Kashghar but he agreed to bid his cousin farewell because he understood that '*baz gardad ba asli khud hama chiz, zar-i safi-u nuqra-u airzin*' ('Everything goes back to its source, pure gold, silver or tin').[13]

The most crucial period of his life, however, was spent with Ahmad Khan's son, Abu Said, who left an indelible stamp on the character of this budding talent and soldier of fortune. At the luxurious court of Sultan Said, Haidar Dughlat spent twenty-four years merely in acquiring knowledge, 'many accomplishments and much learning'[14] under the 'direct supervision (instruction and guidance)' of the Sultan.

He describes how 'in the affairs of the state, in important transactions, in planning campaigns and forays (*kazaki*) in archery, in hunting, in the training of falcons and in everything that is useful in the government of a kingdom', the Khan (Abu Said) was (his) instructor and patron'. As for the most lucrative and popular art of his times, that of battle, he participated in numerous wars and his valour and strategy have been recorded both by him and by others.

Haidar Dughlat proudly recollects how at the time of the distribution of presents (possessions) and the subsequent departure of the Sultan's son, Rashid Khan, Sultan Said had showed him special honour, telling him 'to fasten on his (Rashid's) sword and quiver for him, and help him to mount his horse; it may be a good omen, and in the art of war he shall be your pupil'. Haidar performed this service and the Khan repeated the *fatiha* and instructed Rashid not to forget that Mirza Haidar had fastened on his sword for him and that he (Rashid) was Haidar's pupil. He then asked his son: 'should any one ask you whose pupil you are in the art of war what answer will you make'? and on getting the answer he wished, the Khan informed everyone that Haidar Dughlat was his own pupil.[15]

Mirza Haidar was a good general and showed the utmost courage and bravery in Sultan Said's expeditions against the Kirghiz, Uzbegs and others. In 1527-8, Sultan Said Khan sent the Mirza with his son Rashid Khan to Balur 'a country of infidels', situated between Badakhshan and Kashmir, where they both 'conducted a holy war successfully and returned victorious, loaded with booty and covered with glory'.

Immediately afterwards, Mirza Haidar was despatched with Rashid Sultan to drive out Aiman Khwaja from Aksu in which he succeeded. 'Having set in order the military and civil affairs', he left Rashid Sultan in Aksu and himself re-entered the service of the Khan. When Said Khan wanted to conquer Tibet, Mirza Haidar was sent in advance and several forts were taken and many subdued. Sultan Said had undertaken many incursions on Ladakh which his men had failed in till Haidar Dughlat was appointed to accompany Sultan Said's second son prince Sikandar Mirza.[16] They occupied Nubra (a region of Ladakh) in July 1532 and marched towards Maryul near Leh. When Sultan Said arrived he was suffering from *damgiri* (asthma); further Ladakh was no place to quarter more than a thousand soldiers in winter. At that point, Haidar Dughlat decided that since Kashmir could easily support the entire army and since the Khan was not in good health, he should instead proceed to Baltistan in Ladakh along with 1,000 soldiers while Haidar would march towards Kashmir with the remaining 4,000. On his way to Kashmir, the Mirza managed to get the support of several Ladakhi chiefs who joined him with their forces.[17] Many Balti Tibetans along the way became loyal companions who guided them through difficult defiles, till Haidar finally reached Zoji La in January 1533.[18]

There exists a controversy regarding the strength of Mirza Haidar's army. According to Haidar Malik, Mirza had 14,000 cavalry and 20,000 infantry whereas Nizamuddin says that he had merely 12,000 soldiers. Others say that total number of Mirza Haidar's forces did not exceed 5,000 of which 3,000 were Khan Said's followers and 2,000 were raised by Mirza himself. An advance guard of 400 chosen soldiers was sent under Tuma Bahadur Qabuchi to face the Kashmiris who had assembled in the Lar defiles.[19] The attack on the Kashmiris at dawn took them unawares. They fled in different directions, hotly pursued by Mirza Haidar's forces, and finally took shelter in the fort of Hanjik[20] (near Srinagar). This preliminary success encouraged the Mongols, who marched forward to occupy Naushahr where people surrendered easily. Mirza Haidar was, however, sceptical about the intentions of his newly-found supporters. He fortified the palace of Sultan Zainul Abidin Rajdan[21] and spent three or four weeks there, and then marched towards Maraj.

Some chroniclers have exaggerated the destruction and devastation wrought by the Mongols in the region, comparing it to the havoc created by Chingiz Khan, particularly the fact that they 'did not distinguish between Muslims and non-Muslims' and that 'their invasion compelled the terrified people to take shelter in the defiles or in the uphills'. They were blamed for setting fire to villages and towns and massacring men, women and children. They did not spare even the grand buildings and magnificent remnants of the past.

It is said that after the reign of terror let loose by the Mongols between January and March 1533, the Kashmiris had no strength left in them to make any reprisals.

However, the exhortations of the *ulama* infused a new life into Kashmiris. In the true fashion of the age, the call for a holy war was given and a *fatwa* decreeing the war against the Mongols not only desirable but 'obligatory' was also issued. The love for 'martyrdom' was the best incentive for believers. The Kashmiris put up a stiff resistance. Attempts were made to disrupt the Mongol advance, to destroy their baggage and harass the Mongols through guerilla warfare. Mirza Haidar avoided an open confrontation but his caution yielded no fruit. The Kashmiris repeatedly made incursions, eventually provoking the Mongols into a war which took place at Baghi Bavan. Mirza Haidar's forces consisting of 500 cavalry, led by Baba Sharq Mirza, was repulsed by Malik Ali Chadura who succeeded in putting the wounded commander to flight.

Nevertheless, Daim Ali and Mirza Haidar tried to save the situation by attacking them on the right and left respectively with their *hazaras*. After some initial success, and despite their courage and brave fighting, the Kashmiris lost the field. Many of their generals (including Malik Ali Chadura) were killed and the army sought refuge in flight.[22] Undeterred by this defeat, the Kashmiri forces led by Kazi Chak and Abdal Magre continued their sudden attacks and continuous raids which ultimately tired out the Mughal forces.

Mirza Haidar was probably at his wits' end. Instead of using his own judgement or relying upon wise counsel, he gave in to the advice of disloyal and less sensible nobles. In a *kangash* which was organized by him before battle in the Mongol fashion, he sought the suggestions of his comrades in arms. Mir Daim Ali, who had already proved his bravery and loyalty, failed to convince the Mirza about the feasibility of an attack on the Kashmiris who had been harassing the Mongols from their mountain refuges through their '*chupao*' (guerilla) tactics. Mirza Ali Taghai, on the other hand, made the pernicious suggestion that the families of the Kashmiris be attacked. In his view this was bound to compel the commanders to descend from the mountains to defend their kith and kin. It would then be easy to destroy each of the two groups separately.

Haidar Dughlat accepted Taghai's advice even though it was fraught with danger. Since the Kashmiri forces were now divided, it was possible for them to attack and surround the Mongol forces from all sides, and the Mongols found themselves being hounded from place to place. Mirza Haidar had to pay the price of trusting an unfaithful adviser. Recording his thanks to the Almighty that he finally emerged safe and managed to exterminate the army of Kashmir and the kings, Haidar laments that he would have subdued the whole of the country, had it not been for some of these malignant persons who by their words and actions threw this in disorder and who rendered further reduction impossible.

Ali Taghai repeatedly stressed the difficulties involved in the venture and impressed upon the Mirza that he should give up the campaign. The soldiers were homesick and exhausted with the unending and fruitless march, when even the booty was not guaranteed. The humiliating situation and the treachery of Ali Taghai must have been painful for Mirza. Yet he refused to listen to the advice of Daim Ali to put Ali Taghai to death. A peace with the Kashmiris was patched up and Mirza Haidar was able to ensure that the terms of the treaty were in no way degrading for his patron Sultan Ali. It was settled that the *khutba* was to be read in the name of Sultan Said and suitable presents were to be sent to him. The ruler of Kashmir Muhammad Shah's daughter or niece was to be married to Prince Sikandar Sultan, son of Sultan Abu Said.

There were, however, two clauses favouring the Kashmiris. All the Kashmiri prisoners of war were to be released by the Mirza and rich presents, woollen clothes, etc., were to be offered as *peshkash* to Muhammad Shah. Finally, in May 1533 the Mughal forces withdrew, leaving a devastated and ravaged Kashmir where every sign of agriculture had been trampled over by the warring armies. A severe famine broke out which is said to have lasted for more than an year.[23]

Another invasion of the territories of Kashmir was not possible immediately as the Kashmiris had become wiser and avoided wars, ensuring a strong united rule to ward off danger from the Mongols. Sultan Muhammad, his successor Shamsuddin (1537-40), and the king-maker and prime minister Qazi Chak somehow managed to hold the state together till its division into three equal parts—governed by Qazi Chak, Sultan Ismail Shah (son of Muhammad Shah), and Saiyid Ibrahim. Besides, the situation in Moghulistan had also altered. For various reasons, Abdur Rashid Khan suspected that Mirza Haidar was sympathetic towards Sikandar, and was somewhat unkind towards him. The Mirza's unsuccessful attempts to conquer Tibet and Ladakh had also exhausted him. Mirza Haidar had no desire to risk his life any further; it seemed safer to go to Badakhshan.

After a hazardous journey, the Mirza reached Badakhshan but his hopes were belied, there was no possibility of getting asylum anywhere and he finally decided to proceed to Lahore to join Kamran.[24] In 1536, Mirza Haidar started from Kashghar and joined Mirza Kamran in Lahore travelling via Badakhshan. When Kamran marched against Kandahar the same year, he left Mirza Haidar as *naib* to take charge of Lahore.

For Mirza Haidar and his Mongol allies it was a time of hectic activity. While Humayun faced the threat from Sher Khan and was busy 'in arranging his troops, and conciliating his brothers and relatives and amending their secret dispositions', Kamran maintained his 'stubbornness in the path of discontent'. Even while Kamran had come after a long absence due to professed illness, he refused to leave his men behind.

Kamran brought Mirza Haidar with him to Agra. Abul Fazl records that the Mirza 'enjoyed this privilege of serving His Majesty and had been treated with abundant favours. The hour of crisis and point of predicament arrived for Mirza Haidar. When Mirza Kamran made his own ailment an excuse and laboured to induce him (Haidar) to accompany him. Abul Fazl syas that: 'The Mirza showed himself favourably inclined towards Kamran and proceeded to excuse himself (to Humayun), and out of want of consideration brought forward the matter of leave.'

Humayun observed: 'if kindred be the point for consideration, you are equally related to us both; if loyalty and truth be regarded, the tie to me is closer. If glory and manliness be sought, you should accompany me for I am marching against the foe. As to what M. Kamran is representing about his illness, you are not a physician nor a druggist that you should go with him. What the Mirza imagines about Lahore's being a place of safety, is idle—for if anything is clear as the result of his holding back from this expedition, it is that he will not find a corner of safety in India. Your action cannot be divested of two difficulties. Should I succeed, what face can you put on the matter or what respect will you have? You will not from shame be able to lift your head from the ground, so that death will be preferable to life. If, which God forbid, the result be otherwise it will be impossible for you to remain in Lahore. Whoever has suggested such a thing to M. Kamran is either wrong in his brain, or he is treacherous and has concealed the truth and entered on the path of flattery. . . . In fine, M. Haidar happily found the path of good counsels and gloriously associated himself with the army of honour.' Other sources, however, confirm Mirza Haidar's loyalty towards Humayun also. In an hour of crisis, he not only stood by Humayun but tried to enthuse and infused new spirit among this disheartened group of desperados through his optimistic view of future.

Haidar Dughlat fought in the war against Sher Khan. When the battle order was drawn up, he was stationed on Humayun's left, and on his right were twenty-seven bannerets (*tugh*-bearing *amirs*). After the defeat and flight of Humayun towards Punjab, Haidar joined him on 28 May 1540 in Rohtak. When the future course of action was being debated, and varied opinions were put forward, Mirza Haidar gave sage and brave cousnsel: 'It is proper that all the Mirzas should settle down after securing the slopes from the mountains of Sirhind to those of Sirhind.' His suggestion was that the Mughals should try to hold the lower ranges between the Indus and Kashmir, i.e. from Sirhind in the south-east to Rawalpindi on the north-west. With a resolute courage and confidence, Haidar Dughlat reassured the desperate men: 'I engage that with a small force I will in two months get possession of Kashmir. When that news comes, let every man send his belongings to Kashmir, for there is no safer place. It will take Sher Khan four months to arrive and he will not be able to bring into the hill country the gun carriages and cannon which are the support of his warfare. In a short time the Afghan army will be ruined.' As against this, Hindal and Yadgar Nasir Mirza were of the view that they should go to Bhakkar to subdue that country. Kamran's advice was the worst: that they should all should stay in the mountains while he (Kamran) himself accompanied their families to Kabul, and after seeing them to safety there he (Kamram) was to join the debate of princes as he had his own designs. Abul Fazl says that Kamran sent Qazi Abdullah, his *sadr*, to Sher Khan with overtures of friendship seeking 'the fulfilment of his desires with the help of enemies' and also wrote a letter to the effect that 'if Punjab were secured to him as formerly, he would soon bring affairs to a successful issue'. As feared the attempts proved to be abortive. The envoy behaved treacherously and the exchange of embassies only served Sher Shah's ends. On the Mirza's advice, Humayun thereafter 'resolved to attempt Kashmir and sent a body of troops in advance with Mirza Haidar to that province'.[25]

Thus the Mirza had another opportunity to intervene in the politics of Kashmir as petitioins from Abdal Magre and Regi Chak against the king-maker Qazi Chak were brought to him at Lahore by Khwaja Haji. All Mirza Haidar's pleas to invade Kashmir fell on deaf ears, and his attempts to persuade Kamran to undertake the venture was no more successful as the latter was preoccupied with the greater task of suppressing Hindal's rebellion. Although Haidar Dughlat had to accompany Kamran to Agra, he did not give up hopes of conquering Kashmir. He raised an army led by Baba Jujak, who unfortunately lacked the courage and capacity for such a gigantic task. Khwaja Haji accompanied him. The force however did not proceed beyond Lahore as by that time the news of the Qanauj war, followed by Humayun's defeat (17 May 1540), provided a reason for postponing the invasion. However, when Humayun returned to Lahore, Abdal Magre and Regi Chak approached Haidar once again through Khwaja Haji to undertake the campaign against Qazi Chak—a task which they themselves were incapable of undertaking. Once the battle was won for them, they expected Haidar to leave the field to them.[26]

The political situation in Kashmir considerably favoured this venture; many nobles like Khwaja Haji, Abdal Makri, Zangi Chak, and others were opposed to the de facto ruler of Kashmir, Qazi Chak, and had come to

Lahore 'in order that by their intimacy with Mirza Haidar they might obtain an army from Kamran and so get possession of Kashmir'. Once again, the Mirza was deputed for this diplomatic mission; 'though M. Haidar exerted himself', says Abdul Fazl, 'their wish was not fulfilled'. At this critical juncture, when Humayun was let down by his brothers (as Hindal 'raised a disturbance by having the *khutba* read in his own name and Kamran marched from Lahore to Agra), Mirza Haidar by great exertions contrived to raise an army and to despatch it from the capital Agra under the charge of Baba Jujak who was one of Kamran's superior officers'. Dughlat had planned that this force should march towards Kashmir led by the Kashmiri nobles and occupy the land. However, both because Baba Jujak was negligent in setting out, and news of the disaster of Chausa which was 'a blow to eternal dominions, became widespread. The expedition had to be postponed and the Kashmiri *amirs* waited at Naushahra, Rajouri and hill tracts for another opportunity to come their way.'

Humayun on his part shared the optimism of Mirza Haidar and in this hour of need encouraged him to take up arms against the Kashmiris. He assured the Mirza that Sikandar Topchi and Khwaja Kalan would both join him and that Humayun himself would also follow them. Since these two officers had not helped Humayun in his hour of crisis, Humayun's faith in them is somewhat surprising.

When Mirza Haidar reached the vicinity of Naushahra, these nobles came forward to assist him. At Bhira came Abdal Makri and Regi Chak. Mirza Haidar had only a small detachment of retainers in his own pay and Humayun had only 4,000 horsemen. While his adversary, Malik Ghazi Chak—the ruler of Kashmir—had 3,000 or 4,000 infantry and 50,000 horsemen and had proceeded to check the advance of the Mirza at Karanbal.

To the discomfiture of the Mirza, neither Sikandar Topchi nor Khwaja Kalan came to his aid, but ran away—and this was a blow to Humayun who also gave up the idea of joining Mirza's expedition. So, instead of facing the enemy, Haidar Dughlat thought it advisable to change his route and went by Punch which had been left undefended. (Having heard about the Mirza's march and the assistance given to him by Abdal and Regi) Qazi Chak had his forces to Kapartal pass. However, 'a schism occurred' in the army, and even when Humayun's officers came, Khwaja Kalan Beg abandoned the campaign possibly at the instigation of M. Kamran, and joined Kamran at Bhera. Muzaffar Topchi also deserted and fled to the Sarang hills. According to Abul Fazl, 'none remained with Mirza Haidar save a few old servants and the troops whom Humayun had appointed for his assistance. These were 400 men only given to him by Humayun at Lahore. However, Haidar Dughlat succeeded in conquering Kashmir as Qazi Chak fled to Sher Shah. The Mirza entered the valley on 22 November 1540 'without a battle or struggle' and 'safely crossed mountains and descending into the Kashmir plains, at once occupied Srinagar'.[27]

Abul Fazl explains the reasons for Haidar Dughlat's easy victory. In the first place, there was 'much strife and dissension and confusion and anarchy in Kashmir'. Secondly, Haidar was 'warmly supported by the eagerness of Kashmiris' who were tired of misrule and perpetual uncertainty. Thirdly, the place had for a long time been without 'an established ruler', and the ministers ruled the country, under the nominal rule of a puppet king. Thus, a person called Nazuk Shah 'having a name that was no name' (*ism-i ba musamma*) was made the 'reputed sovereign'. Abul Fazl rightly records that 'under such circumstances in whatever direction there might not be union, or plan, or counsel, or judgement to that quarter did the affairs of the country drift'.[28] The Kashmiri chroniclers support the above-mentioned version. Qazi Chak was therefore in no position to face the enemy and fled to Sher Shah.

However, Haidar Dughlat, having installed a Kashmiri—Nazuk Shah—as ruler with another Kashmiri, Abdal Magre as *wazir*, aroused the hostility of certain Kashmiris. Immediately after the conquest of Kashmir, Abdal Makri and Zangi Chak, finding themselves 'strong enough busied themselves with the affairs of the kingdom, and gave several *purgannahs* to the Mirza'. Although Mirza Haidar divided his lands into three portions and gave two portions to his allies, Abdul Magre and Regi Chak, retaining only one part for himself. The Kashmiri chiefs were unhappy over the turn of the events. They were unpleasantly to find that the Mirza intended remaining in Kashmir. Qazi Chak had meanwhile approached Sher Shah and received from him 5,000 horsemen and two elephants led by two brave Afghans, Adil Khan and Husam Khan Sherwani.'[29] Qazi Chak then marched towards Kashmir via Hirapur in 1541. The death of Abdal Magre, a seasoned soldier and ally, was serious setback for D.H. (His *jagirs* were bestowed upon his son Husain Magre by Haidar Dughlat.)

Haidar Dughlat collected his forces and with his two allies, Husain Magre and Regi Chak, marched towards Watanar. He was joined by Idi Zaina. The first encounter was indecisive, and skirmishes took place every day, for over a month till the rains followed by floods stopped the fighting temporarily. Qazi Chak withdrew his forces to Girdar while the Mirza came to Kother. A fierce battle was fought and despite having a small force of only 3,000 men, Mirza Haidar defeated the joint forces of Qazi Kak and Sher Shah of 5,000 cavalry and several thousand infantry. The defeated chiefs including Qazi Chak, Daulat Chak, Saiyid Ibrahim, and the Afghans, were put to flight and sought shelter in India. Like Chingiz who rewarded brave soldiers, Haidar Dughlat also treated Malik Naji well—he had been severely wounded and preferred to surrender.

Contradictory accounts of this campaign are given in the *Akbar Nama* and other sources and even the names seem to have been confused. According to the *Akbar Nama*: 'it was the winter quadragesima and there was heavy snow. When Kazi Chak saw that M. Haidar was disposed to make himself independent he, using the craft and perfidy which are indispensable to Kashmiris, left Kashmir and went before Sher Khan. For his object in bringing in M. Haidar was his own aggrandizement and when that was not achieved but when on the contrary things assumed a different shape, he withdrew his hand and entered on another scheme. He now tried another course and gave Sher Khan the sister of Ismail (the son of Muhammad Shah). When he had made himself acceptable by this means, he took Alawal Khan, Hasan Khan Sarwani and others to the number of 2,000 men and came to Kashmir.'

Haidar Dughlat records that the role of Kashmiris was not very helpful from the beginning. As soon as they heard of the evacuation of Lahore, both his supporters—Iskander Topchi and Mir Khwaja Kalan, deserted him—the former took shelter with Sarang Sultan in the foothills of Hind, and the latter left Sialkot and joined the fugitives from Lahore. Even when he had conquered Kashmir 'ascending the throne of Kashmir (*julus-i darulmulki* Kashmir)' in the season of Sagittarius, 'the eyes of the enemy turned dark'. Qazi Chak along with other chief men of Kashmir left, 'vainly imagining that Sher Khan by force of arms could change the decree of God, appealed to him for aid'.

Circumstances, however, favoured Mirza Haidar. Immediately after receiving reinforcements from Sher Khan, Qazi Chak advanced towards Kashmir, leaving behind his children under the care of Malik Abdal and Zangi Chak. Almost immediately Malik Abdal Makri who was his right hand man of Qazi Chak had paralysis, and died of dropsy, leaving Zangi Chak alone. Haidar Dughlat makes a cryptic reference to this calamity which befell on his enemy. He wrote 'in a word, after various difficulties had been surmounted which it would be tedious to relate in detail, we left our families in the fort of Andarkul and went out to meet and oppose (the enemy) with a vacillating hand'. Abdul Fazl, recounts that 'the people of

Kashmir all deserted him (the Mirza) and but few persons remained with him. He spent three months in the mountain defiles and then on 16 August 1541 a battle took place and he gained victory.'

The description of this war is fully recorded by Haidar Dughlat. Since Indarkot (perhaps renamed Andarkul or the inner lake by Haidar Dughlat) was an impregnable site. Haidar Dughlat was no longer worried about his family, although the enemy's forces, comprising partly the Afghan auxiliaries and partly 'faithless' Kashmiris consisted of more than 5,000 horses. Over a period of three months, several attacks were made on their strongholds and several times open confrontation took place, 'till at length Qazi Chak having formed a junction with the auxiliaries of Sher Khan, marched boldly out of the hill district (*baladast*) which was fortified and turned into a place for attack'. Malik Qazi Chak had obtained two elephants and 5,000 cavalry led by Husain Shirvani and Adil Khan. The forces of Mirza Haidar met him and his Afghan allies between Danahdyar and Kawah Malik.

Haidar Dughlat recounts that, the Kashmiri forces 'who from their outward appearance looked as if they were to be defeated and must disperse in flight, held their ground. On the side of Haidar Dughlat, the Mughal army maintained its position. The battle ensued all of a sudden and unexpectedly, hence, only 250 men were present there together with a few Kashmiris who had joined the Moghuls, raising the number to 300 as all others were scattered in different directions. The enemy's forces constituted 5,000 cavalry, two elephants, and a body of infantry more numerous than the cavalry.' Haidar Dughlat's army 'attacked their rear and started looting and plundering their baggage and stores. Many were slain, some fell into captivity. The battle was so desperate that should I enter into the particulars, the reader would imagine I was exaggerating.' On 2 August 1541, the army of 5,000 cavalry and several thousand foot was routed. The place came again into the possession of Mirza Haidar. The *khatib* (preacher) of Kashmir, Maulana Yusuf, found the chronogram in '*fath mukarrar*' (the second or repeated victory). Abul Fazl explains that the first victory occurred on 1 March 1533 when the Mirza had come to Kashmir over the pass of Lar (Baltistan), as the agent of Said Khan, the ruler of Kashghar; but in May 1533 he had then made peace with the Kashmir ministers and with the nominal ruler, Muhammad Shah, whose daughter was given in marriage to Iskandar Sultan, the Mirza's son, and the Mirza returned by the way he had entered. H.D., however, says that he had earlier entered Kashmir and gained victory there.[30]

Initially, Mirza Haidar must have felt insecure in a new place and struggled to maintain good relations with Kashmiri nobles. He had won a number of Kashmiri supporters whom he honoured with rewards. They were consulted on all important and insignificant matters concerning state, administrative and political affairs and socio-economic issues. Gradually, however, H.D. grew overconfident and started behaving like a king. His arrogance and superiority, and particularly his deliberate act of ignoring those who had stood by him in the hour of need angered the nobles. When Regi Chak started showing his displeasure, the Mirza played Husain Magre and Idi Zaina against him. Hearing of the Mirza's intentions to punish him, Regi fled to Rajauri to join Qazi Chak in 1543. Infuriated by this, Haidar ordered that his house be torn down. The revenge did not prove to be disastrous. In 1544, Regi came to Gulmarg with Qazi Chak but was taken unawares by the Moghul forces who drove them out to the Punjab hills after a successful night attack. Qazi Chak himself died on 12 September 1544 at Thanna. Regi then invaded Kashmir once again only to be defeated by a detachment sent by Haidar Dughlat. The head of the rebel was brought to Haidar Dughlat.

Mirza Haidar's relations continued to be amicable with his two other allies, Husain and Raina. He now felt strong enough to undertake further campaigns. Although he did not depose the nominal ruler, Nazuk Shah, his defacto authority provided him with enough resources and military power to recover the lost territories which had once formed part of Husain Shah's Kingdom of Kashmir.[31]

His next expedition was planned to Kishtwar. The Mirza himself remained at Jhapur near Kishtwar, and his vanguard led by Bandagan Kuka, Muhammad Makri and Idi Yahiya Zaina marched towards Dahlot about a three day journey. On reaching the village of Dahlut, they found the enemy already ranged in battle formation ready to face them. There was a indecisive encounter which did not prevent their onward journey. Since it was too windy, to cross the river, they had to take another route to Kishtwar. After making a diversion and reaching Dhartas a severe storm laden with dust arose, and the day became dark. The towns people attacked them and killed Bandagan Kuka and Muhammad Magre, along with five others. So many Mongols were killed in the encounter that the place was thereafter called as 'Mughal Mazar or Muhgal Maidan'. After suffering 'a thousand exertions', the army joined Mirza Haidar Dughlat, who had to return unsuccessful.

This reversal did not dampen Haidar. He next made ready an army to invade Tibet. He managed to occupy Lansur and several other large citadels. He advanced on Tibet in 955 and conquered Rajaori and Great Tibet (Ladakh), and in 956 subdued the fort of Danel.

Without mentioning the sources, the editor of *Tarikh-i-Rashidi* gives a somewhat different account. After Mirza Haidar's conquest of Kashmir, Malik Ghazi and his Afghan allies fled to Bahramgalla. In 950, Mirza Haidar made himself secure in the fort of Indarkot. In 951, Zangi Chak had also fled to Ghazi Chak and the two had started for Srinagar, 'determined to root out Mirza Haidar'. Bahram Chak, son of Zangi Chak, reached Srinagar before them, but he was 'easily put to flight by two of Mirza's generals and his disorganized troops [fell] back on the main army'. Zangi Chak and Ghazi Chak thereupon retreated to Bahramgalla.

Since Ghazi Chak and his son Muhammad Chak died of fever and ague in 952, and the following year Zangi Chak was also slain and his head along with that of his son Ghazi, were brought before the Mirza, most of his opponents were now eliminated. But the turn of events soon added to Mirza's problems as some misunderstanding cropped ignited the Kashmiris. In Lar, the head of Khwaja Ujh—son of Masud Chak—was also brought to him. Khwaja Ujh had been a source of trouble for over seven years, and had only recently agreed to come to terms with the Mirza. He was lured by the assurances given by Mirza Mirak that everything would be all right if he agreed to come to the assembly. On his arrival, he was stabbed by Mirak, who pursued him into the jungle, and took his head to Mirza. Idi Zaina was enraged at this and protested that 'after an oath and covenant had been made, the slaughter of an innocent man was unjustified and unwarranted'. Mirza Haidar himself had the similar feelings but he could not undo the action of his lieutenant and had to give an evasive reply that he 'was not party to the circumstances of the death' he was not at all answerable.

Such a manner was sure to arouse enemies and was responsible for his unpopularity among Kashmiris. Apart from the treatment meted out to Ujh by his own courtiers, the Mirza's own attitude towards Daulat Chak irritated the latter and his followers. In 956, Adam Ghakkar requested, Mirza to pardon Daulat Chak who was brought to the tent with full assurances of pardon. But the Kashmiris felt that Mirza failed to show any respect or honour to Daulat Chak who was so displeased that he took away the elephant he had brought as a present for Mirza. The courtiers wanted to pursue him but the Mirza out of his inherent goodness prevented them.

Haidar Dughlat's nepotism, favouritism and special patronage to the

Mughal *amirs* and his own favourite chiefs further angered the Kashmiri nobles. Apart from this, the sources complain that Mirza had started behaving like a despot, concentrating all authority in his own hands and selecting his officers and governors from one particular section of his own favourites. Earlier, the Kashmiris had a share in the activities of the state, but now they complained that they were no longer consulted even by way of courtesy. They were also feeling that they were being deprived of privileges and were no longer given high posts. Such an attitude alienated even the most loyal Kashmiri nobles.

The anger was soon expressed in varied ways.[32] Daulat Chak, Ghazi Khan and Jai Chak went to Haidar Khan who had fled from Islam Shah to Rajori. When Islam Shah came in pursuing him (Haidar Khan) up to Madawar, the Kashmiris seized this opportunity to approach Islam Shah, wishing him to be the King. Although Islam Shah had not, perhaps, entered Kashmir, the nobles are said to have struck coin in his name in anticipation of his rule, 'having the formula "struck in Kashmir" engraved' on the reverse.

Elias has seen two such coins of Islam Shah which in his view were either in pursuance of 'the common practice to strike coins anticipating events which did not come to pass' or, the date on this coin being 957, 'it may have been struck by Haidar Dughlat himself as a compliment to Islam Shah'.

The reason for such an amicable gesture had been variously described in the sources. Some chroniclers record is given in the sources. It is said that when Haibat Khan Niyazi, governor of Lahore, was defeated and hotly pursued by his master Islam Shah Sur in the outer region of Kashmir, Mirza Haidar feared an Afghan onslaught on his newly-conquered territory. Sandwiched between the Moghuls and the Afghans, Haibat Khan was in difficulties. When Daulat Chak and Ghazi Chak approached him to join them in driving the Mirza out of the Kashmiri lands, Haibat Khan was clever enough to ignore their overtures and preferred to bargain with Mirza Haidar. He sent a Brahmin envoy to Mirza Haidar who was perhaps so alarmed by this gesture that he bought his safety by showering money on Haibat Khan. The latter no longer aspired to conquer Kashmir and left for Birna near Jammu. The Kashmiri chiefs were disappointed and once again went to Islam Shah for help.

The danger of an Afghan–Kashmiri alliance was averted by Mirza through an exchange of friendly embassies and showering costly presents, including saffron, upon Islam Shah, who reciprocated the gesture with equal warmth through political expediency, as his own power was not unchallenged.[33] This diplomacy could not however avert the constant danger threatening the insecure and unstable kingdom of Mirza.

The rivalry and enmity between the Kashmiris and the Mughals were the main reasons for Haidar Dughlat's fall; Haidar Dughlat underestimated the Kashmiris and favoured the Mongols excessively. The events which followed have been variously interpreted by the chroniclers. Some of them record that when trouble broke out in the outer hills, Mirza sent an army under his cousin Qara Bahadur to quell the disturbances. Another version holds that Mirza Qara Bahadur was appointed governor of Bhirpul (or Bharmal) and certain Kashmiri nobles (like Idi Zaina, Husain Makari and Khwaja Haji) were ordered to accompany the prince. Instead of supporting and assisting Qara Bahadur they returned to Indarkut, and thence to Baramulla and rose in rebellion. The much-trumpeted cause of this uprising was that they did not like the attitude of the Moghuls in the forces. On reaching Mankot, the Kashmiri chiefs decided to attack the Mughals. They left Qara Bahadur and sent a detachment to the hill top to cut off supplies. The Mughals who 'were unacceptable' to the Kashmiris warned Mirza Haidar about the impending revolt—to which an over-confident Mirza gave the reckless and complacent reply that 'they were no less ready than the Kashmiris to rebel'. Husain Makari sent his brother Ali Makari to Mirza Haidar, offering excuses on bahalf of the Kashmiris and requesting him to summon the army. Haidar Dughlat was unaware of the Kashmiri resentment. He told them that the Kashmiris were 'in no need for panic and not so powerless and that there was no necessity for calling in the army'.

At the same time, either by some contrivance or by accident a fire broke out in Indarkot. Mirza Qara and his followers were keen to re-build their houses and only then proceed to Bhirpul, but Haidar Dughlat allegedly did not approve of this. The enraged Kashmiris led by Idi Zaina, left the Moghuls and when they reached Bhirpul they took along with them Husain Makari, Ali Makari, and others to save them from the Moghuls. The next morning, the people of Bhirpul took up arms against the Moghuls who infested the mountains. Saiyid Mirza took shelter in the fort of Bhirpul. About eighty noted Moghuls were killed in the encounter, and Muhammad Nazir and Qara Bahadur were captured. The remaining army reached Bahramgalla.

A vexed Haidar Dughlat reacted sharply to this setback by ordering that all silver vessels were to be melted and turned into coins in order to raise soldiers. The nobles were to be won over: Jahangir Makari was pardoned and Husain Makari's estates were returned to him. Tradesmen now owned horses and were fitted out as soldiers. The exodus of Kashmiris and their miserable plight pained Mulla Abdullah who decided to visit the place to bring about peace. Haidar Dughlat might himself have asked him to use his good offices to pacify the people. Saints were greatly respected people in Central Asia and their influence was often used by the rulers in such difficult circumstances. However, the infuriated Kashmiris pounced upon Mulla Abdullah and slew him, in their frenzy, the Kashmiris swooped upon the Moghuls who sought refuge in flight. They were pursued by the Kashmiris who plundered their luggage and killed some of them. The remaining Moghuls strengthened the fortification of Bhirpul citadel.

Idi Zaina decided to proceed personally to Punch while a small detachment of about 500 horse led by Husain Magre, Naji Malik, and Khwaja Haji, were sent to besiege the fort. The Moghuls were outnumbered by the Kashmiris who were also receiving regular reinforcements and supplies. Qara Bahadur lost all hope. In a state of desperation, he decided to seek peace. Although chiefs like Saiyid Mirza and Mirza Ali Kuka tried their best to dissuade him and showed willingness to fight their way to Ghakkar, Qara Bahadur had no desire to suffer such misery. He came out of the fort in the hope of negotiations but the Kashmiris fell upon him. At this point, the army darted out and managed to escape.

Qara Bahadur, Qutub Ali Kuka, Muhammad Nazir and several others were brought before Idi Zaina. Qasim was killed in Baltistan and Muhammad Nazir was imprisoned in Rajauri. The Kashmiris left Bahramgalla and came to Hambarapur, Mirza Haidar was thus compelled to take up arms against them and rushed to Indarkot. At that time, Haidar Dughlat had only 1,000 men with him and his Moghul followers had an additional force of 700 men. They stood in battle array in a place at Shihabuddinpur. Daulat Chak and Ghazi Chak went to Hambarapur to help Idi Zaina, and on their return they assembled at Khampur. Mirza Haidar's forces were tanged on the plains of Khalidgarh near Srinagar. Fath Chak (whose father Khwaja Bahram had been killed by the Mongols) brought 3,000 men to Indarkot, they burnt all the places constructed by Mirza Haidar in the Safa gardens. When Mirza Haidar received this news, he said, 'I have not brought this from Kashghar; yet I might by the grace of God again built it'.[34] The enraged Kashmiris sought revenge. Jan Ali burnt down the palace of Zainul Abidin in Suryapur which angered the Mirza so much that he ordered his army to set fire to the palaces of Idi Zaina and Nauruz Chak in Srinagar. When Mirza Haidar took up his position in Khampur, the opposing forces stationed themselves at Adnipur, at a distance of two *kos*.

Haidar Dughlat had resolved to march against Idi Zaina when revolts broke out in Baltistan, Ladakh and Pakli. The governors of these places, namely, Mulla Qasim, Mulla Baqi and Abdullah Samarqandi, were defeated by the rebels. Koka Mir, who had been sent to Kishtwar to suppress the rebels, was also put to death along with his 1,500 soldiers in the *pargana* of Adavin.

Hearing about the disaster, Haidar Dughlat moved towards Srinagar and halted at Aunpur as the Kashmiris, led by Idi Zaina, were stationed in the fort of Manar near Khampur. At this time, as Mirza Haidar had a small force consisting of only about 700 or 800 horsemen, he thought it best to plan a night attack on the fort. Various sources tell us that Mirza Haidar had gone to survey the surroundings of the fort to assess the situation, leaving his small army behind and taking only thirty men with him. Of these only seven soldiers were with him when he was struck by an arrow when he was trying to enter the fort.

Different versions of Mirza Haidar's death have been given by the chroniclers. Usually, Saiyid Ali's account referred to above is said to be most reliable as he had participated in the campaign. Although he was not an eyewitness of Haidar Dughlat's tragic death, he was a careful writer and must have verified the fact that Mirza Haidar was killed by an arrow.[35]

END OF HAIDAR DUGHLAT

There were, however, certain significant factors which led to mutual suspicion and discord. The Kashmiris seemed to have developed imaginary fears and attributed to Mirza Haidar some kind of chauvinism. During his ten years' rule in Kashmir, Haidar Dughlat is said to have 'felt as if he was in exile', and consistently suffered from homesickness. The thought of his own country never left his mind. But this does not mean that he failed to assimilate and identify himself with Kashmir and adopt it as his own home, its people could not have reacted to him but with suspicion. Haidar Dughlat's total faith in his own kith and kin—the Mongols—and the denial of equal opportunities and the honour of his confidence to the newly-conquered people which was bound to result in his isolation.[36]

Abul Fazl gives four valid reasons for his downfall.[37] According to him, Haidar became unpopular owing to his own 'frigid and insipid bigotries, the result of imperfect development', due to which 'the essentials for Kashmir, viz., unanimity and fidelity found a bad market'. It is significant that Abul Fazl holds Haidar Dughlat responsible for creating this atmosphere of religious fanaticism and schism as in the author's view the *jugis* of Kashmir were far from being communal. Abul Fazl records: 'And to this day there is an odour of bigotry about the Kashmiris, for there is a powerful influence in association and especially is a strong impression produced by the ways of princes who are vigorous. It is to be hoped that by the blessings of His Majesty Akbar, the King of Kings, truth and chastity (*haqq-u haqqaniyat*) spiritual and temporal, may attain unity, and that the articles of worship and religion may become current, unadulterated by hypocrisy and bigotry',—a dream which was fulfilled by Akbar.

Another reason was his 'capital and most inauspicious mistake' of reading the *khutba* and striking coins in the name of Nazuk Shah in the fashion of Kashmiri ministers, even after his own full victory, instead of having impressed the *darahim* and *dananir* and the pulpit rostra with Humayun's name.

Abul Fazl's complaint is not entirely sustainable. It is generally accepted that Haidar Dughlat had maintained an attitude of loyalty towards the Mughals. Haidar was neither aware of Humayun's whereabouts nor was he sure of Humayun's intentions and future plans. Abul Fazl himself records that 'apparently he was temporising and was giving currency to disloyalty, for when Kabul was taken he honoured himself by having the *khutba* read in His Majesty's sacred name'. It is also possible that Haidar Dughlat did not feel secure enough to ignore Nazuk Shah. The step, however conciliatory, exposed Haidar Dughlat's weaknesses. It should be noted however that in certain sources, it is written that *khutba* was read in the name of Humayun.

Thirdly, the Mirza (whom Babur described as a faithful Muslim) is said to have 'transgressed the law of justice'; instead of acting as 'dominion's watchman', Haidar 'took to living for his own lusts and pleasures. He let fall from his hands prudence and the bearing of burdens, those two arms of felicity'. These comments of Abul Fazl not only contradict Babur's assessment but have not been corroborated by any other source.

The Mirza's skill and sagacity could not contain the seditious Kashmiris, who in friendly garb did the work of enemies. Their best stroke was separating his army from him, and scattering his capable servants. Some were sent to Tibet, some to Pakli, and some to Rajori. Idi Zaina and Husain Makri (son of Abdal Makri) won over Khwaja Haji, the Kashmiri Baqal, who was manager of the Mirza's affairs. They drew a great many to their side and marched against the Mirza. Ghazi Khan and Malik Daulat Chak also joined them. Near Khanpur (between Hirapur and Srinagar), they made a night attack on the Mirza who was approaching the quarters of Khwaja Haji to release Qara Bahadur, then a prisoner of war. The Mirza lost his life at the hands of Kamal Dubi though some say that it was one of his servants who unknowingly shot him with an arrow.

Abul Fazl simply records that he was killed in 958, by some treacherous Kashmiris. In another tradition, it is recorded that Kamal Kuka killed him with a sword though except an arrow shot through his heart no other wound was visible on his body.

Haidar Malik reports that Mirza Haidar had set out with a group of soldiers to explore the situation in the enemy's camp. While on his way, the Mirza was confronted by a butcher, who asked where he was from. The Mirza replied that he was neither a Persian nor a Kashmiri, at which the butcher took him for a Moghul spy and shot him to death. But the story does not seem to be true. Nizamuddin presents a totally different version of his death. According to him, the unpopularity of Haidar's men had led to a confrontation between the Mughals and the Kashmiris. Mirza Haidar was determined to undertake a night attack upon his enemy. The night was very dark and cloudy, and it was difficult to see. When Mirza entered the tent of Khwaja Haji 'who was the soul of rebellion', the agent of the Mirza, namely, Shah Nazar, a cuirassier of Mirza Haidar, shot at him. He said: 'when I shot an arrow, the voice of Mirza fell on my ear saying "you committed a fault". I then knew that the arrow had accidentally struck the Mirza'.

At dawn, the Kashmiris learnt that some Moghul lay slain in the camp. When Khwaja Haji saw the body, he immediately recognized that it was Haidar, though he was still not dead as he 'held up the head from the earth nothing but the last breath remained. He moved his eyes and gave up the ghost.' Haidar Dughlat was buried in the grand building at Andarkul which had once served as his dwelling place and was later converted into his memorial.

After this, the Mughals lost heart; they retreated to Inderkot, leaving the dead man to the mercy of his enemies. The Chaks wanted to mutilate Haidar Dughlat's body but Husain Magre and Saiyid Muhammad Baihaqi insisted on burying the body near the tomb of Sultan Zainul Abidin, and some of them protected it for a month. Having first buried the corpse, they went in pursuit of the fleeing Mughals to Inderkot which they defended for three days. On the fourth day, Muhammad Rumi loaded the cannon with copper coins and fired them on the enemy. Every one who was struck with them died.

Finally, Mirza Haidar's wife, popularly known as Khanmai, and her sister Khanji, could no longer tolerate these difficulties and told the Mughals that 'inasmuch as Mirza Haidar had departed from our midst, it would be better to make peace with the Kashmiris'. There was no hope of reinforcements or replenishment of provisions in the citadel. Having no option left, the Moghuls despatched Amir Khan to the Kashmiris to sue for peace.

The terms of surrender were negotiated and settled. Husain Magre's suggestion to put an end to the enmity with a fallen foe was magnanimously accepted. Qara Bahadur and all other captives were released. The Kashmiris, who had long awaited this situation gladly gave them an undertaking that they would not persecute the Mughals any more. When the gates of the fort were opened, the Kashmiris fell upon the treasury of Haidar Dughlat and plundered it taking away the 'beautiful and delicate garments it contained'. The Kashmiris also promised not to harrass the family of Mirza Haidar'. Some Mughals like Sabir Ali and others who passed through Ladakh were killed by the Ladakhis. The Mirza's family was taken to Srinagar and placed in the hands of Manuja. They were then sent via Pakli and Kabul to Kashghar. The Kashmiri chiefs divided the region among themselves. Daulat Chak received Deosar, Ghazi Khan took Wali, Yusuf Chak and Bahram Chak got Kamraj; Khwaja Haji took one lakh shawls. The government of that province fell into the hands of Idi Zaina who became the defacto ruler under Nazuk Shah, 'a kind of shadow of a King'.[38]

HAIDAR DUGHLAT AND THE MUGHALS

Haidar Dughlat had many good qualities which endeared him to each of his patrons. Loyalty was a trait which added lustre to his character, as his deep devotion to Sultan Said and Babur well illustrates. At one point, Babur was 'displeased and irritated' when the Mirza asked for leave to go to Andijan to join the service of Sultan Said, despite his deep attachment to Babur. The Mirza left for Andijan though he recorded his repentance later on thus: 'In my childish folly I did not (as was my duty to do) pay attention to the Emperor's consent'.

When Sultan Said brought up the issue of Aiman Khwaja and (being ill advised by Ali Taghai) was somewhat sceptical about Mirza's faithfulness and his support, the latter referred to the equal relationship which had existed between him and each one of them (Khan and Khwaja) and assured the Khan about his personal loyalty in these words: 'Rather in there, is the advantage on our side that I have been in your service for twenty-three years, and you have always singled me out for fatherly care and brotherly love. How then shall I exchange the Khan's cause for that of the Sultan? I will forward any measure that may be for the benefit of your (Said Khan's) state by all the means in my power.' These assurances were reinforced with actions.

Courage and bravery were other qualities which Mirza Haidar possessed. Even when he was too young to actually take part in the fighting, he appeared on the battleground with his small retinue to assist Babur, who ordered that Mirza should get the first *juldu* (reward for this bravery) of his retinue. When he conquered Kashmir, he continued to maintain shadow rulers for some time, presumably for two reasons: both to keep himself free for campaigns and, secondly, to emulate the traditions of Timur whose gallantry had greatly inspired him. Besides, the Kashmiris could be better controlled by their own ruler rather than by an alien. When Humayun conquered Qandahar and Kabul with the help of Persian forces, Haidar Dughlat adopted another strategy. He invited him to occupy the places he had conquered which could serve 'as an impregnable position from which the Emperor might pour down his troops for the conquest of India'. Abul Fazl says that Haidar Dughlat even read the *khutba* and had the coin struck in Humayun's name—a fact borne out by the numismatic evidence.[39]

Yet his attachment to the two ruling houses brought two different responses. While Yunus Khan (Mirza Haidar's maternal grandfather) himself loved and patronized him, his two sons failed to inculcate the same confidence and affection towards themselves which their father had created in his protege. For the house of Timur, however, his great achievements were a routine affair. For instance, the conquest of Kashmir, one of Mirza Haidar's achievements, won exuberant praise from Yunus Khan but little appreciation from the Mughals who considered it to be merely a routine conquest on the ruler's behalf. Haidar Dughlat, however, sufficiently understood and valued his successful endeavour which was undoubtedly another feather in Mirza Haidar's cap. Haidar quoted his patron Yunus Khan's words to reiterate its significance and to glorify his achievements in the following words: 'Hitherto no one of the conquering Khakans, from the time of Chingiz Khan to the present day, has laid the hand of dominion upon the collar of Kashmir. But now, by Haidar Dughlat's laudable and strenuous efforts, the pulpits of Kashmir have been decorated with the titles of the Mughal Khakans. The Sultans of Kashmir who in former times owed allegiance to none and the governors who were dependent on them alone are now subject to the Mughal Khans. For this mighty achievement, not only I, but all the Moghal Khans owe you a debt of gratitude, as do also my nobles and especially my own children for whom such a glorious name has been won.'[40]

In the Mughal sources, however, Haidar's memorable victory was just another addition to many other indirect achievements of Humayun. The difficulties and pain suffered by Mirza during this campaign are brushed aside in a few sentences. Even the fact that the significance of the conquest of Kashmir was greatly enhanced because it happened at a time when Humayun was without a territory to fall back upon did not stir the Mughal historians to record its importance. For instance, in his *Ain*, Abul Fazl casually remarks that 'during his stay in Kashghar, Mirza Haidar had accompanied the son of Sultan Said on several expeditions to Kashmir and had thus acquired some knowledge of the people and the state of that province. During his stay at Agra, he tried on several occasions to persuade Humayun to take possession of Kashmir. When Humayun retreated to Lahur after his second defeat at the hands of Sher Shah, he sent Mirza Haidar with a small corps to Kashmir.'

With a sense of superiority, Gulbadan Begam also records that it was His Majesty (Humayun) who had appointed Haidar Dughlat to conquer Kashmir. Since Sher Shah was thundering in the vicinity and Humayun was in a difficult situation, he wished to go to Kashmir. However, news of Haidar Dughlat's victory had not yet reached the Emperor, and the nobles counselled that if the place was not conquered, 'it would—with Sher Khan in Lahore—be a very difficult time'. Haidar Dughlat, however, says that Humayun was unable to reach Kashmir (in spite of his endeavours) as 'he could induce no one to accompany him'. Hindal Mirza, Yadgar Nasir Mirza and others carried him off to Thatta and Bhakkar to attack Mirza Shah Husain. Subsequent events prove that it was merely the far-sightedness of Mirza Dughlat which in the long run saved Humayun from a very difficult situation, even though he could not provide timely help to Humayun. It seems that Haidar Dughlat was unaware of the developments which took place thereafter as he says that, being deserted by Yadgar Nasir Mirza and Sultan Kasim Husain and having suffered 'endless hardships and incalculable misfortune, Humayun passed to Irak, but up to the present time it is not known what has become of him'. Kamran, however, remained at Kabul and 'in despair from the buffetings of fortune'. It is clear that Mirza Haidar Dughlat's loyalty to Humayun continued even in the days of his adversity.[41]

Although Haidar Dughlat held Humayun responsible for the fatal mistakes leading to his fall, he considered him to be a sovereign 'than whom there have been few greater Sultans' and prayed that he have 'similar well-being and wisdom' as his father, Babur, who had mounted the throne of Samarqand after having suffered ruinous defeats, yet later on 'all the world felt his influence, while his name remains among the immortal Sultans'. This veneration for Humayun persisted throughout his life. In 1548, Haidar Dughlat had sent a supplicatory letter through Samandar, a servant of Humayun, when Humayun was at Ushtargram. Since Samandar brought this letter to Humayun, it is surmised that the Mirza's letter was in response to one from Humayun. The Mirza's letter was full of praise of the climate, flowers and fruits of Kashmir and 'pressing entreaties that Humayun should visit that lovely region'. In addition to this, there were 'fitting expressions about the conquest of Hindustan and incitements were held to the world conquering genius'. Haidar Dughlat's sincerity was highly appreciated and Humayun 'sent a diploma of victory full of favourable expressions to the Mirza. Humayun also mentioned therein his secret designs upon India'.[42]

While the role of Shah Tahmasp in the recovery of Humayun's lost throne in India is recorded, Haidar Dughlat's supportive attitude and selfless devotion is nowhere mentioned. No detailed account of his extraordinary achievements have been given by any of the Mughal chroniclers. His family continued to be included among the Oughlans (Khanazad) and gained no special place in the upper hierarchy of the Mughal ruling group. Very few assignments were bestowed upon the Dughlats. Haidar's cousin Qara Bahadur mayhave been chosen for the conquest of Kashmir merely because he 'was acquainted with the country'.

Either due to Haidar's well-known loyalty to Humayun or due to his own sensitive and responsible nature, Akbar is said to have given him due importance. On his return from Kashmir on 31 October 1592, Akbar halted at Andarkul to pay his respects to the departed soul.[43]

HAIDAR DUGHLAT'S PERSONALITY AND ACHIEVEMENTS

Haidar Dughlat possessed immense courage, physical and mental vigour, an adventurous spirit, generosity and magnanimity. He was an excellent warrior, but at the same time humane and affectionate. Nevertheless, he is said to have lacked Babur's far-sightedness, sagacity and political wisdom and, therefore, lost what he had gained with great difficulty. In assessing Haidar Dughlat's character and achievements, the compulsions he had to face and difficulties of his situation should not be overlooked. Given his limited opportunities, his performance is not dismal. Haidar Dughlat showed his ability in administration. The reconquest of lost territories restored his kingdom what it had been during the reign of Sultan Zainul

Abidin. As a good ruler, he did his best for the development of trade, agriculture and industry.

In Kashmir, Mirza Haidar Dughlat 'ruled as an absolute king for ten years, although he ordered that the *khutba* be read and coins be struck in the name of Humayun'. Although he retained a nominal ruler Nazuk Shah, he enjoyed full authority over civil and military affairs. He created his own nobility and appointed governors of his own choice. Rajaori was given to Muhammad Nazir and Nasir Ali, Pakli to Mullah Abdullah, and Little Tibet (Baltistan) to Mulla Qasim. Mulla Husain was appointed governor of Great Tibet (Ladakh). Like Timur, Mirza Haidar dreamt of an Empire, where men of talent could assemble to embellish the court, and he fulfilled his aim.[44]

Haidar Dughlat was well-versed in the art of administration even before he took over Kashmir. While still in his teens, he had been exposed to all kinds of experiences, to hardships, and to the vicissitudes of fortune. This bred in him the qualities of understanding, steadfastness and perseverance. The insecurity strengthened his instinct for survival, sharpened his physical and mental capabilities, his abilities to seize every opportunity which presented itself before him. Although he did not have a royal background nor an ancestral kingdom, his patrons bestowed upon him atleast some facility and possibility of progress.

The Mongol ruler Sultan Said Khan of Moghulistan guided him at every important stage of his life. He entered the court of Said Khan in September 1512 and 'remained in his service till the Khan's death on 24 June 1533. During this period, the Mirza was 'distinguished by his regard and liberality'.[45] The description given by the Mirza of his life at court is highly graphic and informative as the following excerpt shows:

'From that date to the day of the Khan's death, in Zulhijja 939, I remained constantly in his service, and was all the while distinguished by his regard and liberality. In short, until he conferred upon me the rank of *kurkani*, I was never absent from him. At night, whereever his bed was spread, one was also spread for my convenience, at his side. At royal banquets, the right hand of my fortune was joined to the left hand of the Khan's favour. Whenever a consultation was held, my uncle was sure to be at the head of the meeting [*sar-i-daftar*], but he gave me precedence over my uncle; nay more, he did so at the request of my uncle, who used frequently to point out to the Khan that [although] I was only the son of his brother, still he recognized that my precedence over him was not only proper, but necessary. When he rode out, I always rode at his side; and when he went hunting, he used to instruct me in the sport [and initiate me into its secrets and subtleties]. He used to lead the hunt himself, for he was a keen sportsman. He never allowed me out of his sight, but used to persuade me to go hunting with him, and if ever I showed any reluctance, he would compel me to enjoy it. He used to set me various tasks to do, at the same time pointing out what benefit I should derive [from doing them], and would say: 'Until young men begin to perform duties, they can never gain experience. [Otherwise] in important affairs and in large assemblies, in mosques and in the battlefield, where the leaders of the people, whether Khakans or Sultans or Amirs, take part, they become confused, and meet with opposition from their people. But when young men practise themselves in the business of their elders, they gain insight into the particulars of their various duties, and in all such matters as wars and the like, they acquire a certain confidence. Their self-reliance gains for them the esteem of the people, which strengthens their authority. In the performance of these duties they learn to recognize their own merits and demerits, and to judge of the best modes of action.'

'While in the service of my father and my uncle, I had these principles indelibly engraved upon my heart, and they used to make me perform numerous duties, that I might turn the advantages derived from them to the best possible account. What I learnt from my elders I now am teaching you, that you, in turn, may also profit by it.'

'Till the age of twenty-four, I was employed in every kind of service, and all that the Khan gave me to do, both great things and small, I carried out single-handed. But if, even in the councils of the Amirs in which I had my special place, an opportunity of some service presented itself to me the Khan would forbid my performing it saying "in the battlefield you must remember your rank, so that you may not fall in the estimation of the people". When I was between twenty-four and twenty-five years of age, he bade me desist from all these service, and said: "All that I have given you to do, you have done well. Now you can return to your favourite pursuits." Thereafter, till the age of thirty, he entrusted to me the affairs of the army. But he caused me to be attended by men of judgement and experienced Amirs, and instructed me never to deviate from what they considered right, but to follow them in all matters. When several campaigns [*lashkar*] had been carried through in this way, he gave me leave to speak my mind in debates and plans of action. Up to the age of thirty I had never received this permission, nor had I ever spoken in an assembly, but had always remained silent. After sanction was accorded to me, however, I spoke much, and whenever I used to speak in the assemblies, the Khan would say to me: "Explain this matter more fully, give us your proofs and your reasonings." If I explained myself well and said what was fitting, he would praise me and desire the people to applaud; and when I did not say exactly what was right, he would add: "What he means to say is so-and-so"; and thus would improve my words and satisfy the Amirs.'

'When some time had passed in this way, he said to me: "I have now learnt to rely on you thoroughly"; he then entrusted to me the entire management of the army and the direction of the government, giving me, in these matters, absolute freedom of action, together with sanction to issue mandates and *firmans*.'

On several occasions, Mirza had the opportuinty to handle the law-and-order situation and to organize administrative affairs on behalf of his patrons, Sultan Said Khan and Babur. During the turmoil in Badakhshan, when Khan Aba Bakr planned to invade the territory and his (Sultan Said's) own son's flight forced him to leave Kashghar, Mirza Haidar was left in Kashghar, where he 'busied himself with the management of all that was important in the affairs of that country'. He gained a great deal of experience of administration and state affairs were gained by him in this process. When Khan Said himself gone to Kashghar 'in order to gather all the people together, and to see if any agreement could be brought about between themselves and the Uzbegs', he left Mirza Haidar 'in Moghulistan to ensure law and order among the inhabitants'. Haidar remained with Rashid Khan till the Khan's return.[46]

This close association with state affairs gave Haidar Dughlat keen insights into the strategies of political expediency which stood him in good stead later. As ruler of Kashmir, Haidar Dughlat seized the opportunity to develop friendly relations with neighbouring regions to ensure peace, during his short reign of a decade. In 1547, when an ambassador came to the Mirza from Kashghar, Mirza went accompanied by some of his nobles as far as Lar to meet them. In 1550, Mirza Haidar sent presents of saffron to Islam Shah of through Khwaja Shams Mughal. Islam Shah returned the ambassadors and sent presents of yarn, silken cloth and precious goods through his own envoy. Mirza Haidar in turn sent back Yasin 'laden with shawls and saffron to Islam Shah'.[47] This attitude helped him in maintaining peace in the region.

Inspired by the example of his brother-in-law—the Uzbeg ruler Ubaidullah Khan Uzbeg—whom he idolised, Haidar Dughlat had requested his spiritual guide Maulana Muhammad Qazi (d. 1515) to prepare certain rules of conduct for kings. It was at his request that a moral treatise was also compiled by Shaikh Shahabuddin Mahmud Khwaja Nura. These books were prepared primarily and exclusively for his own use. The religious and moral ethos of Kashmir had left an indelible stamp upon his mind and shaped his outlook in such a way that his policy could easily be termed, even by medieval chroniclers, as tinged with orthodoxy or even bigotry.

His capacity to rule, to manage political and administrative affairs was not thwarted by the intriguing nature of companions such as Ali Taghai, nor was his vision of an ideal state ever blurred. Beset by the constant conspiracies of his Kashmiri and Moghul followers, torn by the conflicts of his own emotional nature, Haidar Dughlat was faced with numerous challenges. Despite all this he proved himself to be a good ruler.

Abul Fazl says that during ten years of his rule in Kashmir, Mirza Haidar Dughlat 'applied himself to its administration and clothed that charming land, but of desolate (*hukmi kharabi dasht*) appearance with cities and civilization. He sent for artists and craftsmen from all quarters and laboured for its renown and prosperity. Especially Music was in brisk demand and varieties of instruments were introduced. In short, the outward condition of that country, that is, its worldly state, acquired solidity. The villa known as Bagh-i Safa was also created by him.' According to Jahangir, Mirza Haidar's court was celebrated for its skilled musicians.[48]

He was a man of imagination, and known for his innovative and refined experiments in food and dress. He had immense admiration for Zainul Abidin, whom he emulated in every sphere of his activity. Like other Turco-Mongol and Timurid rulers, he looked for talent in every part of his world, inviting craftsmen and artists from all over the region. He also revived the arts which had suffered a setback due to incessant civil wars and disturbances.

Haidar patronized men of learning and arranged for the education of children both in the countryside and in towns. As Abul Fazl has noted, he was a lover of the arts and patronized musicians, poets, architects, learned men and painters. In Central Asian fashion, numerous mosques were constructed in Srinagar with bath-houses which kept the prayer rooms so warm in winter that even in very cold weather people could pray and relax there. Magnificent gardens were laid out by him in Andarkul. He is said to have invented new architectural motifs and introduced new types of doors and windows. His contribution in the development of saffron cultivation had been recorded by the historians.

But Haidar Dughlat's reputation and permanent fame rests on the books he wrote and the contribution he made to the development of the fine arts. Like other princes of his age, Mirza Haidar was a prolific writer and an excellent poet. He wrote prose and poetry in both Persian and Turkish with equal ease and competence. He compiled his *Tarikh-i-Rashidi* in chaste and eloquent Persian, and wrote another book the *Jahan Nama*, a metrical treatise on geography in Turki, which he is reported to have prepared during his stay in Badakhshan in 1508-9.

In the opinion of Ahmad Razi, a critic writing in the sixteenth century, Haidar Dughlat's *Tarikh-i-Rashidi* 'enjoys universal esteem'. The reader is immediately enchanted by the lucidity, frankness and pleasant style of writing and is engrossed by the recital of rapid events, the day-to-day experiences of an adventurer, a soldier of fortune who was in the thick of the fray and whose description of the hazards he faced in childhood is as absorbing as the adventurous exploits of his youth are thrilling. The author shares all his woes with his readers with the same intensity as he does his joys and his frivolous activities, his happy moments and moments of sober reflection. Haidar Dughlat was greatly influenced by the Arabic style of writing history in which truthfulness and *usul-i isnad* are as important as the descriptions of a geopolitical and socio-economic nature. The *Tarikh-i-Rashidi* is in fact a fine blend of autobiography, memoir and with his readers of history. The author, makes no effort to be diplomatic in presenting facts. The work, therefore, belongs neither to the category of 'intentional records' nor to official biographies.

While admitting that 'the rank and dignity which historians attain to, is not so high that one should have a craving for it', Mirza Haidar nevertheless fully realized the significance of history and its importance as a subject, its value for the reader, the writer and the teacher. Emphasizing the importance of this subject from ancient times, he highlighted its sanctity by adding that one of the three portions of the Holy Book deals with 'historical matter, such as the lives of the Prophets. Thus, we see, one-third of this book is intended to teach the history of past generations; and therein lies the clearest proof of the excellence of the science of history. Moreover, all are agreed concerning the utility of this science; and most nations, nay, all the peoples of the world, have studied it, and have collected and handed down traditions of their forefathers, of which they give ample proofs and upon which they rely.'[49]

It was not only a genuine urge which made Mirza Haidar compile his valuable history of the Mongols. There were some additional and very valid reasons for his venture. History writing was one of the most popular professions of the medieval age: not only did it satisfy the literary thirst of men of letters but it was equally appealing to the sober-minded intellectuals, the politically-conscious elite, or the curious commoner. It was an essential exercise for the Mongols as there was no information or historical record giving their own point of view regarding events which sometimes clearly damaged their position or spoiled their image as rulers, conquerors or as human beings.

The accounts available for understanding Mongol history have come down to us usually from hostile sources which claimed to have 'suffered greatly' at the hands of the requisite nuisance of medieval times, i.e. the army. These works exaggerated the destruction caused by the Mongol army, reducing the position of Chingiz to the most 'dreaded destroyer' of civilizations. Although there were Mongol works also, namely *Notse Tobtso* (*The Secret History of Mongols*) and *Altan Topchi* or *Altan Daptar*, these were written in the Mongolian language and were therefore inaccessible the posterity. Besides, the first work was (as the name itself suggests) kept a secret for quite a long time even after its translation into Chinese. Although the Mongols had a particular kind of script called *phags-pa*, their official records were maintained, and even the laws of Chingiz Khan were compiled in the Uighur language, perhaps because of the grandeur and sanctity attached to the Turks and the awe in which they were held by the less sophisticated Mongols. Even the genealogy of the Mongols is supposedly constructed by describing them as the descendants of Alonqova, or belonging to the same stock as the Turks. Under these circumstances, some retelling of Mongol history was immediately needed.

Several works and general histories prepared during the medieval period contain detailed accounts of the Mongols, although no exclusive work dealing with the Mongols and their history was written in Persian, either under Chingiz Khan or his early successors. Mirza Ulugh Beg had compiled a history of the Mongols titled *Tarikh-i ulus-i Arabi* in the first half of fifteenth century, which has been lost. An anonymous manuscript preserved in the British Museum seems to be a history of the four *ulus* and tempts the reader to believe that it could be the same work reported to have been lost. Yet, it is in effect another version of the *Tarikh-i-Rashidi* (or the *Tarikh-i Hafiz Abru*) since the study of and picking up facts from other sources is a common feature of history writing in those days.

The dearth of written material on the subject could have grave consequences. As Haidar Dughlat laments: 'For much time has already passed since the Khakans of the Moghuls were driven out from the towns of the civilized world, and have had to content themselves with dwellings in the desert. On this account, they have written no history of themselves but based their ancestral records upon oral traditions. At this present date 951 (AD 1544), there remains not one among them who knows these traditions, and my boldness in attempting this difficult work is due to the consideration that, did I not make the venture, the story of the Moghul Khakans would be obliterated from the pages of the world's history.'

Haidar Dughlat wrote the first part of his historical narrative *Tarikh-i-Rashidi* in Kashmir during the year 1544-5. Further additions were made between March 1546 and February 1547. In this work, the prolegomena of Yazdi's *Zafar Nama* have been extensively used. The second part is said to have been compiled earlier, i.e. in 1541-2. The *Tarikh-i-Rashidi* is said to have been completed in February 1547 in Kashmir five years after Haidar Dughlat ascended the throne of that 'paradise on earth', though events of later years are also found in it.

It is of great interest that Haidar Dughlat should have taken upon himself the gigantic task of compiling a history of the Moghuls and their Khans which he recognized fully well 'can be of little interest to any but the Moghuls themselves'. He admits: 'My object is not to extoll my own merit, but simply to write a memoir, that the history of the Mughals may not be entirely forgotten; and that if by chance, any of the Mughal Khans should wish to know his genealogy, he shall be able to find it in this book.' Fully conscious of the fact that 'the Moghuls have become a most isolated and paltry people,' and 'remote and insignificant of tribes' and that none but 'a Moghul could be interested in this history', Haidar had 'not shrunk from doing the best' in his power, 'to compile this work with all his professed lack of literary capacity.'

This attitude shows how strongly Haidar Dughlat must have felt about the failing fortunes of his kith and kin. It was certainly not in his power to resuscitate the dying dynasty, but he could at least fulfil his duty of recording the history of the Mongols to keep their name alive. Haidar Dughlat's modesty makes him desist from offering the standard apology for mistakes or blunders in his work as he believes that his 'book is full of mistakes from the beginning to the end.'[50]

Haidar Dughlat laments that when 'the Mughal power was high, many eminent men flourished and some wrote their people's history. . . .' In his time 'no vestige of these men survives and none knows anything concerning them. For during this long lapse of time, all have become strangers to the old customs and ways of learning. Since the conversion of the Mughals to Islam, more especially no history of them has been written. But the learned men of Transoxiana, Khurasan and Iraq who have written the annals for their own kings, have made mention of the Moghuls just where it had suited the context, while they have paid no attention to them when not connected with their own country.'

Among these histories he mentioned the *Jamiut Tawarikh* of Rashiduddin, the *Tarikh-i Guzida* of Mustawfi, *Zafar Nama* of Yazdi, *Tarikh-i Manzuma* of Abdur Razzaq, and the *Ulus-i Arabi* of Ulugh Beg, and remarks: 'Among these, I have sought carefully for any mention of the Mongol Khaqans but found nothing very connected (*batartib*).' From his early years, Haidar Dughlat 'was much drawn to the study of the history' of his forefathers and in those days 'there was still alive some of the Moghul amirs and nobles (some over one hundred years of age, some under). But it never occurred to my father or my uncles to commit to writing what they had heard concerning the Khaqans, from their parents, and other trustworthy sources. And now they have all been dead for some time.' On this account, Haidar Dughlat 'resolved to prepare an account of the Mongol after their conversion to Islam basing my facts upon histories and reliable traditions, in addition to what I have myself witnessed in my own times'.[51] . . . 'I . . . notwithstanding my ignorance and want of skill, felt it my duty to undertake this difficult task.' He was particularly conscious of the fact that the history of the later Mongols had for some reason been altogether ignored. Sharafuddin Yezdi had compiled the valuable prolegomena to the *Zafar Nama,* comprising a history of the Moghuls and their Khaqans, from Chingiz Khan till Tughlaq Timur Khan, whose name and achievements however flickered only 'where context required it.'

Haidar Dughlat had, therefore, started his work with the reign of Tughlaq Timur Khan. This particular exordium he chose for three reasons: that the earlier history (before Tughlaq Timur) was already written in 'other excellent history, e.g. the Zafarnama' and its repetition 'would be like digging a well on the margin of the Euphrates'; that no other ruler had attained so great a degree of pre-eminence, or acquired so extensive a dominion as Tughlaq Timur Khan; and finally, that he was one of the Moghul Khans who was converted to Islam, and that during his reign the Moghuls, 'having withdrawn their necks from the yoke of unbelief entered into that state of freedom in Islam enjoyed by all Musulmans. For these reasons, this history is dedicated to his illustrious name and his most noble memory.'[52]

It is of interest that despite such exuberant expressions of appreciation and regard for Tughlaq Timur, Haidar Dughlat named his book *Tarikh-i-Rashidi*. For this he gives three reasons, only the third of which seems to be valid. The first two reasons are indicative of his deep emotional attachment to Tughlaq Timur Khan, but the third one shows the compulsions which forced him to dedicate it to some other person. The three reasons are that 'it was Maulana Arshaduddin who converted Tughlaq

Timur to Islam; secondly, that although before the time of Tughlaq Timur, Barak Khan and after Barak Khan, Kabak Khan had become Musulmans, neither these Khaqans nor the Moghul people had a knowledge of the *Rushd*, or 'True Road to Salvation'. Their natures had remained base, and they had continued on the road that leads to Hell. But a full knowledge of the *Rushd* fell to the lot of the enlightened Tughlaq Timur and his happy people. And in as much as the beginning of this history will deal with this matter, the suitability of the title *Rashidi* is evident.

Thirdly, since at the present date, Abdur Rashid, the last of the Mughal Khaqans, is reigning and since this book has been dedicated and written for him, the reason for the title *Tarikh-i-Rashidi* is apparent. While showing his great love for Tughlaq Timur who was his 'only instructor' in 'most of the pursuits and studies', Haidar Dughlat clearly and frankly admits: 'Although I have received from his sons the worst possible treatment, I will return them good for evil; and whether the Khan's son (Abdur Rashid) accept this small work or reject it, I will all the same, dedicate it to him, in order that he may have a remembrance of me and that the world may have a remembrance of him. And the title of the book is derived from his illustrious name.'

The combination of aggrieved expressions and expedient determination to dedicate the work to Abdur Rashid, indicates Haidar Dughlat's diplomatic skill, his regard for protocol, propriety, and the expediency that governed his emotional but noble soul.[53]

Although some valuable works were produced on Mongol history several decades later, at the court of the Ilkhanids of Iran, chroniclers like Rashiduddin Fazlullah, Banakiti, Juvaini, and others have surveyed events from the vantage point of the reigning Khagan Ogedei, presenting them in a very derogatory manner, presumably to boost the image of Touloui and his family. Other works on the Mongols suffer from one defect or the other. For example, Fakhruddin Banakiti's work *Tarikhi Banakiti* is a general history and gives only a sketchy account of the Mongols. Although *Tarikh-i Wassaf* is extremely valuable for its rich material and useful supplements, its language is florid, hyperbolical, and studded with Arabic phrases and puns which makes its study interesting but difficult. Other books like *Rauzat-us-Safa Habib-us-Siyar* are by-and-large remakes of already available information, though they often supplement them. The Travelogues fill the gap though they have to be studied with much care and circumspection. The historians whose accounts present the Mongols in their true colours, highlighting at least some of their merits alongside their demerits, include Minhajus-siraj Aljuzjani and Hasan Sijzi, besides

Babur and Abul Fazl who had appreciated Chingiz Khan exclusively.

Haidar Dughlat's book thus fills a lacuna: many areas of Central Asia which remained historically obscure were brought to the surface of knowledge by his efforts, e.g. his description of Kashghar. Although he does not conceal the fact that he had extracted certain portions from the *Jamiut Tawarikh* (which he calls *Mujammil ut Tawarikh*) of Rashiduddin, he had added considerably to the information already available on Kashghar. He also included in his work the first part of Yazdi's *Zafar Nama*.

Haidar's *Tarikh* consists of varied kinds of information gathered from different sources. Before writing his history, he seems to have had consulted people extensively about the subject. Sometimes, he forgets these details. Regarding Kashghar, for instance, he records: 'I have questioned some of those who have seen something of that country but I can recall nothing of what they told me.'[54] At other times, he puts down the facts immediately.

Haidar Dughlat's History covers a very large area which extended from Western Turkistan, Bukhara, Farghana, province of Semirech Kashghar Zungaria (Ili), Eastern Turkistan, Ladakh, Tibet, Baltistan, Gilgit and the nearby regions of Chitral, Wakhan Badakhshan, Afghanistan, Kashmir and northern India, containing references to even more distant regions. Haidar's work differs from other contemporary writings in that he restricts himself exclusively to the Mongols. Other personalities or events which are discussed by him appear only in the context of the Mongols. Babur's account of India is occasionally referred to as Babur (who denounced the Mongols but praised Chingiz Khan's achievements) was very much part of the Mongol line, on his mother's side.

Haidar Dughlat has great command over language; his book is full of candid descriptions and felicitous expressions, as well as puns and flourishes. For instance, commenting upon the three nobles, Haidar, Shah Muhammad and Baba Sultan who served Sultan Said for nine years, Haidar wrote: 'Like the three dots under the letter, *'sīn'* in Said, we were never separated nor did we leave his service on any pretext. Our worldly goods we shared in common and were participators in each other's praise and blame.' Kashghar is described thus: 'it is a sort of purgatory between the paradise of Towns and the Hell of Deserts'. The usage of His excellence in writing is best depicted in proper phrases, words studded in the most careful and well thought out manner and cryptic sentences carrying vast meanings. His succint comment 'It was the season of Shaibani Khan's rise', brings alive the political scene very vividly. Referring to Shaibani's invitation to his father, Haidar Dughlat wrote of his father's 'safety being more slender than a spider's web'.[55]

Surprisingly, Dughlat chose to write his work in Persian, though in his time the Turkish language was widely read and valued in Central Asia, particularly after Ali Shir Navoi's literary attainments. Even Babur wrote his autobiography in Chaghtai Turkish. The motivating factor in choosing Persian was mainly the surroundings in which he was writing his book. In India, Turki was neither understood by the people, nor commonly used by the ruling family, despite the efforts of the Mughal rulers to teach this language to all their children. Gulbadan Begam, Bayazid Bayat, Mir Khwand, Khwand Mir, and other writers preferred Persian, which was the language of the elite in the region. The comment that Haidar Dughlat was 'using a foreing language, and it is for this reason, perhaps, that his style is wanting in the simplicity which characterizes that of Turki writers' needs reconsideration. Persian was more deeply rooted than Turki in Central Asia. Haidar Dughlat's Persian is not like that of Wassaf, Juvaini, Banakiti or Rashiduddin. His style is interesting but the language is simple which makes reading it a joyful experience.

The editor's criticism of Haidar Dughlat's 'loose usage of terms[56] and names of countries, people; weakness of chronology; and the looseness with which numbers and measurements are used and the want of systematic arrangement' are an exaggeration of occasional mistakes. Moreover, such characteristics were a common malady of medieval times. The loose usage found in other contemporary writers had created havoc with historical facts. Haidar Dughlat should in fact be credited with the honour of being the first chronicler who had tried to depict the history of the Mongols in the true perspective. Although his emotional attachment to his people was the main factor in inspiring him to compile this history, Haider cannot be blamed for habitual distortion or deliberate subjectivity. It is only human that Haidar Dughlat should pour forth his anger or shower praises when his emotion overcome him.

Haidar Dughlat's work has considerable significance for us. There are a few aspects of Mongol or Mughal history which have only been tuoched upon by Haidar Dughlat. There is for instance no detailed account of the reasons leading to Babur's surrender of Khanzada Khanam to Shaibani Khan. Babur himself refers to this event in the most cryptic manner saying that in those days of adversity, Khanzada Khanam fell into the hands of Shaibani Khan. Haidar Dughlat, however, gives the details (which are confirmed by Gulbadan Begam): Shaibani had demanded Khanzada

Khanam and Babur gave her up in ransom or in exchange for his own life and escaped.

Where Babur tried to gloss over the issue of his accepting Shiism, Haidar Dughlat gives a very detailed account of the events and circumstances leading to Babur's expulsion from Central Asia, which was primarily due to his association with the Persian Shah Ismail. Mirza Haidar has given a picturesque description of the joyful reception given to Babur and people's subsequent disenchantment with him on account of his affiliation with the Shah.[57]

The book also has very information on different aspects of the Central Asian social structure: its tribal organization, customs, traditions, food habits and so on. The fact that the Qazaqs continued their pastoral economy and cattle-breeding even when the Uzbegs, as stressed by Shaibani, graduated to a more settled pattern of life that is confirmed by Mirza Haidar. The best assessment of Qazaq life and culture is presented by Haidar Dughlat through the words of Kasim Khan: 'The Qazaqs are men of the desert, and here there is nothing in the way of riches or formalities. Our most costly possessions are our horses, our favourite food their flesh, our most enjoyable drink their milk and the products of it. In our country are no gardens or buildings. Our chief recreation is inspecting our herds.'[58] Similarly, the verdict that 'All the Mughals have become Musalmans but the Kirghiz are still infidels,' speaks volumes about the conditions of that age.[59]

Although epithets such as *Karawanas*, *Jetah*, *Kazaqs*, *Qauchin*, *Imak* are frequently mentioned in our sources, the *Tarikh-i-Rashidi* is one of the few works which provides explanations for these unfamiliar terms and titles. Sometimes Dughlat Haidar gives very specific information relating social structure and social groups. For instance, he refers to four classes in Kashghar and Khotan: namely the Tuman, Kuchin, Imak and the custodians of religion. On the other hand, the division of the horde has been described rather inaccurately. 'One of the four hordes', says he, 'is that of the Moghuls, who are divided into two branches, the Moghul and the Chaghatai. But these branches, on account of their mutual enmity, used to call each other by a special name, by way of depreciation. Thus the Chaghatais called the Mughals Jatah, while the Mughals called the Chaghatai Karawanah.'

While Ladakh is almost always mentioned as Tibet, certain other terms have been properly, explained by him, e.g. 'In the Turki language they called a *Karawul* (picqueter guard) '*Yazaq*'. In his account of Tibet and the custom of its people, he describes at length the Lamas, Shakia Muni, the tenets of their religion, the mode of salvation, philosophy and places of worship. The account of Kashmir is marked by some inaccuracies, although the geographical details are by and large correct and the architectural details, particularly his description of 151 temples reflects Mirza Haidar's knowledge of architecture. Many of his statements cannot however be trusted wholly as sometims his restricted access to places and limited knowledge about the world leads him to categorical make wrong statements. For example, he claims that jade is found in the rivers of Yarqand and Khotan, and that no trace of it 'is to be found in any other part of the world', though jade is to be found even in Burma, Western China and other places. Similarly, his surprising view that he never heard of the disease of *damgiri* outside Tibet, though the disease was common. Babur condemned the storms of dust and sand—the *aandhi* as if it was a new and painful experience for him. Haidar Dughlat, however, says that 'Although Hindustan is notorious for this phenomenon (*sifat*) yet in Kashghar it is still more prevalent.'[60]

Another defect is that Haidar Dughlat sometimes conceals facts and obscures the issues. Although he does mention that Sultan Abu Said had invited Yunus Khan and placed him on the throne, the fact that Yunus Khan's elder sister whom the Sultan had married only a little while earlier,[61] must have been the prime mover is ignored by him.

Haidar's faith in the will of God, predestination, etc., is reflected throughout his book. He writes, for example, 'But how excellent a thing it is that the Almighty has power to check the violent and, if he so wills it, to restrian the hand of the cruel; so that without his consent, the tyrant cannot touch a single hair of any man's head.' Again, 'Since the decree of the will of the Almighty had not been issued for my destruction but for my preservation, Shahi Beg Khan with all his boastings and power, was not able to touch one hair of the head of that helpless child whom he wished to kill.'[62]

The theme of punishment for evil deeds runs through Haidar Dughlat's work. In his view, Humayun 'had endured such suffering and misery as have fallen to the lot of few Emperors. . . . It is thus written in "Sunna": that when the affairs of a great ruler go to ruin, he is himself the cause. If, as is rarely the case, the ruler be spared these calamities, his escape must be certainly attributable to his good sense.'[63]

His history is not merely a collection of facts presented as history. He intervenes and gives his own assessment of events, and his own verdict on episodes. Describing the evil deeds of Abdur Rashid Khan—the Mongol ruler—he criticizes him for his intimacy and friendship with the Uzbeg

Shaiban, a former enemy, and for doing his best to exterminate the Uzbeg, Qazaqs who were old friends. All this, he declares, was 'base action'.[64] Haidar Dughlat has in fact been rated as a 'better historian' than Babur. His history 'carries with it a conviction of honesty', and he is by and large honest in assessing his own character. Giving an account of the end of Shah Muhammad Sultan (son of Mahmud Khan and grandson of Yunus), Haidar Dughlat refers to the reproaches showered upon him by his maternal aunts and their daughters, blaming him for disregard of his blood connection with Barlas which led to the death of Shah Muhammad. 'Such were the taunts and reproaches they poured on me; nevertheless fate willed that I should pay no attention to the true words of my relations. I returned falsehood for truth and would not hear of retaliations.'[65]

It is thought that Haidar Dughlat's good qualities 'were offset by his religious fanaticism. In his zeal to preserve orthodox Islam, he banned Shiism and the Shafaite school. Haidar Dughlat had apparently extracted a decree from the Indian *ulama* that the Nurbakhsh Shias were heretics and their suppression and even destruction was justified if they refused to accept the teaching of Abu Hanifa. Large-scale persecution and the murder of many of their leaders angered a vast section of Kashmiris. The other Sufi orders were also banned on the grounds that the Sufis led immoral lives, ate and drank forbidden things, interpreted dreams, claimed to produce miracles and prostrated themselves before one another. In his anxiety to introduce and confine everyone to his own idea of religion, Haidar Dughlat lost much popular support. The Kashmiri nobles particularly disliked this disregard of individual faith and joined hands to plan his overthrow.[66]

Although it cannot be denied that, like other Central Asians, Haidar Dughlat was an orthodox Sunni Muslim of the Hanafite school, he had also inherited the legacy of liberal traditions. In the beginning, Haidar Dughlat was extraordinarily kind towards the followers of the Nurbakhshia sect, perhaps because the Mongol rulers generally respected the saints, and attached equal importance to all religions 'eschewing bigotry and preference of one religion over another'. Besides, political expediency also necessitated close contact with religious divines who had a great following and whose verdict was respected by the common man. Like Timur, Babur, and others, Haidar Dughlat also paid a visit to the tomb of Mir Shamsuddin with the fervour of a devotee. The followers of the Nurbakhshia sect including Regi Chak were highly respected.

The revolt of Regi Chak, however, made him realize once again that the Chingizide principle of the oneness of religions was to be replaced by that of uniformity of religion, if the Kashmir region was to be held and governed by him strongly.[67]

Exaggerated stories of Mirza Haidar's bigotry have been spread to malign him. It seems that, like Ghazan Khan (who gave up his staunch faith in Buddhism and embraced Islam with fervour simply to win over his Muslim subjects), Mirza was also forced by the exigencies of the situation to take to orthodoxy. To please the orthodox section and gain popularity among them so as to perserve his rule in Kashmir, he acceped the advice of Maulana Jamal and Shaikh Umar and banned the Nurbakhshia order. Even the tomb of Shamsuddin was destroyed. In 1545, Hazrat Rishi was put to death. Several Nurbakhshi saints (like Sufi Daud and Mulla Haji Khatib) were either executed or, like Qazi Mir Ali, were exiled and their homes destroyed. Shaikh Shamsuddin's son, Shaikh Daniyal, who was a pious and highly respected man in Kashmir also fell a victim to, Mirza's wrath. His trusted lieutenant, Mulla Abdullah, had persuaded him to spare Daniyal as his execution was likely to boomerang on the Sultan. But this wise counsel was brushed aside with the confident assertion that such a step would ensure the stability, prosperity and well-being of the kingdom.[68] Shaikh Daniyal, who had fled to Skardu, was summoned back in 1549 and imprisoned. On 14 March 1550 charges of reviling the first three caliphs were brought against him, and he was hanged on the strength of *fatwas* given by Qazi Ibrahim, Qazi Habib, and Qazi Abdul Ghafur. The followers of the Nurbakhshia order took his head and body and later buried in the tomb of his father.[69]

Mirza Haidar's hasty and unwise decision on this point proved disastrous. His own companions, Malik Idi Zaina and Malik Muhammad Naji themselves Shias were pained by this ruthless persecution of their co-religionists. Others like Nazuk Shah, Husain Magre, and Khwaja Haji also disliked such inhuman acts. They were already angered by Haidar Dughlat's haughtiness and favouritism of his kinsmen, the Mongols.

Haidar Dughlat's attitude towards Islam was actually that of the average Muslim who offers prayes, keeps the fasts, is afraid of God and fearful of the Day of Judgement. His orthodoxy is indeed a matter of conviction with him where tinge of bigotry unintentionally appears. He says categorically: 'Of those Moghuls who were not Musulmans, I have not mentioned more than the names; for an infidel, though he attains to the splendour of Jamshed and Zohak is not worthy of having his life commemorated.'[70]

He claimed to have waged holy wars. Those who are acquainted with the medieval sources and political strategies of medieval rulers know the precise significance of holy wars. Although it cannot be denied that Haidar frequently expressed religious sentiments, these stem more from the tenor of the age and political exigencies than with his own individual beliefs. Babur says that during his later years (in or about 1527) , Haidar Dughlat became an orthodox Muslim who 'lived lawfully' (*taib*) and had 'found the right way (*tariqa*)'.[71]

Haidar was born and bred in Cenral Asia at a time when Sufism was the most popular philosophy and way of life. He himself records that it was customary for every prince in those days to have one spiritual guide. The most popular saint in those days was Hazrat Maulana Qazi who 'was living in Farghana and all the amirs of every degree used to wait upon him and profit by the blessing of his converse.' Haidar himself dutifully and happily 'waited on him frequently and he continued to shower' upon Mirza the 'same kindly favour as he had done when Haidar was a child in Uratippa.'[72] It was this connection that Haidar valued most. The question of his personal hatred for Sufis or Sufism in general, therefore, does not arise.

On the other hand, Haidar Dughlat gives a very horrifying description of the sect of Chiragh Kush (Ismailis?). His hatred for their tenets resulted in his taking the extreme step of religious genocide—a symptom of imperial heurosis. A person who since his birth had breathed Sufism in it can not ignore it. The information provided by the chroniclers regarding Haidar Dughlat's bigotry and the hostile perspectives of the subjugated should not be overlooked. But if such facts are put forward by family historians, the matter undoubtedly carries some grain of truth.

NOTES

1. Haidar Dughlat, *Tarikhi Rashidi* (*TR*).
2. Amin Ahmad Razi, *Haft Iqlim*, vol. II, p. 368. Eng. tr. by Denison Ross, Patna, 1972, pp. 75, 125, 133, 294, also see Introduction, i-xxvii.
3. Babur, *Babur Nama* (*BN*), pp. 21-2; *TR*, p. 294.
4. *TR*, 125, 133, 210-12; also see Introduction, i-xxvii.
5. Ibid., p. 210-12.
6. Muhibbul Hasan, *Kashmir under the Sultans*, Calcutta, 1959, 125.
7. *TR*, 80, 125-33, 161, 207, 210-12, 341; Gulbadan Begam, *Humayun Nama* (*HN*) Eng. tr. by Beveridge, Delhi, 1972, 97.
8. Ibid.
9. *TR*, 205-9, 215, 228.
10. Ibid., 157-8, 205-9, 215, 277-9.
11. Ibid.
11. Ibid., 207-9.

12. Ibid., 423-4, 437; *BN*, Turkish text, 10-11, Eng. tr. by Beveridge.
13. *TR*, 228-30; *BN*, Turkish text, 10-11.
14. *TR*, 3-4.
15. Ibid., 141-2; *Haft Iqlim*, II, 368.
16. *TR*, 417.
17. Ibid., 417-21.
18. *TR*, 423. There is a controversy regarding the date of Mirza Haidar's departure. The date given by Abul Fazl is not correct.
19. Haidar Malik, *Tarikh-i Kashmir* (*TK*), f.139; Nizamuddin, *Tabaqat-i Akbari* (*TA*), III, 370.
20. *TR*, 423-4, 437.
21. Ibid., 437; *Baharistan Shahi* (*BS*) (BS), 98-9.
22. *TR*, 135-8; *BS*, 98-100.
23. Ibid., 135-7; 439-41; *BS*, 98-102, *TA*, III, 465.
24. Ibid., pp. 450, 473, 481-2, *BS*, 107, ANI 359.
25. *BS* 102-6, *TR* 472, 482, Abul Fazl, *Akbar Nama* (*AN*), Vol. I, 346-8, 350-60, 402-6, pp. 513, 26. *BS*, Abul Fazl, *Ain-i-Akbari*, 107; *TR*, 473, 481-2; *AN* I 359.
27. *AN*, 402-6; *TR* (Eng. tr.) 478-89; Banerjee, *Humayun* II, 16; Hasan, *Kashmir*, 130-3.
28. *TR*, 47-85; *BS*, 100-10g; *TK*, 145; *AN*, 403.
29. *AN*, 403; *BS*, 107-10; *TA*, III, 468; *TR*, 484. Some chroniclers record that only a small force was given to Qazi by Sher Shah.
30. *AN*, 402-3; *TR*, 482-6.
31. *BS*, 107-11; *TA*, III 467-9.
32. *TR*, Appendix A, 483-91; Hasan, *Kashmir*.
33. Ibid., *HN*, 146; *Ain* I, 512-13.
34. Ibid.
35. Ibid.
36. *TR*, 469, 490-1; *AN*, 204-6, 406; *TA*, III 475, 718 fn.1.
37. *AN*, 198-9, 402-6; *TA*, III 475, 718 fn; *TR*, 490-1.
38. *SA*, 53, WK46, *TH*, II, 130, *TA*, III, 478; *TR*, 228-30, 244, 267-8, 421.
39. *AN*, III, 959-90; *TR*, 243-4, 267-8, 392; Lane Pool, *Catalogue of coins of Muhammedan States of India*, p. x/viii; Erskine, *History of India*, vol. II, pp. 366-7.
40. Ibid.
41. *HN*, 146; *Ain*, I, 512-13; *TR*, 483-9; *AN*, 284, tr. 541.
42. *TR*, 484, *AN*, 284, tr. 541.
43. Ibid., *AN*, III, 959-60.
44. *Ain*, I, 513; *TR*, tr., Appendix A, pp. 487-91.
45. *TR*, 260-77.
46. Ibid., 355, 377.
47. *TR*, Appendix A, 488-91.

48. *AN* 198; tr., 404-585; *Tuzuk-i Jahangiri,* II, 148.
49. *TR*, 1; Razi II, 368.
50. *TR*, I, 48-149; Editor's note, 7.
51. *TR*, 150-7.
52. Ibid., 2-4, 150-1.
53. Ibid, 4.
54. Ibid, 294.
55. Ibid, 207, 303.
56. Ibid, Introduction, 4-8.
57. *TR*, tr. 196, 239.
58. *TR*, 276.
59. Ibid, 148, 217-18, 276.
60. Ibid, 148, 301, 350, 413.
61. *BN*, 10, tr., 20.
62. *TR*, 210-11.
63. Ibid, 484.
64. Ibid, 27, 146.
65. Ibid, 383-4.
66. *BS*, 111-20; *TR*, 435-6; Farishta, 646-7.
67. Ibid.
68. *BS*, 111-12; *TA*, III, 472.
69. Ibid., Rafiuddin Ahmad, *Nawadirul Akbar Pir Hasan Shah, Tarikh-i Hasan*, f.127, Muhammad Ạzam, *Waqial-i Kashmir*, f. 45.
70. *TR*, I, 148-9; Editor's Comments, 10-16, 71; *BN*, 10-11, 21-2.
71. *BN*, 10-11, 21-2.
72. *TR*, I, 148, 217-18, 341-2.

Mirza Haidar Dughlat's Tribal Antecedents

Dughlat and Oirat

Although there is no record of any divisions of the Oirat tribe in Altan Topchi, Ming annals refer to three tribes which had constituted the Oirat tribes in the early fifteenth century. Sanang Setzen also confirms that there were 'Durben Oirats' (the four Oirats) namely Kergud, Baghatud, Khoit and Oghelet. Like Setzen, Chinese Chroniclers of seventeenth and eighteenth centuries also describe four oirats 'Sz O-Lat'e but the names as recounted are totally different: These were Choros (Dzungars), Durbet, Turgut Khoshat. It is interesting to note that the oral traditions of Kalmuks also carry these names for 'four Oirats'. If Pallas is to be believed the Kamkuks or Oelots are said to have been divided into four tribes (viz., Khoshot, Derbet, Soongar and Targot) and the fifth one *khoit* was added to the list by Pallas at a later stage. Galsang Gamboyeff explains the term Oirat as Oi'Orat (Oi home-orat forest) i.e. people living in the forest.

Uspensky makes us believe that Durben meaning four in Mongol language 'was also the name of a Mongol tribe, which as he proves from a statement of Rashiduddin in the days of Chingiz Khan was allied to the Oirats'.

(Howorth, *History of the Mongols*, 1876, vol. I, Chap. IX, p. 558; Bretschneider E., *Medieval Researches*, vol. II, London, pp. 169-70)

Apart from the oral traditions, Sheng Wuki further adds to the confusion by saying that: 'The O-Lute are of Meng gu (Mongol) extraction. when the Mongol dynasty in China had been overthrown the Mongol people split into three branches. One of them lived south of the desert and continued to be called Mengu; another brand lived north of the desert, and they called themselves Korhk (Khalkhas). Both the ruling Khans of both tribes are descendants of Chingiz. A third branch dwelt westward. They do not descend from Chingiz, but they trace their origin back to Huan Taishi and Yasien Kahan of the wala and the Wa-la-are the same tribe we now call O-lu-te Dughlat and the four wei-late (oirats).

Secret History refers to the Dorben people and gives the story of their origin from the two brothers namely Duua Soqor and Dobun Mergen. At the advice of Duua Soqor, Duben Mergen had married the best maiden Alonqova who bore two sons namely Bugunutei and Belgunutei. When Duua Soqor died, his four sons not looking upon their uncle as a kinsman, despised him and separating themselves, journeyed forsaking him. Taking the clan name Dorben—those became the Darben people.

(Cleaves, Francis Woodman, *The Secret History of the Mongol Dynasty*, Harvard, 1982, pp. 1-3, Shenq Wu Ki, Chap. III, 'Emperor Kanghi expedition against the Dzunars'. Bretschneider, 169-72)

There are two comments by Juvaini which highlight the significance of Oirats though no reference to its sub branches or divisions is found in this work also.

Juvaini categorically states that the Oirats were one of the best known of the Mongol tribes, and to that tribe belong most of the maternal uncles of the children and grand children of Chingiz Khan, the reason being that at the time of his first rise to power the Oirat came forward to support and assist him and vied with one another in their alacrity to tender allegiance, and in recognition of their services an edict was issued concerning that tribe to the effect that the daughters of their amirs should be married to the descendants of Chingiz Khan; and he likewise bestowed upon the chief of that tribe a daughter of his own called Checheken Beki. Banakiti says that Chechekan was married to Turelchi Gurgan son of Qutuqna one of the rulers of the Oirat qaum. This is the reason why all the princes take their wives from the Oirat.

(Juvaini *Tarikh-i-Jahankusha*, text 242, Eng. tr. A.J. Boyle, pp. 50-6; Banakiti, *Tarikhi-I-Banakiti*, 364)

Juvaini affirms that 'when Chingiz Khan's case prospered, the stars of his fortune were in the ascendant, he despatched envoys to the other tribes also and all that came to tender submission, such as the Oirats and the Qunghrat or Qonqurat were admitted to the number of his commanders and followers and were regarded with the eye of indulgence and favour'.

Dughlat

In one of the later works, Dughlat is described as one of the finest aqwam (peoples) of Qiyat tribe though the etymology of this name is not yet clear. Dughlats were renowned for the nobility of their pedigree and lineage (*sharafati nasb-o-hasb*) and propinquity and affinity (qarabat-o-waslat) of this qaum (people) with the Great rulers. Some of the most famous amirs who emerged out of this qaum (people) were:

AMIR DAUD DUGHLAT

He was one of the *Muazzam Umara* (dignified highly placed amirs) of Timur whose elder sister Qutlugh Turkan Agha was married to him. He accompanied Timur in the wars against the amirs of yasuri and those of Chaghatai Khans and in every battle he distinguished himself as a good brave and manly warrior.

AMIR QAMARUDDIN DUGHLAT

He was one of the *Umari Kabbar* of this (qaum) and was famous throughout Moghulistan for his large following (having numerous il-o-ulus). During the reign of Khizr Khwaja Khan Chaghatar, there was no amir like him. In 799 he himself came to Transoxiana. Several times Sahib-i-Qiran amir Timur invaded his territory. In gallantry and courage, he was unique and proved his worth in bravery and showed his mettle in the attacks on the Barlas. Once he abstained from participating in one of the battles of Sahib-i-Qiran whose men pursued him hotly. From amongst these amirs, Auj Qara Bahadur reached Qamaruddin. Qamaruddin shot an arrow on the horse which fell down immediately. When Auj Qara drew his lance and wanted to pursue him, amir Qamaruddin turned back and said that: In gallantry I liked your performance hence I do not want that any harm should reach you from my side. Now you better return as you have already shown your loyalty to the salt of your master otherwise you would face injury at my hand. He shot through the *sangikhara* (rugged and hard stones) which he had in one hand. Auj Qara was surprised and returned. He started praising him. Amir Qamaruddin spent his entire life in overrunning and devastating the countries. Once Sahib-i-Qiran had sent an army to fight against him also. Amir Qamaruddin had one son named as Amir Jahan Shah who had his yurt in Moghulistan at Sangin Tash. In 918 when Shahzada Ulugh Beg son of Shahrukh turned his reins towards Moghulistan, Amir Jahan shah came to fight along with his own aimaqs. The qaum of Kerait then appeared with the Barlas amirs. The *kalantars* of Kerait were all killed. Amir was defeated due to the lack of companions. Again he fought a war in his own yurt against Sultan Owais Barlas and faced defeat. When the Gurgani army of Barlas arrived, Amir could not join Sher Muhammad Chaghatai because Khizr Khwaja (son of Sutlemish Uzhruq) and Amir Khudadad were taken to Samarqand by the order of Ulugh Beg. Amir Jahan Shah received a victory in the war. As soon as the reinforcement reached there Jahan Shah initially desisted from the war. However, a battle ensued between him and amir Iskandar Shah and Wali Muhammad Barlas and finally he remained victorious. Muhammad Husain Mirza Dughlat belonged to this qaum. In 899, he became son-in-law of Umar Shaikh Mirza, son of Abu Said Gurgtan. Amir Sultan Muhammad commonly known as Muhammad Hesari and Sultan Husain Dughlat were the amirs having large territories and horde (*sahib-i-il-o-ulus*) in the days of Zahiruddin Muhammad Babur. Saiyid Muhammad Dughlat was an amir of Chaghatai Khan who was killed in the Uzbeg war. Both Sultan Husain Muhammad Hesari and Sultan Ahmad Mirza Dughlat were the nobles of lower rank (*Umrai Kichik*) of Chaghatai Khans of Tashkent. In 980 he was appointed at the order of Qaan to help Muhammad Babar Badshah against Sultan Ahmad Tambal taking with him his own tuman and the tumans of others which had been invited for the purpose. Mirza Haidar Dughlat was an Amir of Kashghar. In 948, he went to Kashmir at the order of Humayun and occupied it. In 958 he was killed there. Mirza Abdur Rahman Dughlat was his brother. It is also worth mentioning that Dughlat is often written after dropping *alif* and sometimes it is written by dropping *dal* then it becomes 74 Oghlat though the correct pronunciation is Dughlat. Dughlat is a *Sharif Qaum* (people of noble origin).

AWIMAQ-I-OIRAT

Oriat is an awimaq-i-sharif. It originates from the Qiyat tribe though the reason for the name is not known. In the early years of Chingiz Khan's reign, Bozanjari considered this qaum also to be a branch of Naimans and stood up to fight against him. When Qaan took his army to Irtish, these people first tried sword and later on sought safety in submission. Being helpless they served as Ghacharchis. In the reign of Qubilai Qaan there arose a hakim known as Tingiz from this qaum. He had numerous *il-o-pulus* (territorial and tribal strength). Qubilai Khan had nominated him to fight against his own brother Irtiq Boqa whe happened to be one of the umra-i-muazzam (nobles of dignity) of that age. From 75 among the descendants of Tingiz Oirat, in the age of Abu Said Bahadur Bozanjari King of Iran and Khurasan was Amir Ali Badshah Oirat who was the maternal uncle of Sultan Abu Said Khan. In 730 Sultan Musa Khan who happened to be the son of Taraghai (son of Hulaku) was raised to the throne. Sultan Abu Said Khan was killed. Thereupon Urpa Khan from the descendants of Irtiq Buqa was elevated to the *masnad.* Amir Ali Oirat who had hereditary enmity with the descendants of Irtiq Buqa was victorious in a war against him. In 736 he was killed in the war between Muhammad Khan Amir Hasan Elkani Jalair. The Oirat Amirs were dispersed. From this qaum Shaikh Ali Oirat became the ruler of Ardabil. In the reign of Sahibi Qiran Qizil Mir Ali Oirat was one of the respectable amirs of this qaum. Sariq Umar Oirat who ruled over Takrit rendered excellent service. When Sultan Ahmad Jalair was defeated in the battle by Qaraquyunlu Turkomans, Amirs of this qaum held sway and ruled over Moghulistan after a short time following death of Timur Qaan. The countries of Khita and China went out of the hands of Mughals and fell into the hands of successors of Ogedei. Except Qaraqoram and lands of Qalmaqs there was no place left unconquered hence Oirat Aimrs became very strong. That Wilayat was also brought out of their possession and for quite a long time Oirat ruled over it.

From this noble people originated nice venerable noyans. Arghun Aqa Oirat was so good that due to his respect and high standing he was called aqa (big brother). In the time of Ogedei Khan he was appointed as ruler in the balda of Khurasan and he was included in the list of Bitikchis and became a high noyan (noyani suzurg), from the Urugh of Chingiz Khan. Several rulers were looked after and served by him. Throughout the long span, he spent a fine righteous life. He ruled Khurasan with all grandeur and pomp for thirty-nine years and showed justice and beneficence. When Hulaku was appointed in Iran Khurasan and Iraq-i-Ajam as governor in 951 by the order of Mangku Khan, Arghun Aqa proceeded towards the army of Qaan. Arghun Aqa, Jormaghun and Taichu noyan who were holding the charge of the Wilayats of Iran and Iraq were brought under the sway of Hulaku Khan. Hulaku Khan, however, allowed Arghun Aqa to continue in Khurasan as before and showed kindness towards him. All the affairs of Iraq, Siestan, Azerbaijan were entrusted to him. Arghun Aqa enjoyed the support and occupied and dominated over the region. Geral Malik Oirat sent his own son and other descendants to Hulaku to serve him and show obeisance. The Sultans of Moghuls and all the high and low among the Moghuls held Arghun Aqa in high esteem. After a reign of 39 years Arghun Aqa died in 676. A chronogram stating that in the year 676, on Monday 20th Zilhijj the diadem of fortune was removed from the face of just sovereign. One of the several sons of Amir Arghun Aqa was Amir Nauruz Beg Oirat who distinguished himself in good qualities, righteous character, learning, wisdom, bravery and generosity in which he was unique. Since it was necessary that after Hulaku Khan there should be one governor of Khurasan hence Ghazan Khan Bozanjari son of Arghun Khan was bound to stay in Khurasan. Amir Nauruz Beg spent his time in the service of Ghazan. At a time when Arghun Khan Boqa was executed (*ba Yasa rasanid*), Amir Nauruz Beg raised the opposition and went towards east and invaded Ghazan Khan though he lost his way and fell in the yurt of Buqa Yarghuchi. He however was victorious (76) in his war against him and extended his power. He raised the prince Gesu on the throne and wrote down *yirlighs* in his name. When Ghazan Khan came to know of this incident he took courage to remove Amir Nauruz Beg. In this war he was defeated by the army of Ghazan Khan and thereafter went to Qaidu Khan in Moghulistan. Qaidu showed clemency and Kindness and ordered that the Chaghatai Walis should also be helpful towards him. Amir arranged his army and marched towards Khurasan. Prince Qutluq Shah, Qutluq Timur, Ghazan Khan Bahadur were appointed for his removal. A severe battle ensued between them. Amir lost in the game of war and rushed to Siestan. In 694 he came to agreement with Aurang Timur (the son-in-law of Qaidur Khan) with whom he overran the army of Maisur Ughlan. Due to sheer enormity of numbers of enemy he turned his reins from the war and wrote a *yirligh* in the name of Aurang Timur and besieged Nishapur. In the meantime, Aurang Timur also grew afraid of him and aimed at him. Amir Nauruz became aware of his intentions and ran away. He sent an envoy Ghazan Khan and asked for forgiveness. Ghazan Khan valued these expressions of obedience and (out of expediency) sent a *Yirligh* of conciliation and encouragements. Amir came and they opened negotiations with each other.

When Baidu Khan deserted Gaikhatu and killed the ring leaders, Ghazan Khan discussed the matter with Amir Ghazi who assured him that through the might of sparkling sword they may place the ruler on the throne and the enemies would all be annihilated. Yet this could be possible if only the prince ensures out of expediency that the dust of paganism be cleared by the waters of Islam. The prince himself had a clear inclination towards this religion. Shaikh Sadruddin Hamwi recited the holy *kalima* and chastened their hearts from heresy. Many of the Moghuls adopted the religion of Muhammad that very day. The prince was given the title of Sultan Mahmud Ghazavi Khan and gave the message to Baidu Khan to surrender the ring leaders so that they may be punished as per Yasa of Chingiz Khan and marched towards them with a large army. Amir Nauruz Beg proceeded towards the Tukal the vanguard of Baidu Khan and achieved a victory. Baidu Khan and Ghazan Khan exchanged letters and messages and met each other. Ghazan Khan sensed the elements of rebellion and saved himself from this whirlpool. Amir Nauruz came as an envoy to Baidu and explained that we did not feel secure from the treachery of enemies and had to leave without permission. Now, if Fars and Iraq are left to us he would be included in the list of relatives. Baidu Khan, however, did not grant leave to Amir Nauruz. Through his own magnificent power and contrivance and through promises of capturing Ghazan Khan, he managed to take leave only to return with a very large force of Ghazan Khan to defeat Baidu. Most of the Amirs of high standing were not happy with the ways of Baidu. They accepted the promises of Nauruz Beg and joined the banner of Ghazan Khan. Baidu Khan tried to escape but he was made captive and Amir Nauruz Beg put him to death by the order of the king. All the worship places of Nazarenes and fire worshippers/Magis which had sprung up and dotted the area were devastated. Immediately after his accession, Ghazan Khan ordered that all the high and low should accept Islam and any person who showed reluctance was to be beheaded.

In the middle of the coin, Kalima was inscribed. The *altamgha*, *paiza* and *yirligh* were patterned in this way, Khan entrusted the organization of army, administration of finances and country to Amir Nauruz. The son of Burraq Oughlan, Chaghatai invaded this side. Due to certain changes, the king became worried and wary of administrative burden within a few weeks. But Amir Nauruz borrowed money from the grandees of Tabriz to organize the army. In the vicinity of Herat, he fought a war against the Chaghatai and became victorious. All the opening and closing of affairs of *diwans* and *altasmgha* which is a high *mansab* was entrusted to Amir Haji Beg Oirat, brother of Amir Nauruz Beg. At this juncture the Khan ordered that the Amir should go to Khurasan for management of the affairs and the rebellious amirs decided to attack and kill him while he was on the way. Through his good fortune he became aware of the conspiracy and was hiding in the place. The nobles like Islamic Arslan Durlaka and Barlaka had decided that the first mentioned nobles should kill the king and the last mentioned should put amir Nauruz to death. When Suka proceeded for the night attack, amir Nauruz came out from his ambuscade and defeated him. The king also had a fight against the rebellious amirs whom he put down with a heavy hand. In this tumult the five princes of Bozanjari Aimaq and thirty-eight highly placed amirs lost their lives within a short span of one month.

(Mirza Muhammad Abdul Qadir Khan,
Awimaq-i-Mughul, Amritsar, 1902, pp.72-4)

Awimaqi Dughlat

Dughlat, occasionally Duklat, a Mongol tribe whose name, according to Abu 'l-Ghazi (ed. Des,maisons, St. Petersburg, 1871, i, 65) derives from the plural of the Mongol word *dogholong* (-lang) 'lame'. The tribe appears to have played no part in the early period of the Mongol Empire, though it is supposed always to have supported Cingiz Khan (Rashid al-Din, ed. Berezin in *Trudi vost. otd. Imp. Russk. Arkheol. obshcestva,* vii, 275, xiii/ text 47, 52; tr. L.A. Khetagurov, Moscow-Leningrad 1952, i/i, 193). At that time the tribal apparently emigrated in its entirety out of Mongolia; there is at least no Mongol tribe of that name today.

The Dughlat did not attain political significance until after the disintegration of the Ilkhan Empire [q.v.], from which time Muhammad Haydar Dughlat (Haydar Mirza, [q.v.]), a member of the tribe, provides information about them in his *Tarikh-i-Rashidi* (ed. N. Alias and E. Denison Ross, London, 1885). But his information is not everywhere reliable and, in the few places where the tribe is mentioned in other sources, contradicts these. According to Haydar a member of the Dughlat, Tulik or perhaps his younger brother Buladji (the form Pulader printed in the edition of Abu-l-Ghazi 56 ff., does not appear in the manuscripts), is supposed in 748/ 1347-8 to have placed Khan Tughluk Temur on the throne at Aksu in the Tarim Basin. The latter in turn is supposed to have expressed his gratitude to the Dughlat by granting them 'nine powers' and thus to have stabilized their power in the Tarim Basin. Haydar Dughlat claims to have seen this document 'in the Mongol language and script' in his childhood, but says that it was lost during the reign of Shaibani Khan, d.916/1510 [q.v.] (*Tarikh-i-Rashidi* 54 f. 305). But the inaccurate chronology of this historian in the pertinent notices tends to provoke strong doubt as to the genuineness of the document. Between 769/1368 and 794/1392 (?) power in Mogholistan (as eastern interior Asia starting at about Semiryec'e was at that time called) was wielded by Kamar al-Din Dughlat (Sharaf al-Din Yazdi, *Zafar Nama* ed. Bibl. Ind., Calcutta 1887-8, i,78ff.) a brother of Buladji according to the *Tarikh-i-Rashidi*. After an early period of cooperation with Timur (q.v.) he was forced by the latter, after a long struggle, to flee across the Irtish into the Altai (Yazdi, i, 494ff.) two of his brothers remained in the service of Timur (Yazdi, i, 104, ff., 650), whose sister was married to a member of the Dughlat.

After 1392 Kamar al-Din's nephew (?) Khudaydad, nominally major domo, was in fact the ruler of Mogholistan. The Chingizid (q.v.) Khans whom he put on the throne were nothing but puppets. Khudaydad demonstrated his readiness to reach a settlement with the Timurids (q.v.) ostensibly owing to their common Islamic faith, and met in 828/1425 Ulugh Beg [q.v.] without battle in Semiryec'e (Abd al Razzak Samarkandi, Matla al-sa-dayn, Ms. Leningrad, 157, fol. 230). In view of this agreement the Khans of Mogholistan had to accept the division of their land among the brothers and sons of Khudayad (*Tarikh-i-Rashidi* 100). His eldest son Muhammad Shah was appointed tribal chief (Ulus Begi) by Khan Wais (ca. 1418-29) and took up residence in Semiryec'e (*Tarikh-i-Rashidi* 78). His younger son was driven out of the western Tarim Basin by the Timurids (1416) Samarkandi in Notices et extraits xiv, i, 296) and died even before his father did. His son Sayyid 'Ali finally retook Kashghar and ruled there for 24 years (died 862/1457-8, according to his tomb in Kashghar; see *Tarikh-i-Rashidi* 87, 99). He was succeeded by his two sons Saniz Mirza (until 869/1464-5) and Muhammad Haydar (until 885/1480), both of whom performed great services in the development of the region. Then Abu Bakr Mirza, the son of Saniz, drove his uncle and Khan Yunus of Mogholistan out of the western Tarim Basin, after which he took up residence in Yarkend and defended himself in 904-5/1499 against an attack by the Khans of Mogholistan. Not until 920/1514 was he eliminated by Said Khan.[1]

In addition to the principal line other branches of the Dughlat repeatedly established small principalities, occasionally at war with the former. Muhammad Haydar for example, the grandfather of the historian Muhammad Haydar, fought in alliance with the Chingizid Yunus and with the Timurid Ahmad Mirza against Abu Bakr Mirza (see above). His sons Muhammad Husain and Sayyid Muhammad Mirza vacillated continuously between the two dynasties and were even from time to time in the service of the Uzbeks. The former was finally killed in Herat at the command of Shaibani [q.v.] in 914/1508-9. His brother fell victim in 1533 to the hatred of Khan 'Abd al-Rashid of Mogholistan, who had come to power in the same year (*Tarikh-i-Rashidi* 106ff. 305, 450), Muhammad Husayn's son, the historian Muhammad Haydar Mirza, in 1541 his position as a governor of left service of the ruler of the Tarim Basin to proclaim his independence in Kashmir (see Haydar Mirza).

With the elimination of this line and the end of Abu Bakr's (see above) rule in 920/1514, the independence of the Dughlat in the Tarim Basin came to an end. They continued to support the Chingizids there and wielded considerable power into the seventeenth century.

A tributary of the 'Great Horde' of Kazakhs between the Ili and the Jaxartes bore the name Dulat into the twentieth century, obviously derived from Dughlat. At the end of the nineteenth century, they included almost

40,000 tents (see N. Aristov, *Zametki ob etniceskom sostave Tyurkshikh plemen i narodnostey,* St. Petersburg, 1897, 77).

Bibliography: the sources are mentioned above. Studies include W. Barhold, Zwolf Vor-lesungen iiber die Geschichte der Turken Mittelașiens, Berlin 1935, 209-14 (French tr. Paris, 1945); idem; *Four studies on the history of Central Asia*, tr V. Minorsky, i, 1956, 54; R. Grousset, L'Empire dies steppes, Paris, 1939, index p.p. Ivanov, Ocerki po istorii Sredney Azii (Outlines of the history of Central Asia), Moscow 1958, i, and ii; v. 5 index. The last two works named contain further detailed bibliography.

(B.B. Barthold Sochinenija, vol. II, Moscow ed.,
also see B.B. Barthold, *Encyclopaedia of Islam*, new ed.,
vol. II (C-G), London, 1965, pp. 621-2)

NOTE

1. *Tarikh-i-Rashidi*, 293.

Mirza Haidar Dughlat's Views on History Writing

'It is the practice of historians to recount everything as they find it, whether worthy or unworthy of mention. For it is not their object to write down the good qualities of princes, and to omit all their bad actions, but rather to reproduce all facts without discrimination, in order that they may leave behind them a record of the people of this world. Thus all men in power, as well as others, reading their histories, may profit by their advice, and may see what have been the various fruits and results of praiseworthy habits, on the one hand, or blameable actions on the other: also that they may accept the lesson to be learnt from observing the way in which the memory of different princes has been preserved, and may, in short, incline to good deeds and avoid evil ways.

'I would lay before the wise and critical that I, the least of God's servants, Muhammad Haidar, known among my intimates as Mirza Haidar, son of Muhammad Husain Kurkan, have been continually possessed of the thought that the rank and dignity which historians attain to, is not so high that one should have a craving for it. Still, there can be little doubt that this poor history (which has been driven by the whirlwind of pride and the waves of ignorance and intoxication, from the sea of incapacity upon the shores of small literary attainment) may be regarded as of some value by the divers in the ocean of excellence, who have concealed in the shells of perfection, the pearls of poetry and the precious stones of prose. According to the saying: "Necessity makes lawful that which is forbidden", and because certain important events in the annals of the Moghul Khakans have been entirely forgotten, I was induced, as far as time should permit, to narrate some of the most trustworthy facts in their history.

'When the Moghul power was high, many eminent men flourished; and some wrote their people's history. Now, for more than a hundred years nothing of the sort has been done—no trace of these men remains, nor of their writings. Nor does any sign remain of their property and civilization, except here and there a ruined tower or fortification; and in some towns, the relics of a monastery, a college, a mosque, a portico, or a minaret, still exist, because their foundations being of stone, or for some other reason, God willed that they should endure. No vestige of these men survives and no one knows anything concerning them. For during this long lapse of time, all have become strangers to the old customs and ways of learning. Since the conversion of the Moghuls to Islam, more especially, no history of them has been written. But the learned men of Mavara-un-Nahr and Khorasan and Irak, who have written the annals for their own kings, have made mention of the Moghals, just where it has suited the context, while they have paid no attention to them when not connected with their own country. Among these histories may by mentioned the *Mujma-ut Tavarikh*[1] of Khwaja Rashid-ud Din; the *Tarikh-i Guzida*[2] of Khwaja Hamid Ullah Mustaufi; the *Zafar Nama*[3] of Maulana Sharaf-ud Din´Ali Yazdi; the *Tarikh-i Manzum*[4] of Maulana Abdur Razzak; and the *Ulus Arbaa*[5] of Mirza Ulugh Beg. Among these, I have sought carefully for any mention of the Moghul Khakans, but have found nothing very connected [*ba tartib*]. In my early years, I was much drawn to the study of the history of my forefathers, and in those days, there were still alive some of the Moghul Amirs and nobles (some over one hundred years of age, some under). But it never occurred to my father or my uncles to commit to writing what they had heard concerning the Khakans, from their parents, and other trustworthy sources. And now they have all been dead for some time. [On this account] I intend, God willing, to write an account of the Moghuls after their conversion to Islam, basing my facts upon histories and reliable traditions, in addition to what I have myself witnessed in my own times. But not finding that I had capacity or talent sufficient to justify my setting out on this bold venture, I have resolved to begin by making a trial on those events of which I have been an eye-witness, and then, should I by the grace of God succeed. I will proceed with my original plan of writing the history of the Moghul Khakans.'

(Haidar Dughlat, *Tarikh-i-Rashidi*, Eng. tr.
by Denison Ross, Patna, 1973, pp. 129, 150-1)

NOTES

1. The correct title of this work is *Jami 'ut tavarikh*. It is a general history of the world from the earliest times to AH 700, and gives a special account of the Moghuls. (See Dr Rieu's *Catalogue*, I, p. 74.)
2. A general history from the earliest times to AH 730, by Hamid Ullah Mustauff, Kazvini, (Rieu, I, p. 80).
3. A History of Timur.

4. The proper title is *Matla 'I Sa 'adain va Majma ul-Bahrain*, by 'Abdur Razzak bin Ishak us Samarkandi—('Manzum' here, may mean 'well arranged') (Rieu, I, p. 181b).
5. A history of Chingiz Khan, his ancestors and descendants, down to the time of Timur (Rieu, I, p.164).

Comments in *Tarikh-i-Rashidi* reflecting Mirza Haidar Dughlat's personality

'Between Sultan Mahmud Khan and the Uzbeg-Kazaks two battles took place, the Khan suffering defeat on both occasions. The cause of those defeats was that the most distinguished of his generals had left Yunus Khan. For the Khan had, in common with all who succeed to power, the defeat of not knowing the value of men of worth, and of imagining that whomsoever they favour becomes for that reason, a valuable man which is of course impossible. However, in conformity with these pernicious principles, the Khan patronized some of the lowest of his people who were, continually engaged in trying to decry the old and influential amirs. This they carried so far as to induce the Khan to put to death five of the great amirs each of whom was the head of a department (sar daftar), and to extirpate their families. While in their places, five of those base born men were set up. At the time when the difference arose between Sultan Mahmud Khan and the Uzbeg Kazak on account of Shahi beg Khan, and a war ensued, these five base born men were generals; hence the defeat. That dread and esteem of the Khan which by the successful efforts of the five amirs had taken possession of the hearts of the neighbouring Sultans, had now disappeared.'[1]

'When Yunus Khan went to the palace of eternity, he left the kingdom to Sultan Mahmud Khan and the Moghuls according to their custom, placed him on his father's throne. It is a common occurrence that those who inherit what their fathers had left them do not appreciate its worth; thus the new Khan undervaluing the great amirs who had served his father, expelled them and set up, in their stead, weak minded and base men; while his old friends being defeated, old enemies who styled themselves new friends, now gained the supremacy. But in this new order of things the Khan found it difficult to withstand these (new advisers) nay, was incapable of keeping together his kingdom.'[2]

'The duty of the young is obedience; that of adults is favour (inayat). If the young neglect their duty, it is incumbent upon their elders to correct them. At this time the elder brother is in the place of the father.'[3]

'It is the practice of the humane and the usage of the generous (and of these two qualities kings make boast) that when a person at any time renders them some particular service, they reward that person with various presents and favours.[4]

About Ayub Begchik (one of Babur's disloyal nobles) Haidar Dughlat writes: 'He repented his disloyalty; when he lay dying some two years later (920 AH) in Yangi Hisar he told Said Khan who visited him that what was "lacerating his bowels and killing him with remorse" was his faithlessness to Babur in Hisar, the oath he had broken at the instigation of those "hogs and bears", the Mughal chiefs.'[5]

'Now, at that time Tahir Khan had a force of 20,000 men, but his fortunes were on the decline; for his army had formerly counted a million. He began to increase his violence and severity, and on this account he was abhorred of the surrounding sultans and men of note. . . . The people were able to judge of him by the violent treatment he meted out to this brother, (Abul Kasim Sultan) whom he suddenly put to death.'[6]

The Khwaja was an exceedingly pious and austere man, and the Khan longed to wait upon him, in the hope that [in his service] his desire might be realized. So he journeyed from Kuchkar to Yarkand, where he arrived at the end of the winter and waited on the Khwaja. [But] when he explained to him his resolve, the Khwaja remarked: 'Much has been said by wise men on this subject; such as: Remain on the throne of your kingdom, and be like an austere darvish in your ways! And again: set the crown on your head, and science on your back! Use effort in your work, and wear what you will! In reality sovereignty is one of this closest walks [with God], but kings have abused its rights. A king is able, with one word, to give a higher reward than can a darvish (however intent upon his purpose) during the whole of a long life. In this respect sovereignty is a real and practical state. . . .[7] But I will show you one line that my father, Khwaja Muhammad Abdullah, wrote for me.' And he gave the writing to the Khan. It was written: 'The most important conditions, for a seeker of union with God, are: little food, few words, and few associates.' This brief [sermon] sufficed to compose the Khan, and he resolved to pursue the road of justice and good deeds. He began to occupy himself, at once, with what he was able, until the words of Shaikh Najm-ud-Din should be realized. A short time after this, Khwaja Nura came, and the Khan's desire was fulfilled. In the meanwhile Khwaja Taj-ud-Din arrived from Turfan. Subsequent to the death of Sultan Said Khan, he marched against Aksu. Twice he failed and was obliged to retire, and in the year 950 he died (may God illumine his proof!) at the age of about sixty years. Except Yunus Khan, no other Khan of the Chaghatai line attained such an age. He ascended the throne,[8] in the year 907, at the age of sixteen, and reigned forty-three years. No other Chaghatai Khan ever reigned as long as this. Nor did any of the Moghul Khans enjoy so long a life and reign. He adorned his days from the first to the last with blessings and charitable gifts. He passed the whole of his time in the study of the holy law, or the reading of the Koran. I have heard from his intimates that he used to spend about one-fifth of his time in directing the affairs of the State, and all the rest in perusal of the Koran [*tilavat*][9] prayer [*davat*] the prescribed prayers [*namaz*] , and in reciting the names of God [*Ixkar*] . It would be hard to find any one among the Padishahs, or even among the most pious men [*ahl-i-suluk]* who disposed of their time better than he did. And in consequence of this he was blessed with a long life and earthly happiness, such as no one but he, of his line, has ever enjoyed. May God bless his heavenly life as he did his days upon earth! Amen. Oh God of both worlds!'

'He excelled in the conduct of life, in intelligence and prudence, and was skilled in state management and the control and organization of armies. By his nature he was not at all addicted to the customs and ceremonies of Kings, or to the grandeur and magnificence of Khans, but rather tried to do without ceremony, and to live as simply as possible. In no way whatever did he make any distinction between himself and the rest of his people. He knew the Koran by heart, and had a very accurate Reader, who was better versed in the Koran than any one else in the country.

One day the Khan, in a state of intoxication, killed Tubra. It came about in this wise. Tubra was a rude, unpolished man, who had never been in personal attendance on the Khakans, but had always lived in the deserts of Moghulistan and Uzbegistan, engaged in forays [*kazaki*] and skirmishes [*karavuli*]. He was ignorant of the manners of an Amir. He now looked upon himself as one of the pillars of the State, and thought that for him to speak gently or courteously to a prince was but flattery, while flattery was the vilest of qualities; that coarse speech was a sign of power, and that a rough manner and the non-observance of the rules of politeness due to a king, should be regarded as a mark of dignity in himself. The people thought he was insane, and that pride had thickened the fibres of his brain. In spite of fear and apprehension, he had certainly made roughness of speech and rude manners his second nature. One day, at a feast given by the Khan, the wine was passing freely, and Tubra's head became hot with intoxication; reason left his brain, and in its place came pride and wickedness. All those thoughts which, when sober, he kept to himself, he now let free with full force, and began to talk wildly. It was in vain that the Khan expostulated and pointed out to him that his railleries were out of place: that he should not let loose the reins of coarse speech and vulgarity. Tubra retorted in a speech reflecting on the Khan's family. At this answer, the Khan quite lost control over his temper, and the harvest of his patience was consumed; he then and there gave orders for Tubra's head to be struck off and hung over the gate, as an example to all not to forget the respect due to authority.

When Sultan Ali Mirza, who was one of the three, heard of this event, he fled to the Emperor in Samarkand, and joined his brothers, Mir Ayub, Mir Muhammad, and Mir Ibrahim. My uncle, Sayyid Muhammad Mirza, who was their leader, was plunged into the greatest alarm. This event had occurred at Akhsi, while my uncle was at Andijan. The Khan immediately sent off Mir Kambar, in great haste, from Akhsi [to explain the matter to my uncle], saying: Tubra was an ass; but no ass would endure him, even to bucckle on his nose-bag.[10]

NOTES

1. *Tarikh-i-Rashidi*, Eng. tr., p. 119.
2. Ibid., p. 157.
3. Ibid., p. 335.
4. Ibid., p. 144.
5. Ibid., p. 315.
6. Ibid., p. 379.
7. Four lines omitted, containing a quotation from Najm-ud-Din, which points out what a faithful disciple may attain to. and what an unfaithful one must forego.
8. That is to say, the throne of Aksu and Turfan.
9. *Tilavat*—reading and meditating on the Koran. The *Namaz* means the five prescribed prayers or litanies of the day—the Arabic *salat*. *Davat* literally means 'supplication', and is used for private, or spontaneous, prayer.
10. A play on the word *Tubra*, meaning a 'nose-bag' for feeding horses.

Mirza Haidar Dughlat's Family

Haidar Dughlat's wife Mulibb Sultan Khanam was the third daughter of Ilacha Khan, Sultan Ahmad Khan Ulusbegi the maternal uncle of Babur.

(*Humayun Nama*, Eng. tr., p. 7)

'Khan Sultan Ahmad had four daughters. The third daughter Muhibb Sultan Khanim on the death of her first husband was married to his brother, Sultan Mahmud Khan, who was martyred at Akhsi by order of Shahi Beg Khan. Muhibb Sultan Khanim then remained with Kutuk Khanim, daughter of Sultan Mahmud Khan, and who after the devastation of Tashkand, was given to Jani Beg Sultan, as has been mentioned. After my uncle has risen up against Jani Beg Sultan and driven him out of the province of Farghana, Muhibb Sultan Khanam was separated from Kutuk Khanim who was her cousin. On the Khan's return to Andijan she rejoined him. Of all the four sisters, the Khan loved her the best, so that when she came to him, he showed her the greatest regard and affection. The occasion of my marriage, was celebrated by magnificent banquets and entertainments, which were remembered long after.'

(Haidar Dughlat, *Tarikh-i-Rashidi*, Eng. tr. Denison Ross, Patna, 1973, pp. 161, 280)

'At that time (Jumada II 921), the Khan's health was somewhat affected by his excessive wine drinking. He, therefore, went to Moghulistan hoping to restore his health by a change of air. On his return, he paid a visit to me, "To you who are like a son to me, I have given my dear sister, who is a pearl in the shell of the Khanate. My hope is that if a child should be born to you, I may be a father to him as well as you. Thus, a child with two loving fathers, two fathers with one happy child. But since you have, up to this time, no offspring, you must took upon this son of mine (Iskandar) as your child so that what I hoped of you, you may realise in me. If eventually you should have a son, he will be a brother to this child; if you should have no children, you will have no need of another son." Favours and kind words such as these did he express to me and his sister; we accepted them with gratitude, and were in/stituted and presents given.'[1]

NOTE

1. Gulbadan calls her Khanish (*Humayun Nama*, Eng. tr., p. 120) and a Habiba fell in captivity and has brought by shaibani Khan, who later on gave her in marriage to his nephew Ubaidullah. Haidar Dughlat records how this marriage saved his life (*TR*, p. 207) and was later married to Said Khan's daughter (Gulbadan, Eng. tr., 235, No. 21, Bibliographical Sketch No. 2) .

Some Views on Mirza Haidar Dughlat's History

'Haidar's book was finished under Humayun in 953 AH (AD 1547), when its author had reigned five years in Kashmir. It is the most valuable of all the sources for those interested in Babur himself, both because of Haidar's excellence as biographer, and through his close acquaintance with Babur's family. From his eleventh to his thirteenth year, he lived under Babur's protection, followed by 19 years service under Said Khan, the cousin of both, in Kashghar, and after that Khan's death to Babur's sons Kamran and Humayun in Hindustan.'

(Annette Susannah Beveridge,
Translator of *Babur Nama*, pp. 348, 350)

In the year 915 AH (21 April 1509-AD 11 April 1510) 'Occurred also what was in itself a minor matter of a child's safety, but became of historical importance, namely the beginning of personal acquaintance between Babur and his sympathetic biographer Haidar Mirza Dughlat, Haidar like Said came a fugitive to the protection of a kinsmen; he was then eleven, had been saved by servants from the death commanded by Shaibani, conveyed to Mirza Khan in Badakhshan, then sent for by Babur to the greater security of Kabul.

(*Babur Nama*, fill index, S.n. *T.R.*, p. 227)

The battle of Pul-i Sangin had been 'admirably described by Mirza Haidar, who was then a boy of 12 with keen eye watching his own first fight and that fight with foes who had made him the last male survivor of his line. In the evening of the victory, Mahali Hamza and Hamza's son Mamak were brought before Babur, who, says "Haidar, did to them what they had done" to the Mughal Khanqans and Chaghatai Sultans, that is he retaliated in blood for the blood of many kinsmen'.[1]

Mirza Haidar gives an 'admirable account of the battle of Ganges' 17 May 1540 (*Humayun Nama*, Eng. tr., p. 142, f.n. 3)

'Mirza Haidar is the author of the most authentic history of that principality'.

Col. Briggs, translator of *Tarikh-i-Farishta*

Mirza was the 'literary compeer' of Babur.

A.S. Beveridge, translator of *Humayun Nama*

There are often certain inaccurate or incorrect information in *Tarikh-i-Rashidi* probably due to deliberate comouflaging. In about the battle of Kul Malik (April-May) Ubaid had as per information given by Haidar 3,000 men while Babur had 40,000 men. Khwand Mir however, contradicted him by saying that Babur's forces were small, 'the semblance being nearer the fact. Haidar it may be said did not go out on this campaign as he was lying sick in Samarkand for a long time. Khwand Mir's details have the well informed air of things learned at first-hand perhaps from someone in Hindustan', after AD 934. Since Babur's cause was now unpopular' where could he have obtained 40,000 men worth reckoning in a fight? The 'local accretions' too may have been very few.

(*B.N.*, Eng. tr., p. 357, also see *T.R.*, pp. 263, 265)

NOTE

1. *Babur Nama*, Eng. tr., p. 353.

Mirza Haidar Dughlat in *Babur Nama*

Khub Nigar Khanim was his (Mongol Khan Yunus Khan's) third daughter. Her they gave to Muhammad Husain Kurkan Dughlat (899 AH). She had one son and one daughter by him. Ubaid Khan Uzbeg took the daughter (Habiba).[1] When I (Babur) captured Samarkand and Bukhara, she stayed behind and when her paternal uncle, Saiyid Muhammad Dughlat came as Sultan Said Khan's envoy to me in Samarkand, she joined him and with him went to Kashghar where (her cousin) Sultan Said Khan took her. Khub Nigar's son was Haidar Mirza. He was in my service for three or four years after the Uzbegs slew his father, then (918 AH, AD 1512) he asked leave to go to Kashghar to the presence of Sultan Said Khan.

Everything goes back to its source pure gold or silver or tin. People say he now lives lawfully (*taib)* and has found the right way (*tariqa*).

'He has a hand deft in everything, pen-manship and painting, and in making arrows and bows, barbs and string grips; moreover he is a born poet and in a petition written to me, even his style is not bad.'

(Babur, *Babur Nama*, Turkish Text, London, f.11,
Eng. tr. by Beveridge, Delhi, 1979, pp. 21-2)

NOTE

1. Gulbadan calls her Khanish (*Humayun Nama*, Eng. tr., p.120) and a Habiba fell in captivity and has brought by Shaibani Khan, who later on gave her in marriage to his nephew Ubaidullah. Haidar Dughlat records how this marriage saved his life (*TR*, p. 207) and was later married to Said Khan's daughter (Gulbadan, Eng. tr. 235, No. 21, Bibliographical Sketch No. 2).

Mirza Haidar Dughlat in *Humayun Nama*

183. Muhibba Sultan Khanam the daughter of Sultan Ahmad Khan known as Alacha Khan who was the *Tughai-i-Khurd* the big Padshah (and she was later married to Mirza Haidar Dughlat) and Kanash the sister of Mirza Haidar.

184. In those days Mirza Haidar was appointed to conquer Kashmir. In the meantime news reached that Sher Khan had come. Strange restlessness and problem arose. It was decided to leave in the morning. During this period when the brothers were at Lahore and every day the expediency was seen and consultations were held in a Kangash (assembly), not a single decision could be taken. Ultimately, the news reached that Sher Khan had come already. Now, there was no way out-no remedy as they had to leave. Humayun had a claim over Kashmir. He sent Mirza Haidar Kashghari to conquer it. In the consultative assembly, it was pondered over that if Humayun proceeds to Kashmir and (since no news had until then arrived from Kashmir, and) Kashmir cannot be conquered—Sher Khan remains at Lahore—there would be great stressful situation and difficult and odd times.

Khwaja Kalan Beg was still in Sialkot. He came to Humayun along with Muid Beg who brought the petition that Khwaja had fears and Kamran should be watched. If the Emperor hurriedly arrives, the service of Khwaja would be made available. Humayun immediately wore cuircassco and weapons. Thus being well-equipped he turned towards Khwaja and brought him.

Humayun said that he was going to Badakhshan along with his brothers and Kabul belongs to Mirza Kamran. But Mirza Kamran was not willing to move to Kabul and commented that Emperor Babur had assigned Kabul in his own life time, to my mother. Departure to Kabul was not advisable. Humayun answered that Emperor Babur had always said that 'Kabul would not be handed over to anyone and that my sons should not covet that place (Kabul). Since God had granted shelter to all the princes in Kabul from where all the places were conquered and Babur had even written about it in his Memoir and letters giving a testimony to the fact though the kindness and grace of humane action, was accomplished (by Humayun) in the context of Kamran.'

(Gulbadan Begum, *Humayun Nama*, Lahore, 1966, pp. 203-5)

Mirza Haidar Dughlat in *Tarikh-i Alfi*

In the year 940, when Mirza Haidar marched with an army towards Kashmir, the Kashmiris met the Mughal army on their way. Mughal forces planned a night attack on the Kashmiris and emerged victorious. They passed through the narrow defiles—Tangi Lar and arrived in the plains of Kashmir, dispersed the Kashmiris. The city of Kashmir which is famous as Srinagar came under the possession of the Mughals. The Mughals stayed for twenty-four days in Kashmir after which they apprehended some trouble as the Kashmiris had started strengthening fortifications in southern region in the midst of laiogil (earthen mire). They assembled together and soon many more Kashmiris started pouring in from all sides. Feeling themselves unsafe at the hands of the Kashmiris, the Mughals were better advised to leave the town and stay outside in the plains. When the Kashmiris grew bold, and having out numbered the Mughals considerably, they came out from Laiogil, the Mughals sought safety in flight though they were being hotly pursued by the Kashmiris, whenever the Mughals went Kashmiris also appeared. Each of the two forces finally stood face to face with each other. Both of them had preferred to open trenches around themselves. When the war ensued Mirza Haidar and Mughals again achieved success, and the Kashmiris were in difficulty and managed to save themselves after great efforts. Since the families of the Kashmiris were clustered in one place, Mirza Haidar thought of attacking that very spot in order to disperse and further destroy the already bewildered Kashmiris. Kashmiris descended from the hills and dug out deep ditch around their place of stay filling them up with felled trees and branches. Mughals marched towards the place but failed to continue their journey due to mud and mire through which they could not hope to pass easily. They, thereafter halted at that place. Everyday the strength of Kashmiris was being reinforced and the Mughals who were eager to return home persuaded Mirza Haidar to open talk of peace. Thus a kind of agreement was reached by which the Khutba was to be read and coins were to be struck in the name of Sultan Said. Further the *peshkash* and tribute was accepted and the daughter of Muhammad Shah ruler was also given in marriage to Sultan Sikandar.

The Mughals then returned. At Marpol which is situated in Tibet they went to pay their homage to Sultan Said who was still suffering from asthma and was terribly sick. Said Khan thereafter appointed Mirza Haidar to overrun Adar Sang which was the centre of worship for the Chinese and where there were many pagodas. Sultan Said himself returned to Yarkand. On the way, he was again attacked by a bout of asthma. The amirs busied themselves in providing him with medical aid which was possible only if they hurriedly took the Khan out of Tibet. On 16th Zilhijja 931 when they crossed Tibet, the Khan collapsed due to weakness. The nobles who accompanied him sent a messenger to his son Rashid Khan who arrived on the last day of Zilhijja.

In Muharram 941, Rashid Khan sat on the throne of his father and became the ruler of Kashghar and Moghulistan. On that very day, during the meeting with Saiyid Muhammad Mirza Dughlat (brother of Mirza Aba Bakr) who was held in high esteem by Said Khan lost favour. Orders were issued for the murder of Saiyid Muhammad Mirza alongwith his sons and followers (excluding Mirza Haidar Dughlat and his brother who had gone to Adarsang). Due to the disease of horses which resulted in the death and destruction of the enemy's cattle, the Mughal forces succeeded and returned within eight days. Immense booty fell into the hands of Mughal army. Many regions of Tibet even agreed to pay tribute (*bajokharaj*). While returning, they heard the news of the death of Sultan Said, accession of Sultan Rashid and Murder of Saiyid Muhammad Mirza. Rashid Sultan sent an envoy to his brother Sikandar Sultan with the message that the rulership of Tibet and the control over the entire army would now belong to him. It was further ordered that Mirza Haidar Dughlat alongwith his brother was to be kept under surveillance near Iskandar Khan. The perturbed army thereupon scattered and only five persons remained with Mirza Sikandar and Haidar Sultan who could reach Marpol with great difficulty. A group of Mughal army who had earlier fled were forced to return to Mirza Iskandar due to excessive cold and inability to return to their own land. Thus five hundred horses joined Sultan Iskandar. They all spent the entire summer in great suffering. In spring Rashid Khan again sent order that they should not stay in Tibet and could run away to any place they liked though their lives were not to be spared'. Sikandar Sultan, thereafter, separated from Mirza Haidar and went to his brother. Mirza Haidar was left with twenty-five men with whom he decided to move to Badakhshan (via Kuhistan and Tibet). It was with difficulty that Mirza managed to reach Badakhshan where he stayed for quite a long time with his maternal cousin Mirza Sulaiman of Badakhshan. Finally he came to Kabul and from there to Lahore where he attained some position at the court of Mirza Kamran.

In 849 when Shah Tahmasp had occupied Garjistan and made Tabriz his winter quarters, on 10th Muharram of the same year Humayun waged a war against Sher Khan Afghan on the bank of river Ganges and lost the war due to mutual rivalry and slackness of some of his companions. On 1st of Rabi I all the sultans and amirs of the ulus of Chaghatai gathered at Lahore and rushed from there to Multan. In every mind there arose tumult and in every heart there sprang up a desire for kingship. Sultan Muhammad Mirza and his son who were ten to hundred times a bundle of dissension and trouble shooting also went to Lahore and then to Multan. Mirza Hindal and Mirza Yadgar Nasir thought it advisable to go to Thatta and after its conquest and extermination of Mirza Shah Husain Arghun, they looked forward to a plan of easy conquest of Gujarat. Mirza Kamran had his own ideas to hurriedly disperse this group of people and to go towards Kabul alone. Humayun hoped in vain for quite a long time that his brothers would unite and march together against the enemy. When he finally realized that such a situation was never to come he was depressed. One day when the sultans, the amirs and the dignitaries and officers had assembled and consultations were going on, Humayun said that every act is preordained in accordance with the order of Almighty without whose wish nothing occurs. All the nobles who were present there, wrote an agreement and started consultation. Haidar Dughlat who had already conquered Kashmir and consolidated it could serve as a strong base. The advice of the soldier of Kashmir should be accepted and all the baggage and family should be despatched and made safe there (Kashmir). Further, the entire region from the Sind to the banks of Yamuna and Ganges should be carefully guarded, as Afghans were not good counsellors and bringing the top and zarbozan (artillery) to Kuhistan was also difficult. Mirza Kamran who was selfish and wanted to puruse his own designs said that this task was fraught with dangers. The enemy was thundering at the gate. There were apprehensions that if Kashmir could not be subdued the families and soldiers sent there would perish. The best option left was that the Padshah and the Mirzas could either go to Kashmir or to some other place but the entire baggage and family should accompany him (Kamran) to Kabul. Having settled the families and the baggage there at Kabul Kamran promised to return and join the royal cavalcade. Since a few moments back, the suggestion had been rejected, the entire assembly was surprised and dumb founded at the advice which smacked of insincerity and treachery and was directed towards occupation of Kabul and devouring of baggage. They unitedly retaliated by saying that if the families of soldiers proceed towards countries outside India how could the soldiers stay back at peace even though the immense booty could be acquired here. Mirza Kamran settled on what he said and desired and the consultative assembly came to an end. The day passed without any concrete decision and necessary action and the dreaded moment occurred when Sher Khan reached near Sultanpur. Mirza Haidar and a group willing to go towards Kashmir were given leave by Humayun. Khwaja Kalan Beg was also deputed to follow Humayun, Mirza Haidar had hardly reached Naushahr and Khwaja Kalan approached Sialkot when Sher Khan crossed the waters of Sultanpur. On 1st of Rajab, Humayun crossed Lahore and Mirza Kamran reached upto Bhira, Khwaja Kalan upto Sialkot and Mirza Haidar arrived at Kashmir. The Kashmiris were fighting against each other and due to mutual dissensions, a group came and joined Mirza Haidar. With the help of these Kashmiris, the region of Kashmir was occupied easily by Mirza Haidar without waging a war.

On 22 Rajab Mirza Haidar became the ruler of Kashmir.

(Arif Qandahari, *Tarikh-i Alfi*)

Mirza Haidar Dughlat in *Akbar Nama*

In fine, when defeat (*shikasti*), which was to lay the foundation of the righting (*durusti*) of the world, made its appearance, the officers fled without fighting to the bank of the Ganges. which was about four miles (a *farsakh*) distant, and as the requital of their disloyalty and ingratitude, sank in the whirlpool of disappointment, giving the vessels of their lives to the boisterous waters of annihilation in recompense of their unrighteousness. His Majesty Jahanbani mounted with firm foot on an elephant and proceeded across the river. He descended from the elephant at the water's edge and was looking around for an exit. As the bank was high, no way out presented itself. One of the soldiers who had been saved out of the whirlpool came there and seizing His Majesty's sacred hand drew him up. In truth, he then, by help of heaven's favouring hand, drew to himself fortune and power. His Majesty asked him his name and birthplace. He made answer, 'My name is Shams-ud Din Muhammad, my birthplace is Ghazni, and I am a servant of M. Kamran.' His Majesty made him hopeful of princely favours. Just then Muqaddam Beg,[1] one of M. Kamran's officers, recognized His Majesty and enrolled[2] himself among those who had received the gospel of good fortune. Acting upon this, he brought forward his horse, and obtained the news of distinction from royal promises. His Majesty proceeded from there towards Agra, and was joined on the way by the Mirzas. When they came to the environs of Bhangapur,[3] the villagers closed the market against the king's men, and behaved in an unruly manner, attacking everyone who fell into their hands. When the august mind was informed of this, M. Askari, Yadgar Nasir M. and M. Hindal were ordered to attack the villains and to chastise them. Nearly 3,000 horse and foot of the insolent knaves had gathered together. When the royal order arrived, M. Askari delayed to proceed and Yadgar Nasir Mirza gave him some strokes with his whip, saying that it was from his discord that things had come to such a pass. Still he did not take warning, and Yadgar Nasir Mirza and M. Hindal obeyed and went against the crowd. A great fight ensued, and a large number of the ill-fated villagers (*guwaran*) were killed. The Mirzas after giving them a lesson returned, and M. Askari who had come to complain, was reprehended. His Majesty Jahanbani hastened on to Agra. The provinces were in confusion and sedition raised its head on every side. Next morning, His Majesty proceeded to the dwelling of that great exemplar, Mir Rafi,[4] who was sprung from the Safavi Sayyids, and was incomparable for knowledge and wisdom, and was the choice favourite of princes. He took council with him, and the final conclusion of His Majesty was that he should go towards the Panjab. If M. Kamran were helped by the sovereignty of reason and suspiciousness, and should bind on himself the girdle of good service and come actively forward to help, the rift of strife might still be closed. With this right intention, he proceeded to Lahore. M. Askari went to Sambal and M. Hindal to Alwar. On 18th Muharram (26 May 1540), Qasim Husain Sultan joined the king near Dihli through the influence of Beg Mirak, and a large body of men collected for the king's service. On the 20th, he again set out, and on the 22nd, M. Hindal and M. Haidar joined him in Rohtak.[5] On the 23rd His Majesty halted there. The garrison shut the gate of the city in his face, thereby opening the doors of disgrace for themselves. His Majesty addressed himself to the attack and in a short space of time chastised the garrison. On 17th Safar, the army arrived at Sihrind and on the 20th, Mir Faqr Ali closed life's litter while on the march. When the army approached Lahore and were near Daulat Khan's *sarai*, M. Kamran came forward to meet him and did homage. His Majesty alighted in the garden of Khwaja Dost Munshi which is the most charming spot in Lahore, while M. Hindal took up his quarters in the garden of Khwaja Ghazi, who was then M. Kamran's *diwan*. After that, M. Askari came from Sambal and settled himself in the house of Amir Wali Beg. At this time, the fortunate Shams-ud Din Muhammad who had given his hand at the river-bank, arrived and was exalted by princely favours. On the 1st[6] Rabi-ul Awwal 947, all the noble brothers and Amirs and other servants collected but in spite of so many lessons and celestial warnings, these fine fellows (*azizan*) were not taught and did not bind the girdle of sincerity on the waist of resolve. Several times, they gathered together on His Majesty's service, and deliberated made vows and promises of unity and concord, and took the great and godly as their witnesses. Khwaja Khawand Mahmud,[7] brother of Khwaja Abdu-l-Haqq and Mir Abu-l-Baqa frequently took part in the deliberations. At length one day, all the Mirzas, nobles and grandees having been assembled, wrote out a deed (*tazkira*) of concord and unanimity, and to this auspicious minute, all the officers gave their signatures.

When this record of confidence had been executed, the deliberations began. His Majesty gave lofty counsels and uttered excellent words. With his pearling tongue, he said,[8] 'The miserable end of those who deviate from the straight highway of concord is known to all. Especially since not long ago when Sultan Husain Mirza beat the drum of death in Khurasan, he left eighteen[9] capable and fortune-favoured sons and yet, in spite of all their array of wealth, in consequence of fraternal discord, the kingdom of Khurasan (which for so many years had been a centre of peace) became in a short space a centre of calamities and was transferred to Shahi Beg. No trace remained of any of the sons except of Badi-uz Zaman who went[10] to Turkey, and all the sons of the Mirza had been reviled and reprobated by high and low. With what difficulty had His Majesty Giti-sitani-Firdaus-makani conquered a Hindustan—so vast a country! If through your disunion it pass from our possessions into the hands of nobodies (*nakasan*) what will the wise say of you? Now is the time to sink the head into the bosom of good counsel and to exert it from jealousy's collar, so that you may attain headship among mankind, and be a means of gaining the favour of God.'

Everyone of the authors of compact and of the lords of confederacy forgot the recent agreements, and each declaimed according to his own good pleasure. M. Kamran said, 'What occurs to me is that the king and all the Mirzas spend some days unencumbered in the mountains while I take their families to Kabul. When I have put them into safety, I shall return and join you.' M. Hindal and Yadgar Nasir Mirza said, 'At present we cannot fight the Afghans. The thing to do now is to go to Bhakkar and to subdue that country. By its means we shall conquer Gujrat, and when these two kingdoms have fallen into our hands and we have brought the business to an end, the deliverance of this country (India) will be effected in an admirable manner.' M. Haidar said, 'It is proper that all the Mirzas should settle down after securing the slopes from the mountains of Sirhind to those of Sarang.[11] I, engage that with a small force I will in two months get possession of Kashmir. When that news comes, let every man send his belongings to Kashmir, for there is no safer place. It will take Sher Khan four months to arrive and he will not be able to bring into the hill country the gun-carriages and cannon which are the support[12] of his warfare. In short time the Afghan army will be ruined.'

As their words and their hearts were not in unison, the meeting ended without any conclusive speech. Whatever proposals were brought forward, and whatever sound advice His Majesty communicated in the hope that perchance the lamp of wisdom might be lighted for M. Kamran and that he would turn away from his dark ideas and come to the abode of candour, the Mirza did not alter what he had said. All his endeavour was that every one should be ruined, and he counted it a gain that he himself might go to

Kabul and secure a corner for his own enjoyment. He was perpetually occupied with evil thoughts, and fortune-conferring words did not arouse him. Ostensibly he breathed unanimity and would say, 'I shall come forth in some fortunate hour and shall gird on the belt of courage and fight the foe with singleness of heart.' But secretly he was strengthening the foundations of opposition, and this to such an extent that out of wickedness and blindness, he privately sent Qazi Abdu-l-lah his *sadr* to Sher Khan, that he might establish friendly relations with him, and made a contract of affection with him. He sought the fulfilment of his desires from the help of enemies, and he wrote a letter to the effect that if the Panjab were secured to him as formerly, he would soon bring affairs to a successful issue!

After these occurrences. Sher Khan came to Delhi, but did not advance further he saw that what had happened was due to his good fortune, and was apprehensive lest if he went on further, his affairs would retrograde. He was extremely frightened about the combination which he heard was making progress in Lahor. Meanwhile the seditious *sadr (sadr-i-pur-ghadar*) who added vile malice to natural baseness, arrived. Sher Khan whose centre was pivoted in craft, warmly embraced him, and was a thousand times emboldened[13] by the good news of disunion. He gave him an answer in accordance with the Mirza's requests. That wretch (the *sadr*) instigated him to make a hostile advance, and held out prospects of desertion. Sher Khan sent a crafty fellow along with him to ascertain the real state of affairs and then return. M. Kamran received Sher Khan's ambassador in the garden at Lahore, and held a feast on that day. He also by entreaties induced His Majesty Jahanbani to come there. That crude, short-sighted Mirza again sent the same wretch (his *sadr*) to Sher Khan. On this occasion the betrayer of his salt came to the bank of the Sultanpur river, and brought forward disloyal proposals and encouraged Sher Khan to cross the river. Thereupon Muzaffar Turkman, who was stationed on outpost duty near the Sultanpur river, came and reported to His Majesty that the enemy had crossed the river (the Bias) and killed his brother's son Junaid Beg, who from his qualities of mind and body was a *persona grata* at Court.

In the end of Jumada-i-akhir his Majesty Jahanbani and the Mirzas crossed the Lahore river (the Ravi), which was fordable, and marched stage by stage to the Cinab. As His Majesty Jahanbani was resolved to attempt Kashmir, he sent a body of troops in advance with M. Haidar to that province. For, when M. Kamran made a rapid march to Qandahar to contend with Sam Mirza, he left M. Haidar in charge of Lahore. Khwaja Haji, 'Abdu-l-makri,[14] Zangi Chak, and many of the nobles were opposed to the ruler of Kashmir and came to Lahor in order that by their intimacy with M. Haidar they might obtain an army from M. Kamran and so get possession of Kashmir. Though M. Haidar exerted himself, their wish was not fulfilled. When M. Hindal raised a disturbance by having the *khutba* read in his own name, and M. Kamran marched from Lahore to Agra, M. Haidar by great exertions contrived to raise an army and to despatch it from the capital[15] under the charge of Baba Jujak[16] who was one of Kamran's superior officers. His design was that this force should proceed to Kashmir under the guidance of the Kashmiri nobles aforesaid, and take possession thereof. Baba Jujak was negligent in setting out and meanwhile the disaster of Causa ferry, which was a blow to eternal dominion, came to be known. He gave up the expedition, and the Kashmiri nobles tarried in Naushahr,[17] Rajauri and the hollows of the hills in the expectation of some event. But they were continually writing letters to M. Haidar full of the advantages of conquering Kashmir, and the Mirza used to bring these to his Majesty Jahanbani's notice. His holy heart grew daily more and more eager to visit the charming country of Kashmir, and meanwhile he gave permission to the Mirza to proceed in the first place to Naushahra with a body of troops. If the Kashmiri nobles, who were always urging the expedition, should come forward, Sikandar Topci, who was a fief-holder in that neighbourhood, was to join him with his troops. When he got to the passes, Amir Khwaja Kalan, who was one of the high officers of His Majesty Giti-sitani Firdaus-ma-kani, and of whom some account has already been given, was to come and help. As soon as the news of Khwaja Kalan Beg's arrival should reach his Majesty Jahanbani he would proceed in person towards that province. His Majesty was on the bank (the right or west bank) of the Cinab when M. Kamran and 'Askari Mirza went off to Kabul with Khwaja 'Abdu-l-haqq and Khwaja Khawand Mahmud. Muhammad Sultan Mirza, Ulugh Beg Mirza and Shah Mirza on hearing, in the territory of Multan, about the separation, joined M. Kamran on the bank of the Indus. In the beginning of Rajab, 947, M. Hindal, Yadgar Nasir Mirza and Qasim Husain Sultan succeeded by importunity in taking His Majesty Jahanbani off to Sind, though his intention had been to march to Kashmir. Khwaja Kalan Beg, who had promised to accompany his Majesty Jahanbani Jannat-ashiyani, went off from Siyalkut and joined M. Kamran. Sikandar Topci withdrew to the Sarang hills. In the same Rajab, after His Majesty Jahanbani had gone towards Sind at the Mirza's instigation they, after going some stages, left him out of thoughtlessness and the suggestions of Beg Mirak, who had abandoned his service and joined them. Meanwhile Qazi 'Abdu-l-lah arrived with some Afghans. M. Hindal's scouts seized them and brought them before him. The ill-fated Afghans were put to death, but the wretch 'Abdu-l-lah having still some breaths of his life remaining, escaped punishment at the intercession of Mir Baba-Dost.[18] For twenty days the Mirzas wandered in the desert of astonishment. They had no idea what to do or where to go. They were severed from fortune and auspiciousness, and having left dominion's fellowship, they had lost their object. As they had not followed the path of purpose, they were astonished and confounded. His Majesty Jahanbani had gone by way of the desert towards Bhakkar, and was wending his way according to guess and conjecture. They found no water, and there was no grain, but went on under the guidance of endurance and with the rations (*zad*) of reliance upon God. At length one day they heard the sound of a kettle-drum. On inquiry, it was found that M. Hindal and Yadgar Nasir Mirza were three kos away and were pacing the valley of search. His Majesty Jahanbani sent Mir Abu-l-baqa, who had left the society of M. Kamran, and become a companion of the sublime army, to the Mirzas to give them information about the camping ground, and to speak wise words and advise them to come and kiss the sublime threshold. The Mir in accordance with these instructions counselled the Mirzas and acted as their guide to the blessing of service. They proceeded in harmony towards Bhakkar. Khawiss Khan and a large army of Afghans was coming up in the rear, but though the imperial army was very small, the former had not the courage to give battle. In the end of Shaban (last days of 1540) when the camp reached Uc[19] the Amir Sayyid Muhammad Baqir Husaini, who was the frontispiece of Sayyids and of the Ulama of the age, expired and was buried there. His Majesty grieved much for his death, but as this evil earth is a scene of departure and dismissal (*quzashtani u guzashtani*), he displayed that resignation to the Divine command which is the ornament of those whose regard is fixed on the station of submission (*maqam-i-taslim*). When they had encamped near the residence of Bakhshui Langa one of the landholders and grandees of that part, an order of grace and a mandate of favour was sent together with a glorious *khilat* by Beg Muhammad *Bakawal*, and Kacak Beg, and hopes were held out that he should receive the title of Khan Jahan, a flag and a kettle-drum, and he was invited to do loyal service and to send corn to the camp. He came forth to meet the envoys, saluted them, and behaved with.

(Abul Fazl, *Akbar Nama*, vol. II, Chap. XXVI, text 166-72, Eng., tr. by Beveridge, New Delhi, 1979, pp. 354-61)

NOTES

1. Apparently, all that is meant is that he entered Humayun's service.
2. Probably the man mentioned in Babur's Mem. 400 and 401 as a servant of Khwaja Kalan.
3. See Erskine, Hist. II, 192n. The place meant is Bhangaon in the Mainpuri district, and on the Grand Trunk Road. Jarrett II, 184, where it is spelt Bhugaon (note by Mr. Irvine).
4. A.F.'s mother belonged to this family. Cf. Jarrett II, 423, where Mir Rafi is called Mir Rafiu-d-din Safavi of Ij (Shiraz). See also Babur's Mem. 345-9. A.F. speaks in the *Ain* of his being one of the Hasan and Husaini Sayyids. He died in 954. Jarrett l.c. Rafi was one of the doctors who encouraged Sher Shah to break his word to Puran Mall and the garrison of Raisin.
5. In the Panjab, 42 miles north-west of Dihli.
6. Three days after this Humayun had a vision in which the coming birth of Akbar was announced. *A.N.* 13. Cf. Gulbadan's account, f.39b.
7. See *Tar. Rash.* 395. where he is called Hazrat Makhdumi Nura. Abdu-l-Haqq was his younger brother.
8. An exaggeration, which occurs also in the *Tar. Rash.* (B.M. Ms. Or.157, 348b) Sl. Husain had fourteen sons and of these seven (according to Khwand Amir) died before their father.
9. A.F. gives Humayun the credit of this speech, but the *Tar. Rash.* from which he no doubt copied it, ascribes it to Haidar. See p. 478.
10. He too, it seems, went there as a prisoner, having been taken by Sultan Salim. He died many years before this speech was made, of plague, in 926. Possibly the reference was to his son Muhammad Zaman, who served Babar and survived till the battle of Causa in 1539.
11. See *Tar. Rash.* 479n. Mr. Elias is no doubt right in considering that Sarang is not a place-name. There is an Afghan tribe in the Salt Range called the Sarangzai (Temple, *J.A.S.B.*, 1880, pp.101 and 106), and perhaps Haidar M. referred to them rather than to an individual. His idea was that the Mughals should occupy the lower ranges between the Indus and Kashmir, i.e. from Sihrind in the S.E. to Rawalpindi on the N.W. For Sultan Sarang, see Blochmann, 456; and Delmerick, *J.A.S.B.*, 1871, p. 87. He was Sultan Adam's brother and must have died in Sher Shah's time, for it was Sultan Adam who delivered up Kamran to Humayun.
12. Babur's Mem. 416, mentions that the Bengalis, i.e. the Afghans are famous for their skills in artillery.
13. *Lit.* one heart became a thousand.
14. Text, Bakri, but the variant Makri is right. Zangi is Rumki in text.
15. Agra. See *Tar. Rash.* 482.
16. *Tar. Rash*, Cucak Haidar does not say he was an officer of Kamran and apparently he was a Kashmiri. It appears from Nizamu-d-din and from Jarrett II, 390, that there was an expedition before this from the Panjab and that

Kamran sent one, Muhammad Beg into Kashmir but that after plundering he had to return. Apparently this was not long after Humayun's accession.

17. In the Peshawar district.
18. I believe this to be the father of Hamida, Akbar's mother. See Gulbadan who calls Hamida's father Mir Baba Dost. As he was a teacher in Hindal's service, he might naturally intercede for a learned man.
19. That is, arrived opposite Uc for they were travelling down the west side of the Cinab and between it and the Indus.

Mirza Haidar Dughlat in *Akbar Nama*

The story of M. Haidar is as follows: when he had got assistance from His Majesty Jahanbani, he proceeded towards Kashmir, as already related. When he got to Naushahr,[1] the officers whose names have already been given, loyally came forward and did homage, and again showed him how he could enter Kashmir and take possession of it. The Mirza advanced by the passes in reliance on the Divine aid and the royal fortune. Meanwhile a schism occurred in the Emperor's army. As has been already stated, Khwaja Kilan Beg either from his own inclination or at the instance of M. Kamran, abandoned the enterprise and joined M. Kamran, while Muzaffar Topci[2] went off to the Sarang[3] hills. None remained with M. Haidar save a few old servants and the troops whom His Majesty Jahanbani had deputed to his assistance. But as there was much strife and dissension and confusions of the Kashmiris, and on 22nd Rajab, 947 (22 November 1540), he entered by the pass of Punc[4] and conquered Kashmir without a battle or a struggle. For at that time it had been long without an established ruler, and the ministers tyrannously held the country in their own possession, and while giving to one of the claimants the name of monarch, themselves exercised the authority. At that period a person called Nazuk Shah having a name that was no name[5] was the reputed sovereign. Under such circumstances in whatever direction there might not be union, or plan, or counsel, or judgement, to that quarter did the affairs of the country drift. It was the winter quadragesima[6] and there was heavy snow. When Kaci Cak saw[7] that M. Haidar was disposed to make himself independent, he, using the craft and perfidy which are indispensable to Kashmiris, left Kashmir and went before Sher Khan. For his object in bringing in M. Haidar was his own aggrandizement and when that was not achieved, but when on the contrary things assumed a different shape, he withdraw his hand and entered on another scheme. He now tried another course and gave Sher Khan the sister of Isma'il, the son of Muhammad Shah.[8] When he had made himself acceptable by this means he took 'Alawal Khan,[9] Hasan Khan Sarwani and others to the number of 2,000 men and came to Kashmir. Meanwhile Abdal Makri, who was his backer, died of dropsy, and M. Haidar having left his family in Andarkot,[10] which is a very strong place, was in a protected position. The people of Kashmir all deserted him and but few persons remained with him. He spent three months in the mountain defiles, and then on Monday, 20 Rabi'u-s-sani, 948 (16 August 1541), a battle took place, and by God's help he gained the victory. Though the enemy, consisting partly of Afghan auxiliaries and partly of faithless Kashmiris was more than 5,000 horse, yet as their action was based on faithlessness and disloyalty, it did not succeed and they were defeated. Many of the enemy were slain, and a party of them were made prisoner. Kashmir came absolutely into the possession of the Mirza, and the Kashmiri preacher (*khatib*) Maulana Jamalu-d-din Muhammad Yusuf found the chronogram fath-i-mukarrar (victory repeated = 948). Though the use of the word 'repeated' (*takrar*) might be applicable to the present expedition of the Mirza, yet as he himself has pointed[11] out in his history, the references is to the fact that he once came[12] to Kashmir by the pass of Lar, as the agent of Said Khan, the ruler of Kashmir, and got possession of it on 4th Shaban,[13] 939 (1 March 1533). But towards the end of Shawwal of that year (May 1533) he made peace with the Kashmir ministers, and with Muhammad Shah who was then the nominal ruler. The Shah's daughter was given in marriage for Iskandar Sultan, the Mirza's son,[14] and the Mirza returned by the way he had entered.

'When on this (last) occasion a providential victory was gained, and Kashmir was conquered, he for ten years zealously applied himself to its administration and clothed that charming land, but of desolated[15] appearance, with cities[16] and civilization. He sent for artists and craftsmen from all quarters and laboured for its renown and prosperity. Especially was music[17] in brisk demand and varieties of instruments were introduced. In short, the outward condition of that country, that is, its worldly state, acquired solidity. But owing to the Mirza's frigid[18] and inspid bigotries, the result of imperfect development, the essentials for Kashmir, viz., unanimity and fidelity, found a bad market. And to this day there is an odour of bigotry about the Kashmiris, for there is a powerful influence in association, and especially is strong impression produced by the ways of princes who are vigorous. It is to be hoped that by the blessing of his Majesty, the king of king's truth and chastity (*haqiqat-u-haqqaniyat*) Kashmir, spiritual and temporal, may attain unity, and that the articles of worship and religion may become current, unadulterated by hypocrisy and bigotry.

'One of the capital and most inauspicious mistakes of the Mirza was that in spite of such victory he read the *khutba* and struck the coin in the name of Nazuk Shah after the fashion of the Kashmiri ministers. He should have fulfilled his duty of loyalty towards his Majesty Jahanbani and have impressed the *darahim* and *dananir* and the pulpit *rostra* with his Majesty Jahanbani's sacred name. Apparently he was temporising and was not giving currency to disloyalty, for when Kabul[19] was taken he honoured himself by having the *khutba* read in his Majesty Jahanbani's sacred name.

'In 958 (apparently October 1551) he became, in a night attack by the Kashmiris, a traveller to the region of non-existence. The short account of this is as follows:

"The Mirza transgressed the law of justice—dominion's watchman—and took to living for his own lusts and pleasures. He let fall from his hands prudence and the bearing of burdens, those two arms of felicity. The fraud and seditiousness of the Kashmiris which had been subverted by the Mirza's skill and sagacity, again stood up and the hypocritical and wicked faction took the road of deceit and in friendly garb did the work of enemies. Their best stroke was the separating his army from him by stratagem, and scattering of his capable servants. Some were sent towards Tibet, some to Pakli, and some to Rajauri. Idi Rina and Husain Makri, son of Abdal Makri, gained over Khwaja, Haji the Kashmiri pedlar (*baqqal*) who was the manager of the Mirza's affairs. They drew a great many to their side and marched against the Mirza. Ghazi Khan and Malik Daulat Cak also joined them. Near Khanpur, between Hirapur and Srinagar, which last is the chief city of Kashmir and the seat of government, they made a night-attack on the Mirza. He had approached the quarters of Khwaja Haji to release Qara[20] Bahadur, who was a prisoner. Suddenly he lost his life at the hands of Kamal Dubi,[21] though some say one of his own servants unknowingly hit him with an arrow.[22]"'

(Abul Fazl, *Akbar Nama*, Chapter XXXI, Persian text, pp. 196-7
Eng. tr. by Beveridge, pp. 402-6)

NOTES

1. *Tarikh-I Rashidi*, p. 483, Naushahr is in Kashmir and W.N.W. of Jammu. It is not given in the Ind. Gaz. It was the old capital.
2. Ibid., Iskandar. And B.M. Add. 27,247, Iskandar.
3. The Ghakkar country S.W. of Kashmir, Panuc.
4. Text, but there is a variant Punc and Nizamu-d-din so writes it.
5. A.F. puns on the word Nazuk which means slight or slender, and calls it an *ism-i-bi-musammai* (like the 'outis' of Ulysses). There is a variant Barak (qu. Narak), and the coins give Nadir. See Mr. Rodgers' paper, *J.A.S.B.*, 1885, p.114.

6. *Cilla-i-dai*, the forty days of *Dai*, a Persian month corresponding to December. Here *Dai* must be taken to mean winter as the month has 30 days only. The text has *baran*, rain, but *Tarikh-i Rashidi* (485) shows that snow is meant.
7. *Lit.* read on the brow of M. Haidar's conduct the writing of independence (or absolute sovereignty).
8. A former ruler of Kashmir. Apparently, he resigned four times and Nazuk three. Jarrett II. 37-80.
9. Variant 'Adil Khan and in Farishta, but Nizamu-d-din has Alawal'.
10. See *Tarikh-i Rashidi*. 485 n. and Jarrett II. 370, but perhaps Indrakat is the true reading.
11. *Tar. Rash.* 423.
12. *Tar. Rash.* 423 and Jarrett II. 363. Haidar on that occasion entered Kashmir from Baltistan, i.e. from the N.E.
13. Apparently this is not the date of the victory, but of occasion on which the Kashmiris rallied after their defeat, (*Tar. Rash.* 437-9), but Haidar is not very explicit. In the *Ain*, A.F. wrongly gives the date as 930. Jarrett II, 390.
14. Iskandar was not Haidar's son, but Said Khan's (*T.R.*) 341, though Haidar at Said Khan's request regarded him as his own. In the *Ain*, A.F. correctly calls Sikandar (or Iskandar) the son of Said Khan. See also *Akbar Nama* III. 552, 1.8. Probably *pisar-i-khud* is a copyist's error for *pisar-i-khwanda*, i.e. adopted son.
15. *Hukm-i-kharaba dasht. Hukm* seems to be used here in the sense of appearance, of. p.127, 1.4 and p. 196, 1.5 from foot.
16. Apparently an adaptation of the phrase used by Haidar about his predecessor Zainu-l-abidin.
17. *Lit.* for music there was a bazaar (*hat*).
18. *Ta'assubha-i-khunauk-i-binamak. Ta'assub* has etymologically nearly the meaning religion. Cf. p. 334. 1.9. *Khunuk*: A.F. in the *Ain* uses the word with reference to Sultan Sikandar, another ruler of Kashmir. He seems to contrast his bigotry and that of Haidar with the liberal spirit of his son Zainu-l-abidin. See Jarrett II. 387, 388. It is clear from the *Tar. Rash.* that Haidar was a rigid Muhammadan of the Sunni school and a persecutor of Sufis, &c. See Elias & Ross, p. 436. He there takes exactly the opposite view of that of A.F. with regard to Sikandar and Zainu-l-abidin.
19. There are Kashmir coins bearing Humayun's name and dated either 952 or 953. *Tar. Rash.* 24. Mr. Rogers gives representations of three, of which one, No. 33, bears the date 950. Kabul was twice taken by Humayun, once in Ramazan 952 (November 1545), and again in Rajab 955 (August 1548). A.F. apparently refers to this second capture for the mentions that after this event, an embassy arrived from Haidar (*A.N.* II. 284).
20. Haidar's second cousin. See his biography in the *Ma' asir* III. 48 and in Blochmann 460.
21. Text, *Duli*, but the variant *Dubi* is right, for Nizamu-d-din speaks of Kamal Dubi as one of the persons who is supposed to have killed Haidar.

22. See *Tar. Rash.* App. A. 487.
A.F.'s account of Haidar should be compared with Nizamuddin's and Farishta's and also with the *Tar. Rash.* and A.F.'s own statements in the *Ain*. In the latter, he is more favourable to Haidar than in the *Akbar Nama*. The translation (Jarrett II. 340), does not seem quite correct. What A.F., text 584, 585, says, I think, is that the Kashmiris read the *Khutba* in Nazuk's name and that Haidar at one and the same time recognized Himayun. The introduction of arts into Kashmir which A.F. ascribes, in part, to Haidar, is modestly attributed by the Mirza himself to Zainu-l-abidin. *Tar. Rash.* 434.

Extracts from *Akbar Nama*

One of the occurrences of this year was the sending M. Qara Bahadur Khan, the brother[1] of M. Haidar Gurgan, to conquer Kashmir. As it is a proper part of the rules of the administration of justice and of world-sway that whenever a ruler engages in his own pleasures, and spends his time in gratifying his lusts, and does not attend to the cherishing of his subjects and to sympathizing with the oppressed, and to overthrowing the oppressors, the Lord of the Age, to whom Almighty God has given power and made him the governor of the terrene and terrestrials, should for the sake of thanksgiving to God, strive to uproot that tyrant, and to make over the inhabitants of his country to the prudent and just-minded, and should consider that as the preamble of elect devotion; so, acting upon this principle, an order was issued this year that a force be put under the command of M. Qara Bahadur, a relative of M. Haidar, and one who was acquainted with the country, and that he be sent to conquer Kashmir, in as much as the disturbances by intriguing Kashmiris, and the injustice of Ghazi Khan, the ruler of Kashmir, had been brought to the royal ears. A large body of men were nominated to assist Qara Bahadur. At this time, Ghazi Khan, the son of Kaci Cak, was the ruler of Kashmir, for the government thereof had come to him after his father. But the truth is that he was the son of Husain Cak, the brother of Kaci Cak. When the measure of Husain Cak's days was filled, Kaci Cak, either swayed by lust, or influenced by political consideration, took to himself his pregnant wife. Two or three months after the marriage, Ghazi Khan was born.[2]

As Qara Bahadur was not skilful nor laborious, he proceeded on his service after long delay, and arrived at Rajauri in the height of the hot season. Nasrat Khan, Fatah Cak, nephew of Daulat Cak, Lohar, Ankari, Naji Rina, the brother of Idi Rina, Yusuf Cak, son of Ramaki Cak, and Khwaja Haji came and joined him. As they saw that the army was not well constituted, Nasrat Khan, Fatah Cak, Lohar and Ankari[3] fled to Kashmir. The army remained for three months in Lali Khokar, near Bimbhar, waiting for the coming of the auxiliaries. As the leaders of the force were old servants, they took the longer time in arriving. It is not by such slowness and heaviness that the entrance into Kashmir is to be effected, for the roads of that country are of such a nature that if the ruler get news a few days before of the approach of strangers and seize the passes, it would be difficult, or rather impossible, for an army adorned with thousands of Rustams to get possession of the country. Ghazi Khan, who heard of the coming of the army, and some months had passed meanwhile, so strongly fortified the roads and passes that there could be no idea of getting through them. He also sent[4] his infantry down from the hills. M. Qara Bahadur, after fighting for some days near Rajauri, was defeated and turned back. It was not solely the strength of the Kashmiris that effected this. The season of ague, the beginning of the rains and the non-arrival of the auxiliary force were the principal causes of the defeat. A wonderful fight occurred on this occasion. On one side were musketeers, and on the other archers. Though the royal soldiers were few in number, yet by heavenly aid they did great things and gave proof of their courage. Kucak Bahadur, a Rustam-hearted man, specially distinguished himself. At last, as the thing was an impossibility and as the superintendents of fortune had reserved the conquest of this delightful country for another time when the world-cherishing Shahinshah should throw off the veil over his world adorning beauty and undertake the management of affairs without the partnership of the destructive and contumacious, they did not on this occasion gather together the materials of victory. Qara Bahadur made such arrangements as he could and came to the fort of Darra[5] near Rajauri. Kucak Bahadur was wounded with an arrow. He became a prisoner and was brought before Ghazi Khan. As the Kashmiris had seen his valour, Ghazi Khan received him with kindness and made him over to the physicians. But as remedies were of no avail, he took the path of annihilation.[6] Next day, Qara Bahadur arrived at Naushahra. At this time of increasing dominion H.M. the Shahinshah in accordance with the suitability of the time was engaged in Agra, the capital, in rendering thanks for the glorious favours of God and under the disguise of inattention to the affairs of the sovereignty, for every day the notes of fortune and felicity were coming into evidence. In every direction, countries were being conquered, and the news of victories was arriving. From all quarters, the lords of sincerity were congregating in crowds. Dominion was increasing, and fortune was adorning. Understanding was becoming far-sighted, and men were becoming devoted. What place in that holy festival could be held by such news as that of what had happened to Qara Bahadur? And what dust of loss could it raise in that sublime sanctuary?

(Abul Fazl, *Akbar Nama*, vol. I, Chapter XXXII,
Eng. tr. by Beveridge, Delhi, 1972, pp. 197-9)

NOTES

1. The word *baradar* is used here loosely. He really was Haidar's cousin. From an incidental remark of Gulbadan Begam, to the effect that Gulcahra was in Qara Khan's house when her brother Hindal died, it seems probable that Gulcahra had been married to Qara Bahadur. This might account in part for his getting this command.
2. A similar account is given by Nizamu-d-din in his account of Kashmir, and he gives details of Ghazi Khan's reign.
3. The *T.A.*, p. 620 seems to call him the son of Sahu. At p. 624, Lohar is called Deo Hari.
4. The *T.A.* says, he himself stayed at Nauruzkot and sent on his infantry.
5. There is the variant Datara, and several MSS. have Danra, so it may be the Danaor marked in Dr. Stein's map, see *J.A.S.B.*, for 1899 as N.E. of Rajapura.
6. But the defeat was a very serious one. The T.A. tells us Qara Bahadur had a large army and nine elephants, and that 500 Moghuls were killed. The *T.A.* gives particulars of Ghazi Khan's reign. See also Jarrett II. 380.

Mirza Muhammad Haidar Dughlat in *Haft Iqlim*

(484) The two brothers Saltiz Mirza and Muhammad Haidar Mirza whose mother was the daughter of Yunus. Due to his seniority in age, amiability and gallantry, Saltiz Mirza occupied the throne of his father. He entrusted Kashghar and Yangi Hesar to his brother. After sometime, the suspicion against his brother provoked Haidar Dughlat to move out to his friend Dust Muhammad whose sister was married to him. Saltiz Mirza ruled over the territory successfully till he died after seven years in 869. Since his two sons Mirza Aba Bakr of Kashghar and Umar Mirza were minor and could not take over the reins of government in their hands, the dignitaries of the country sent for Mirza Haidar. In the meantime, Dust Muhammad Khan came and besieged Yarkand where the sons of Saltiz Mirza were stationed. After a protracted siege, peace was patched up. The wife of Saltiz Mirza was given in marriage to the invader as part of the agreement. Since the lady took along with her Mirza Aba Bakr, her son, the entire territory of Kashghar fell into the hands of Haidar Mirza. He (Haidar) was a man with the reputation of possessing a balanced character who was a seeker of peace, a well-wisher and far from being a trouble shooter. He ruled for 24 years. When Mirza Aba Bakr came of age, Dust Muhammad Khan betrothed his sister to him and took great care in his (485) upbringing. But being distressed with Dust Muhammad, the prince decided to come to his uncle Mirza Haidar and met him in Kashghar. Since Mirza Aba Bakr was a resolute, brave man and had many young mighty followers, eager to support him in his venture of conquering the land of Yarkand, he sent a man to his uncle and expressed his allegiance. With 3,000 horsemen who were with Mirza, he came and wanted to conquer Khotan where the Mirzas were ruling. From the time of amir Khudaidad, they held the sway of this territory which was inherited by their descendants namely Qul Nazar and Khan Nazar Mirza. The latter had a weapon of iron which resembled to a sceptre and which he used in place of lance and sword. At last when Mirza Aba Bakr started for the campaign the Mirzas sued for peace that year. But a second time, the Mirzas were treacherously put to death and Khotan was easily occupied. The event startled all and

sundry and created fear in the minds of Mirza Haidar's nobles who advised him to be careful in the context of his nephew who could raise the standard of rebellion against Haidar also and that the time had come when some solution had to be sought and Aba Bakar had to be checkmated. When this news reached Mirza Aba Bakr he petitioned, with all sincerity and submission to his mother who had now been married to Mirza Haidar Dughlat after the death of her husband Dust Muhammad. His mother interceded on his behalf and managed to convince Mirza Haidar that Mirza Aba Bakr was afraid of the enmity of nobles and, therefore, hesitated to come though he had every regard, faith and confidence in M. Haidar. The lady further requested that since one of Mirza Haidar's servants had always ruled over Yarkand, if his own son Haidar himself is given the charge there (486) would be no problem. At the moment the aliens are jealous and their skirts are burning whereas in case of her son, the heart is burning. Mirza Haidar was a simpleton and was caried away by the magical artifice of his wife. He not only accepted every word of it but willingly agreed to forgive all the mistakes committed by Aba Bakr. Gradually the matters came to such a pass that even most of the trustworthy amirs were given a cold shoulder and turned out mainly because of instigations of Mirza Aba Bakr and his mother.

When the supporters of Muhammad Mirza were dispersed, Mirza Aba Bakr sat on the saddle of conquest and overran the environs of Kashghar and Yangi Hesar. When such inroads occurred repeatedly, Mirza Haidar went with his 30,000 chosen men to punish him. But Haidar was defeated and had to retreat when Mirza Aba Bakr faced him bravely with 3,000 horsemen. Mirza Haidar reported the matter to Yunus Khan who took this affair lightly and proceeded with 15,000 men to join Mirza Haidar. Mirza Aba Bakr came out with the same 3,000 men to meet the joint forces of Yunus Khan and Mirza Haidar and inflicted a crushing defeat upon them. Haidar Mirza strengthened the fortifications of Kashghar and Yunus Khan returned to Moghulistan. Next year, Yunus Khan came with sixty thousand horsemen to exterminate Aba Bakr. Mirza Haidar also joined with 90,000 cavalry and infantry. They besieged Yarkand. Subsequently, one day Mirza Aba Bakr came with five hundred horses and fell upon the forces of enemy in such a manner that the Moghuls were disgusted with Yunus Khan, deserted him and fled away. Mirza Haidar then gave up the hope of recovery of domain and accompanied Yunus Khan to Aqsu. Thereafter, he remained in the service of Khan. (489) Mirza Haidar went to conquer Kashmir with 4,000 horsemen (493) and subjugated the land. Mirza Haidar had performed many good and laudable actions. He had all along surpassed many in the amiability and pleasantness of nature, and excelled in the correctness of language and expression, sobriety of diction, perfectness of management, bravery, gallantry and in art of fighting. At the advice of Sultan Abu Said he had, therefore come from Kashghar and Tibet to Kashmir and conquered it. A second time, he came from India to Kashmir and ruled over this territory for seven years. He finally gave up his life in Kashmir. His book *Tarikh-i-Rashidi* which is famous throughout the world and was dedicated to Rashid Khan, the ruler of Kashghar is renowned throughout the world.

(Amin Ahmad Razi, *Haft Iqlim*, vol. III, 1010 AH, pp. 473-99)

Mirza Haidar Dughlat in *Tabaqat-i-Akbari*

Nazuk Shah sat on the seat of government; but five or six months had not passed, when Mirza Haidar having acquired power in the country took possession of it. During the period of his rule public prayers were read and coins struck in the renowned name of His Majesty, Jinnat Ashiani Humayun Badshah.[1]

AS ACCOUNT OF THE RULE OF MIRZA HAIDAR

In the year 948 AH, at the time, when Jinnat Ashiani having been defeated by Sher Khan had come to Lahore, Abdal Makri and Regi Chak[2] and some other of the chief men of the Kashmir sent a petition, through Mirza Haidar, containing expressions of their loyalty, and incitements to him to seize the country. His Majesty (i.e. Humayun) gave Mirza Haidar permission to go; and also decided to follow him himself. When Mirza Haidar arrived at Bhimbar,[3] Abdal Makri and Regi Chak came and joined him. There were not more than four hundred horsemen with Mirza Haidar. When he arrived at Rajauri, Kaji Chak, who was (then the *de facto*) ruler of Kashmir, came with three thousand horsemen and fifty thousand foot soldiers to the Karmal[4] pass, and strengthened it. Mirza Haidar abandoned that route, and started by way of Punj. Kaji Chak in his great pride did not guard that road; and Mirza Haidar, crossing the hill, arrived in the Kashmir plateau; and suddenly took possession of the city of Srinagar. Abdal Makri and Regi Chak having secured a footing, took charge of all affairs; and allotted some *parganas* as the Mirza's *jagir*. It so happened that about this time Abdal Makri's days came to an end; and he died after recommending his sons to the Mirza.

After the arrival of Mirza Haidar in Kashmir, Kaji[5] Chak went to Sher Khan Afghan in Hindustan; and brought five thousand horsemen, who were commanded by Husain Sharwani and Adil Khan[6] and two elephants, to reinforce his own troops. Mirza Haidar in concert with Regi Chak, advanced to meet him in battle. The two parties arrayed their forces between the villages of Datarbar[7] and Kawah; and the breeze of victory having blown on the plumes of the standards of Mirza Haidar, the *amirs* of Sher Khan and Kaji Chak were routed. Kaji Chak took up his residence in Bahramgalah.[8] Mulla Muhammad Yusuf the *Khatib* (preacher) of the *Jama* Mosque of Srinagar[9] obtained the date of the victory in the words '*Fath-i-Mukarrar*'.

In the year 950 AH, Mirza Haidar took up his residence in the fort of Indarkot.[10] Owing[11] to Mirza Haidar having entertained suspicious about Regi Chak, the latter fled and went to Kaji Chak; and the two united together, and in the year 951 AH, advanced towards Srinagar with the object of destroying Mirza Haidar's (power). Bahram Chak son of Regi Chak reached Srinagar. Mirza Haidar nominated Bandagan Kokah and Khwajah Haji Kashmiri to crush him, and he was unable to meet them, and fled. When the Mirza's troops pursued him, Kaji Chak and Regi Chak, considering flight the safest course, took up their quarters at Bahramgalah. Mirza Haidar left Bandagan Kokah and others at Srinagar and advanced to conquer Tibet; and seized the fort of Kosur,[12] among the great forts, and some other forts.

In the year 952 AH Kaji Chak and his son Muhammad Chak died of a shivering[13] fever. Mirza Haidar passed the year in peace. In the year 953 AH, Regi Chak fought with the *amirs* of Mirza Haidar, and was killed; and his head with that of his son Ghazi Khan was brought before Mirza Haidar.

In the year 954 AH, an ambassador arrived from Kashghar. Mirza Haidar went to Lar to welcome him. Uja Bahram, son of Masud Chak, who for seven years had fought bravely in Kamraj and had defeated everyone there, made proposals of peace to Khan Mirak Mirza, and made conditions and engagements. Khan Mirak Mirza summoned him after making promises and taking oaths. But when Ujh Bahram came to his *majlis*, he drew a dagger out of his boot, and stabbed him in the stomach. The man, wounded as he was, fled and got into the jungle. Khan Mirak Mirza hastened in pursuit of him, and seizing him cut off his head, and brought it to Mirza Haidar at Lar, believing that Mirza Haidar would be pleased. Idi Zina,[14] after the food had been brought in, rose up in great anger and wrath on seeing the head; and said 'It is not right to kill a person after making conditions and engagements'. Mirza Haidar said, 'I had no information of these happenings'.

After this, Mirza Haidar advanced from Lar to Kishtwar. He made Bandagan[15] Kokah, Muhammad Makri, Makna Mughal, Mirza Muhammad Yahiya and Idi Zina the commanders of his vanguard; and himself remained in the village of Jhalu[16] near (the boundary of) Kishtwar.

The vanguard, after traversing marches of three days in one day, arrived in the village of Dohut[17] which was on their side of the river Marma. The Kishtwara army was on the opposite side of the river. There was a skirmish of arrows and musket shots, but neither party could cross the river. The following day Mirza Haidar's army, turning from the right road, wanted to get into Kishtwar. When they arrived in the village of Dar,[18] a strong wind rose, and it became dark. The Kashmiris came bravely in crowds and attacked them. Bandagan Kokah, who was the leader of Mirza Haidar's army, was slain with many others. When they started from there, Muhammad Makri and his son with twenty-five principal men were slain on the road. The rest, who had escaped death from the sword, came and after suffering much privations, joined Mirza Haidar. The Mirza coming back from there in the year 995 AH, advanced towards Tibet and conquering Rajauri from the Kashmiris made it over to Muhammad Nazr[19] and Sabr Ali. He gave Pakli to Mulla 'Abd-ul-lah and Little Tibet to Mulla Qasim; and conquering Great Tibet appointed a person of the name of Muhsin[20] to be its governor.

In the year 956 AH, Mirza Haidar turned his attention to the fort of Danil.[21] Adam Kakhar came there; and prayed for the pardon of the offenses of Daulat Chak, nephew (brother's son) of Kaji Chak. Mirza Haidar granted the prayers; and sitting with Adam in his pavilion, summoned Daulat Chak to come there. The latter became[22] angry, and rose up, and taking the elephant which he had brought with him as a tribute, went away. Some persons wanted to pursue him, but Mirza Haidar forbade them.

After some time, Mirza (Haidar) returned to Kashmir. Daulat Chak[23] and Ghazi Khan and Hasan Chak and Baram Chak went to Haibat Khan Niyazi, who having been defeated by Islam Khan, had come to Rajauri. Islam Khan had also come to Madwar,[24] belonging to the Naushahra area in pursuit of the Niyazis. He[25] sent Saiyid Khan 'Abd-ul-mulk one of his trusted servants to Haibat Khan; and Saiyid Khan, having introduced matters about an amicable settlement, brought the mother and sister of Haibat Khan to Islam Khan. The latter then turned back, and coming to the village of Ban,[26] in the neighbourhood of Sialkot, took up his quarters there. The Kashmiris mentioned above took Haibat Khan to Baramula,[27] and wanted to take him to Kashmir, in order to do away with Mirza Haidar (with his help). He, however, could not make up his mind to do so; and sending a Brahman to Mirza Haidar, made proposals for peace. Mirza Haidar sent ample funds by the hand of that Brahman; and Haibat Khan, leaving the place where he was, went to the village of Bir,[28] which is a dependency of the territory of Jammu. The Kashmiris[29] separated from him, went to Islam Khan, but Ghazi Khan went to Mirza Haidar.

In the year 957 AH, Mirza Haidar, becoming assured in his mind of the condition of the outskirts of the country, sent Khwajah Shams Mughal, with a large quantity of saffron, as an ambassador to Islam Khan; and in the year 958 AH, Khwajah Shams returned with many presents, and much rich stuffs; and Yasin Afghan came from Islam Khan with Khwajah Shams; and Mirza Haidar gave (many) shawls, and much saffron to Islam Khan's ambassador, and gave him permission to return.

He then appointed Qarra Bahadur Mirza to the government of Baharmal; and sent Idi Zina and Nazuk Shah and Husain Makri and Khwajah Haji from amongst the Kashmiris with him. Qarra Bahadur[30] and the Kashmiris left Indarkot, and took up their quarters at Baramula, and commenced to create disturbances on the ground that the Mughals looked down on them. The Mughals represented this to Mirza Haidar, but the latter did not believe it; and said that the Mughals were not in any way better than the Kashmiris in the matter of creating disaffection and disturbance. Husain Makri[31] sent his brother Ali Makri to Mirza Haidar, to make him acquainted with the treachery of the Kashmiris, so that he might decide to recall the army. Mirza Haidar took no notice and refused to listen to him; and said 'What cause of jealousy should the Kashmiris have against you that they should act treacherously towards you', and did not summon the army back.

On the 27th of the Ramadan there was a great conflagration in the Indarkot; and most of the houses were burnt down. Qarra Bahadur and all the men sent the following message, 'Our houses have been burnt down; if you will give an order we would come and repair our houses and turn our attention next year to Baharmal.' Mirza Haidar did not at all agree to this; and the army had to proceed to Baharmal, whether they liked it or not.

Idi Zina and all the Kashmiris then combined together; and when night came they separated themselves from the Mughals, and came to the pass of Baharmal. They also separated Husain Makri and Ali Makri from the Mughals, and took them with themselves, so that they might not be slain with the Mughals. In the morning, there was a battle between the Mughals and the men of Baharmal, and the former were entangled and confined in the hills. Saiyid Mirza, however, fled to Dabil.[32] About fifty renowned Mugahls were slain, and Muhammad Nazr and Qarra Bahadur were taken prisoners. The rest, who escaped the sword, came by way of Punch to Bahramgalah. Mirza Haidar was deeply grieved on hearing this news and ordered that the broken silver *degs*[33] (saucepans), which are now current in Kashmir, be coined. He also made Jahangir Makri his trusted agent, and bestowed the *jagir* of Husain Makri on him. He also gave horses and money to many of the craftsmen, and made soldiers of them. Just after this news came that Mulla Abd-ul-lah on hearing of the rising of the Kashmiris was coming to meet Mirza Haidar; but when he arrived near Baramula the rebels who had collected in large numbers slew him; and Khwajah Qasim was slain in little Tibet; and Muhammad Nazar was taken prisoner in Rajauri; and the Kashmiris having collected in large numbers had come from Bahramgalah to Hirahpur.[34] Mirza Haidar, having no other alternative, came[35] out of Indarkot, with the intention of engaging them. The total number of men with him was only a thousand. Among the Mughals men like 'Abd-ru-Rahman and Shahzada Lang, and Khan Mirak Mirza[36] and Mir Makta and Sabr Ali[37] and others, who were altogether about seven hundred men, joined him; and they took up their quarters at Shihab-ud-Dinpur.

Daulat Chak and Ghazni Khan and other notable leaders in concert with Idi Zina collected their men, and came to Hirapur, and leaving that place came to the village of Khanpur. Mirza Haidar encamped in the plain of Khalidgarh, which is close to Srinagar. Fath Chak, whose father had been slain by the Mughals, raided Indarkot with Raja Bahram and three thousand men, in order to avenge his father's death, and burnt down the buildings erected by Mirza Haidar in the *Bagh-i-Safa*. When Mirza Haidar heard this news, he said, 'I did not bring these edifices from Kashghar. With Divine favour similar ones can be built'. Sabr Ali burnt down the edifices of Sultan Zain-ul-abidin, which were in Suyyapur, in retaliation of the burning down of Mirza Haidar's buildings, but the Mirza was not pleased at this. (They) also burnt down the houses of Idi Zina and Nauruz Chak in Srinagar. After this Mirza Haidar came and took up his residence in Khanpur. In this village there is a plane[38] tree, in the shade of which two hundred horsemen can stand; and it has been found by trial, that whenever a single branch of it is moved the whole tree shakes. The writer of this history Nizam-ud-din Ahmad was in attendance, when the sublime standards of His Majesty the Khalifa-i-Ilahi went on a visit to Kashmir for the second time; and he saw the tree, and examined it. In short, the Kashmiris moved from Khanpur and came to the village of Adanpur;[39] and the distance (between the two armies) was not more than two *karohs*.[40]

Mirza Haidar then decided that he should make a night attack on the enemy; and he gave direction that Mirza Abd-ur-Rahman, his brother, who was adorned with the attributes of piety and purity, should become his heir; and took the allegiance of his men to him. Then, they all mounted, and started for making the attack. As decreed by fate, there were heavy clouds that night. When they arrived near the tent of Khwajah Haji, who was the cause of the disturbance, and also the *vakil* (agent or representative) of the Mirza, nothing could be seen owing to the darkness. Shah Nazr a cuirassier says, 'At this time I shot an arrow. The voice of Mirza Haidar came to my ears, which said "thou[41] has done an evil thing". I knew that my arrow had hit the Mirza.' It is also narrated that a butcher hit his thigh with an arrow. Another tradition is that Kamal Kokah[42] slew him with the sword; but there was nothing (visible) on his body except a wound caused by an arrow.[43] In short, when the morning came, it was bruited about, that a Mughal, who had been killed, was lying there. When Khwajah Haji and his son arrived at the spot, they saw that it was Mirza Haidar. They raised his head from the ground. There was no more than breath left. The dying man opened his eyes, and surrendered his life to the creator. The Mughals fled to Indarkot. The Kashmiris going in pursuit of them took[44] up the corpse of Mirza Haidar to the Darbadu Mausoleum, and buried it.

The people were sorely grieved at the death of Mirza Haidar. The Mughals got into Indarkot, and fortified themselves in it; and fight went on for three days. On the 4th day Muhammad Rumi shot[45] Kashmiri coins from mortars, and every one, who was hit, was killed. At last, Khanam,[46] the widow of Mirza Haidar, and his sister said to the Mughals, 'As Mirza Haidar has gone away from us, it is better to have peace with the Kashmiris.' The Mughals accepted this, and sent Amir Khan, the architect, to the Kashmiris to conclude a pact. The Kashmiris agreeing to a peaceful settlement gave a letter containing engagements and oaths to the effect that they would not cause any trouble to the Mughals.

The period of Mirza Haidar's rule was ten years.

When the gates of the fort (of Indarkot) were opened, the Kashmiris entered the apartment[47] containing valuable furnitures, etc., belonging to Mirza Haidar and carried away fine and delicate goods. They brought the family and dependents of Mirza Haidar to Srinagar, and placed them in[48] the house of Hasan Matu. They divided the country of Kashmir among themselves; and *pargana* Devsar[49] was allotted to Daulat Chak, and that of Wahi[50] to Ghazi Khan and that of Kamraj[51] to Yusuf Chak and Bahram Chak. One *lakh* of donkey-loads[52] of paddy (or rice in husks) was allotted to Khwajah[53] Haji, the *vakil*, of Mirza Haidar. Daulat Chak gave *pargana* Devsar, which was his *jagir* to his son Habib Chak, and the daughter of Idi Zina was married to the latter. The *amirs* of Kashmir, and more specially 'Idi Zina, having gained complete power, raised Nazuk Shah on the throne, and kept him as a puppet; but in fact 'Idi Zina was the *Badshah*.

In the year 959 AH Sankar Chak, son of Kaji Chak, wanted to go away from Kashmir (i.e. I suppose Srinagar), as Ghazi Khan who called himself the son of Kaji Chak and had much *jagir*. The details of this statement are these: that Sankar Chak was the son of Kaji Chak without any difficulty or doubt, and Ghazi Khan although he was commonly known to be the son of Kaji Chak was not in reality his son; for Kaji Chak, after the death of his brother Hasan Chak, took the latter's widow, who was then with child (who was afterwards named Ghazi Khan); and after two or three months the child was born. Hence Sankar Chak on account of the envy (which he bore) to Ghazi Khan wanted to leave Kashmir and go to Idi Zina.[54] When a rumour of this got about, Daulat Chak and Ghazi Khan sent Ismail Hayat[55] and Harju, with one hundred men to summon Sankar Chak. They told them that if he did not come with them they were to bring him by force. Sankar Chak did not come on their summons, and went to Idi Zina. In the end Idi Zina came to them and made an amicable settlement; and the *parganas* of Kothar[56] and Khawar and Mawar having been allotted to Sankar Chak the disturbance subsided.

At this time, there were four groups who had power in Kashmir (1) Idi Zina with his group; (2) Hasan Makri, son of Abdal Makri with his group; (3) the Kishtwaris[57] whose leaders were Bahram Chak and Yusuf Chak and others; and (4) the Kamis of whom Kaji Chak, Daulat Chak and Ghazi Khan were the leaders. Yehayyi Zina gave his daughter in marriage to Hasan Khan, son of Kazi Chak, the daughter of Daulat Chak was married to Muhammad Makri, son of Abdal Makri: and the sister of Yusuf Chak, son of Regi Chak, Kopwari[58] by name, was married by a *nikah* ceremony to Ghazi Khan. These alliances became the cause of the strength and power of the Chaks; and they, in concert with one another, went away to different parts of the country. Ghazi Khan went to the country of Kamraj, and Daulat Chak to Suyyapur. The Makris went to Bankal;[59] and Idi Zina remained at Srinagar in a sorrowful mood, and devised plans for their destruction.

As the season for egg fruits or *brinjals* now came, Idi Zina ordered that fowls and *brinjals* may be brought so that they be cooked together. This was a dish much[60] liked by the Kashmiris. Then Bahram Chak and Saiyid Ibrahim and Saiyid Yaqub came at his invitation, but Yusuf Chak did not come. Idi Zina had the three guests seized and imprisoned them. Yusuf receiving information of this went away by way of Kamraj with three hundred horsemen and seven hundred foot soldiers, and joined Daulat Chak. When Idi Zina saw that the Kashmiris had united with the Chaks, he released the Mughals, such as Qarra[61] Bahadur Mirza, Abd-ur-Rahman Mirza, Khan Mirak Mirza, Shahzada Lang, Muhammad Nazr, and Sabr

Ali from prison; and showed favour of them; and giving each one of them a horse and armour[62] and some money remained at Chakpur.[63]

At this time, Saiyid Ibrahim[64] and Saiyid Yaqub, in concert with Jarud, who was employed to guard them, fled; and going to Kamraj joined Daulat Chak. Bahram Chak could not escape. On the following day, Ghazi Khan came to Srinagar with three[65] thousand horsemen. Idi Zina sent the Mughals to fight with him; but he broke down the bridge, and so the Mughals could not do anything. At this time Daulat Chak also came, and joined Ghazi Khan in Srinagar, and they joined together and took up a position in the *Idgah*. There were constant skirmishes between the two parties, but Baba Khalil went to Idi Zina in order to bring about a peace. He said, 'You put your trust in the Mughals, and paid no regard to the Kashmiris. This was not right.' Having said words like this he effected a peace between him and the Kashmiris. They then sent away the Mughals with their families and dependents by way of Tibet. Khanamji,[66] the sister of Mirza Haidar went away to Kabul by way of Pakli.[67] The people of Tibet slew Sabr Ali[68] and the other Mughals; and Khanamji reached Kashghar.

Following these events news came that Haibat Khan and Saiyid Khan[69] and Shahbaz Khan Afghans, who were of the Niyazi tribe, were coming to conquer Kashmir; and had arrived in the *pargana* of Banihal,[70] and have entered the hills of Lunkot.[71] Idi Zina, Hasan Makri, Bharam Chak, Daulat Chak and Yusuf Chak combined together, and marched out to fight the Niyazis. The two parties confronted each other, and fought bravely. Bibi[72] Rabe'a, the wife of Haidar Khan, also fought manfully; and struck Ali Chak with her sword. In the end Haibat Khan and Saiyid Khan and Firuz Khan and Bibi Rabe'a were slain and the Kashmiris returned to Srinagar with triumph and victory. They sent the heads of the Niyazis by the hand of Ya'qub Mir to Islam Khan, in the village of Ban, which is near the river Chinab.

After that, hostilities again commenced among the Kashmiris; and Idi Zina, in concert with Fath Chak, Lohar Makri,[73] Yusuf Chak, Bahram Chak, and Ibrahim Chak came to Khalidgarh,[74] and took up residence there; and Daulat Chak, Ghazi Khan, Husain Makri and Saiyid Ibrahim Khan and a band of *Dums*[75] joining together, took up their quarters in the *Idgah*. When a period of two months had passed in this way, Yusuf Chak, Fath Chak, Lohar Makri[76] son of Sahu, and Ibrahim Chak separated themselves from Idi Zina; and joined Daulat Chak. Then Daulat Chak mounted with a large force advanced against Idi Zina; and he being unable to meet them, fled without fighting; and went to the village of Jharo.[77] About this time he wanted to mount a horse, but by accident the horse kicked him on the chest, and he concealed himself in the village of Samnak;[78] and he passed away from the world on account of the pain of the accident. They brought his body to Srinagar; and buried it in the mausoleum[79] of Musa Zina. The *amirs* then rebelled and excusing Nazuk Shah, who had nothing of the government except a name, from that also, determined on ruling themselves.

(Nazuk Shah) ruled nominally for two months, for the second time, after (the death of) Mirza Haidar.

(Khwaja Nizamuddin Ahmad, *Tabaqat-i-Akbari*, vol. II, translated and annotated by Brajendra Nath De, Delhi, 1992, pp.707-25)

Mirza Haidar Dughlat Kashmiri, who had been with Mirza Kamran, remained with his Majesty Jinnat Ashiani; and received favours from him. Mirza Kamran also took away a large number of the Agra troops with him.

On account of these dissensions which took place, Shir Khan became emboldened; and came to the bank of the Ganges and sent a force across the river against Kalpi and Itawah. Qasim Husain Sultan Uzbek, in concert with Yadgar Nasir Mirza, and Iskandar Sultan fought with the Afghans in the neighbourhood of Kalpi, and slew a son of Shir Khan, who was the commander of that army, and a large number of others, and sent his head to the service of the emperor at Agra. The latter then came towards the bank of the Ganges with the object of crushing Shir Khan, and crossing the river opposite to Kanauj, sat down for the period of a month opposite to the enemy.

(*Tabaqat-i-Akbari*, p. 72)

NOTES

1. One MS. omits by mistake the passage from جنت اشياني to محمد همايون بادشاه بود, including the heading about the rule of Mirza Haidar.
2. He is called Zangi Chak in the lith. ed. of Firishtah, Zungy Chuk by Col. Briggs (vol. IV, p. 498), and Zangi Chakk by Rodgers (*J.A.S.B.*, vol. LIV, p.117) and the Cambridge History of India; and the translators of the *Tarikh-i-Rashidi* also call him Zangi Chak; but the name is رنگی چک in both MSS. of the Tabaqat, and more distinctly ریگی چک in the lith. ed. Of course there is very little difference between ریگی and زنگی as written in Persian. रिगमचक्र or रिगमचक्रेश is mentioned by Prajyabhatta in lines 388, 393 and elsewhere. *Raga Cakra* may be transformed to Regi Chak, but cannot be changed to Zangi Chak. Regi Chak is, therefore, the correct name and I have kept it رنگی چک in the text-edition is incorrect.

3. The name looks like بنبر in the MS. The lith. ed. has بنبر and Firishta lith. ed. has بهير Bhir. Col. Briggs (vol. IV, p. 498) has Mein, and Rodgers (*J.A.S.B.*, vol. LIV, p. 117) has Bhir. The Cambridge History of India does not mention the name of the place. I consulted the fountain head for the correct name, but Mirza Haidar is delightfully vague in the *Tarikh-i-Rashidi*, page 183, where he says, 'when I arrived at the foot of the pass (leading to) Kashmir, Kachi Chak ascended (?) by one road and we by another, and without further contention or discussion, we (all) arrived at (Kashmir).' I cannot find any place of the name of Bhir, but Bhimbar or 'Bhimbhar' lies at the foot of the outer hills, in the centre of the tract between the Vitasta and the Cinab, note 180, page 33, Stein's *Rajatarangini*. So I think Bhimbar is correct, and I have kept it. In the text-edition M. Hidayat Hosain has بي .
4. Firishtah has كتل كرتل and Col. Briggs (vol. IV, p. 498) has Kurmul pass. In the text-edition كرتل has been changed to كيرتل. Rodgers (*J.A.S.B.*) vol. LIV) p.117, has transformed Katal Kartal to 'Khabal Kartal (it is called Karnal by Erskine)'; and he has transformed پنج ,which is written as بنج in the MSS and in the lith. ed. of the Tabaqat and as بهج in Firishtah lith. ed., out of all recognition to 'Pabhaj (the Pamij of Erskine)'. Col. Briggs comes very near the correct name and calls it Punnuj. The Cambridge History of India, page 288, does not give the name of the place, where Kaji Chakk was stationed; but gives the correct name (Punch) of the pass, by which Mirza Haidar crossed the hill. It makes the statement that Mirza Haidar's allies "engaged Kaji Chakk's attention by threatening a frontal attack'; but I cannot find any authority whatever for it. Both the Tabaqat and Firishtah simply say that he abandoned that route, and Mirza Haidar (whose wrods I have quoted in the preceding note) whatever he says or means, does not mention any threat of a frontal attack by his allies on Kachi Chak.
5. According to Mirza Haidar (*Tarikh-i-Rashidi*, p. 485), there was an interval of some months between his arrival, and Kachi Chak's bringing the troops from Shir Khan. Mirza Haidar crossed the pass into Kashmir on the 22nd of Rajab. Them the winter came on, and it was not till the beginning of spring that Shir Khan's troops arrived. Just then Abdal Makri was attacked by paralysis and died.
6. The name is Alawal Khan in one MS. and in the lith. ed.; but it is 'Adil Khan in the other MS. and in the lith. ed. of Firishtah.
7. The names are دتربارو and كاوه in one MS. and in the lith. ed., and دنه مارو and كاوه in the other MS. Firishtah lith. ed. has ونه ديار and كاوه. The *Tarikh-i-Rashidi* gives various particulars which are not to be found in the Tabaqat or in Firishtah, but does not give the names of these villages. Col. Briggs (vol. IV, p. 499) has Dhunuj and Gava, and Rodgers (*J.A.S.B.*, vol. LIV, p. 117) has Danahdyar and Kawah. The Cambridge History of India does not give any name. In this text-editon the names are دتربار and موضع كاوه .
8. Bahramgalah has wrongly been changed to پرم كله Parmkalah in the text-edition.

9. The meaning is not clear, some words having probably been omitted. I have, however, supplied the omission by a reference to page 485 of the *Tarikh-i-Rashidi*.
10. According to the *Tarikh-i-Rashidi*, page 485, Mirza Haidar is said to have placed his and his followers' families in the fort of Andarkul, when he was going to fight Kachi Chak and Shir Khan's armies. The traslators say in a note that this must be the Indrakot of Firishtah. Firishtah, however, would not dream of writing Indrakot, he was Indarkot. It may be noted, however, that there is a *pargana* called Andarkoh among those of the Kamraj tract (Stein, vol. II, p. 494). So Indarkot may be correct.
11. Firishtah agrees, but Col. Briggs makes various mistakes. Rodgera's account follows Firishtah. The Cambridge History of India, page 288, apparently follows Col. Briggs about Zangi (Regi) Chakk's becoming suspicious of Haidar's attitude, instead of Haidar becoming suspicious of him.
12. The name of the fort is کوسور and الوسوا in the MS, and کوسوار in the lith. ed. Firishtah lith. ed. has لوسور; Col. Briggs (vol. IV, p. 499) has Looshoo, and Rodgers (*J.A.S.B.*, vol. LIV, p. 117) has Lansur. The *Tarikh-i-Rashidi* is of no help, as it ends with Mirza Haidar's victory.
13. تپ ولرزه instead of تپ لرزه in the text-edition.
14. It is not clear who he was. He was apparently someone is authority, for Mirza Haidar thought it necessary to excuse himself on the ground of his ignorance of Mirak Mirza's acts (Jan Mirak Mirza in the text-edition). He is, however, named, a few lines below, as one of the leaders of the vanguard of the army sent to conquer Kishtwar. Both the MSS. say بعد ارحاضر ساختن طعام. The lith. ed. omits the word طعام. Frisihtah says nothing about anything being brought. If the reading in the MSS, is correct, the production of the head was delayed till the food was brought in, apparently with the object of giving it a special relish. In the text-edition the name is عیدی رینا Idi Raina, but Rodgers (*J.A.S.B.*, vol. LIV, p.118) has Ide Zina.
15. The names are as I have them in the text in the MSS. and the lith. ed. of the Tabaqat, with slight variations. Firishtah lith. ed. omits the third and makes Mirza Muhammad Yahiya Zina one man. Col. Briggs (vol. IV, p. 500) only gives the name of Bandagan Koka, and adds 'with other officers'. Rodgers (*J.A.S.B.*, vol. LIV, p. 118) follows Firishtah, but calls the last man there Yahi Zina. *The Cambridge History of India* does not give any name.
16. The name looks like جهاز and جهانر in the MS. and دوجهابر in the lith. ed. of the Tabaqat. Firishtah lith. ed. has جهاپر Col. Briggs does not mention the place, but Rodgers, following Firishtah, calls it Jhapur. The place is not mentioned on page 21 of the Introduction to Elias and Ross's *Tarikh-i-Rashidi* where the editors speak of expedition against Kishtwar. In the text-edition it is جهالو.
17. The name of the village looks like دوهت and روهت in the MSS. It is دوست in the lith. ed. of the *Tabaqat*, and دهنوت in that of Firishtah. Rodgers (*J.A.S.B.*, vol. LIV, p. 118) has Dahlot. No name is given in the introduction of the

Tarikh-i-Rashidi; but it is said that the advance guard came up with the enemy on the banks of the Kishtawar river. The name of the river is ماربا or مارما, or ماريا in the MS. and the lith. ed. of the Tabaqat. Firishtah lith. ed. has مارما . Col. Briggs does not give the name; and Rodgers says, 'where the river winds'. In the text-edition ديهوت is adopted as the name of the village.

18. The name of the village is دار in one MS. and in the lith. ed., and داد in the other MS. It is Dhar in the lith. ed. of Firishtah, and Rodgers (*J.A.S.B.*, vol. LIV, p. 118).
19. The first name is Muhammad Nazr in both MSS. and the lith. ed. The second name is Sabr Ali in one MS. and جبر علی which may be a mistake for ببر علی in the other, and Mir Ali in the lith. ed. Firishtah lith. ed. has Muhammad Nazir and Nasir Ali. Col. Briggs does not mention the names, and Rodgers gives the names after Firishtah. No names are given in the introduction (p. 21) to the *Tarikh-i-Rashidi*, which contrary to Nizam-ud-din and Firishtah's account, that he seized Rajauri, Pakli, Little Tibet and Tibet in the order mentioned, says that he conquered Little Tibet (or Baltistan), Tibet (or Ladak) and subequently Rajaori and Pakhli.
20. The name is محسن نام in both MSS. and محسن نامی in the lith. ed. Firishtah lith. ed. has Mulla Qasim.
21. The name is دمل and دهلی in the MSS. and ديهل in the lith. ed. Firishtah lith. ed. has دنيل . Col. Briggs (vol. IV, p. 501) has Danel, and Rodgers (*J.A.S.B.*, vol. LIV, p. 118) has Danel. In the text-edition it is دهل .
22. Firishtah surmises that غالباً حنانچه مرضی اوبود اعزاز و اکرام بجا نياوردند as the probable reason for Daulat Chak's anger.
23. Firishtah substitutes Jai Chak for Hasan Chak, and is followed by Rodgers. Firishtah, however, has the name of Haibat Khan correctly, but Rodgers (*J.A.S.B.*, vol. LIV, p. 118) converts it to Haidar Khan, though a few lines further down, he has Haibat Khan Niyazi.
24. The name is Madwar in one MS. and Badwar in the other and in the lith. ed. Firishtah lith. ed. has Madwar. The article از appears to have been omitted before ولايت in the MSS. and the lith. ed.
25. Firishtah (and following him, Col. Briggs) and Rodgers (*J.A.S.B.*, vol. LIV, p.118) say that it was Haibat Khan who sent Sayyid Khan Niyazi to Islam Shah.
26. The name is Ban in one MS. and in the lith. ed. It looks like Man in the other MS. Firishtah lith. ed. and Rodgers have Ban, but Col. Briggs (vol. IV, p. 502) has Bhimbur.
27. The MSS have وامله and the lith. ed. has دابله , but Firishtah lith. ed. has باره موله which, I think, is correct. It is داملة in the text-edition.
28. The name is بير , and بركه in the MSS. and لبر in the lith. ed. Firishtah lith. ed. has هير . Col. Briggs (vol. IV, p. 502) has 'the town of Subzees', while Rodgers (*J.A.S.B.*, vol. LIV, p. 119) has Hir, and says that it is Nir in MS. No. 6571, in the British Museum. هركه has been adopted in the text-edition.

29. Firishtah and Col. Briggs and Rodgers agree, Rodgers (*J.A.S.B.*, vol. LIV, p. 119) says that he has seen two coins of Islam Shah of this time, and adds that the Kashmiris were tired of Mirza Haidar, and wanted to have Islam Shah as their king, and the coins were struck in anticipation of his conquering the country, or they might have been struck by Mirza Haidar himself in compliment to Islam Shah.
30. Firishtah agrees, but Rodgers wrongly translates the words از اندر کوت برامده which are in the lith. ed. of Firishtah as well as in the Tabaqat, by the words 'came back to Indarkot'. The sentence, as it stands, means that Qarra Bahadur and the Kashmiris all commenced to create disturbances, but apparently it was the Kashmiris who did so. Rodger's translation of the words که مغلان ایشانرا در نظر نمی ارند by the words that 'the Mughals (the forces of Mirza Haidar) were not acceptable to them' also appears to be incorrect.
31. Apparently Husain and 'All were not acting in concert with the other Kashmiris. There are slight differences in the wording of the sentences. I have adopted the reading quoted by one of the two MSS, which makes most sense, but I have had to change the last word طلبید which is in both MSS to طلبد. Firishtah lith. ed. has طلبد. Rodgers's translation (*J.A.S.B.*, vol. LIV, p. 119) in which he reads the word غدر as عذر (excuse) appears to me to be incorrect.
32. The name looks like دهل and دبل in the MSS. and ومل in the lith. ed. and appears therefore to be identical with Danil, see page 712 and note 3. Firishtah lith. ed. however has قلعه بهرمل. دهلی in the next-edition is certainly incorrect.
33. There is a word which looks like سهمی or سهی Sahi, in the MSS. and in the lith. ed. which I cannot make out, but which may be 'made of copper', Firishtah lith. ed. has زریکمه in the corresponding passage. سهسی has been adopted in the text-edition.
34. The name is clearly Hirahpur in the MSS as well as in the lith. ed. Firishtah lith. ed. has what looks like Habzapur. Col. Briggs's account (vol. IV, pp. 502, 503) is very sketchy, the whole of the incident from the appointment of Qarra Bahadur (called Kiran Bahadur) to Baharmal (called Bheerbul) to the death of Mirza Heidur being narrated in the space of eight or nine lines; and the name of the place under consideration is not mentioned. Rodgers (*J.A.S.B.*, vol. LIV, p. 120) calls the place Hambarapur.
35. Rodgers translates از اندرکوت برامده as 'came to Indarkot'.
36. جان پرک میرزا in the text-edition is a misprint for خان میرک میرزا.
37. The name is صبر علی in one MS. and the lith. ed., and حرعلی in the other MS. Firishtah lith. ed. has جر علی, but Rodgers has Jai Ali. In the text-edition میرمکنه is a misprint for میرمکته.
38. The name is بید in one MS., and جناربید in the other. The lith. ed. has خبازی. جنار and خبازی may be mistakes for چنار Chinar or the plane tree, while بید is a willow. Firishtah lith. ed has بید and Rodgers has willow. Both plane trees and willows grow in Kashmir, but I should be inclined to think

that the tree in question was a plane tree which is tall spreading tree.

39. Both MSS. have ادن پور . The lith. ed. has ادب پور. Firishtah lith. ed. has ادنی پور and Rodgers (*J.A.S.B.*, vol. LIV, p. 120) has Adnipur.
40. It should be noted, however, that just before this, apparently the two armies were both in Khanpur.
41. The reading in the MSS. are قباحت بولدی and قباحت تولدی and in the lith. ed. صاحب تولدی. These are all incorrect, unless بولدی or تولدی is same word in the dialect of Kashghar. Firishtah lith. ed. has قباحت کردی which I have adopted. The whole affair is mysterious. Although it was dark the cause of the death could have been ascertained. Then, why was the corpse, or in fact the man, who was on the point of death left lying where he had fallen.
42. The name is کمال دوته in the MSS and کمال دوبی in the lith. ed. I cannot find any meaning of دوته or دوبی . Firishtah lith. ed. has Kamal Kakah and I have adopted it. The reading in the MSS. is followed in the text-edition.
43. One MS. has زخم تیر و تبر و خندر دیگر , which is of course incorrect. The other has زخم تیر چیزی دیگر , which appears to be correct. The lith. ed. is also incorrect; it has زخم تیر و تبر چیزی دیگر . Firishtah lith. ed. has the same reading as the second MS., and this is followed in the text-edition.
44. It is curious that the Mughals did not even attempt to carry away the Mirza's dead body; and it was left to the Kashmiris to bury it. The MSS. as well as the lith. ed. say that they buried the body in در بدو مزار . I cannot find out what this burial place was. Firishtah only says that the Kashmiris seeing the body of the Mirza buried it.
45. There are slight differences in the readings.
46. She is so called in the MSS. and in the lith. ed. Firishtah lith. ed. calls her خانمی and it calls the Mirza's sister خانجی.
47. The word is توشک خانه , which according to the dictionary is a wardrobe, and which Rodgers calls the treasury. It is really what I have called it in the text. There is or at least was some years ago, what was called a *Toshakhana* correctly *Tushakkhana* of the government of India, in which the articles offered to the Viceroy at the Durbars were kept.
48. I have not thought it necessary to point out all the mistakes in Rodgers's paper, but I cannot pass this over. The words both in the Tabaqat and in Firishtah are اهل و عیال میرزا را در سری نگر اوردند و در حویلی حسن متوجادادند but متو of the Tabaqat is منو in Firishtah. My translation is based on this text, Rodgers (*J.A.S.B.*, vol. LIV, p. 12) has, 'the family of the Mirza was taken to Srinagar, and placed in the hands of Manuja'.
49. Given as one of the S.E. *parganahs*, see list on page 369 of the *Ain-i-Akbari*, (Jarrat, vol. II).
50. It is written as رهی in both MSS and the lith. ed. Firishtah lith. ed. has وهی, and I have taken this in preferences to رهی, as it is probably identical with Vihi, one of the *parganahs* east of Srinagar (*Ain-i-Akbari*, Jarratt, vol. II, p. 368).
51. Kamraj is called a tract containing 16 *Mahals*, page 370 of the *Ain-i-Akbari*

(Jarratt, vol. II) but there is a *parganah* also of the name of Kamraj included in the S.W. *parganahs* of the Kamraj tract.

52. یک لک خروار شالی i.e. a *lakh* of donkey-loads of paddy is transformed into 'a lakh of shawls' by Rodgers (*J.A.S.B.*, vol. LIV, p. 121).
53. *Tar. Rash.* 460 and 482.
54. It is not at all clear where he was.
55. The name is written as اسمعیل ریابت in one MS and in the lith. ed. In the other MS the last half of the name is written as هابت without any dots above or below the second or third letters. This second part is distinctly written as هانت in Firishtah lith. ed., and Rodgers has Hanit. اسمعیل هابت has been adopted in the text-edition.
56. The names of the *parganahs* are not very easily decipherable. They look like کوبهار و کهادر وماور in one MS. In the other they are the same except that the first is کولهار. In the lith. ed. there is apparently only one name کوبهادره باره. Firishtah lith. ed. has کونهار و کها در و ماور and Rodgers (*J.A.S.B.*, vol. LIV, p. 122) has Kothar Khawin and Maduru. In the list of *parganahs* in the *Ain-i-Akbari* (Jarratt, vol. II, p. 369) there are two *parganahs* Khattar and Khawarparah, and I think it very probable that Shankar Chak got these. In the tabulated list of Kashmir Parganas in Stein's *Rajatarangini* (vol. II, pp. 493, 494) I find Kutahar, but no trace of any of the other. In the text-edition the names are کوبهار و کهادر و ماور.
57. The name is written very differently in the different MSS., etc. The MSS. have کشتواریان, and کهاواریان; while the lith. ed. has کهتواریان. Firishtah lith. ed. has کپوریان. Col. Briggs (vol. IV, p. 503) has Kapoories, and Rodgers (*J.A.S.B.*, vol. LIV, p. 122) has Kapuris. I prefer Kishtwaris as it means the people of Kishtwar, while the others have no meaning at all.
58. The name is written as کوپرانی and کوپواری in the MSS, and کیواری in the lith. ed. Firishtah lith. ed. has کتواری. The name is not given either by Col. Briggs or by Rodgers.
59. Firishtah lith. ed. has باکل and Rodgers has Pakul, but the MSS and the lith. ed. of the Tabaqat have بانکل Bankal, which is the name of a *parganah* in S.W. part of Kamraj. See page 371 of the *Ain-i-Akbari* (Jarratt, vol. II) where it is Bankal, one of the south-west *parganahs*.
60. The word is مقرر in both MSS. and the lith., ed. of the Tabaqat. Firishtah lith. ed. has لطیف و مکرر.
61. The names are as I have them in the text in the MSS and in the lith. ed., with slight differences. In the Firishtah lith. ed. some of the names are different.
62. The word used is سرپا in one MS and in the lith. eds. of the Tabaqat and Firishtah, and سروپا in the other MS I cannot find either Sirpa or Siropa in the dictionary. Rodgers has translated the word as armour, and I have adopted his translation. There is a Bengali or Hindi word *Siropa* (शिरोपा) which means an article of dress, e.g. a scarf, which can be worn as a mark of distinction; for instance, in certain places of pilgrimage various different kinds of *Siropas*

are given to the pilgrims, according to the amounts offered by them to the presiding deity of the temple. *Siropa* may also mean something covering the head and feet.

63. The name of Chakpur of one MS and in the lith. ed. of Firishtah. In the other MS. and in the lith. ed. of the Tabaqat it is چک پرتو Chakpartu.
64. This passage with which Firishtah agrees word for word has been translated by Rodgers. (*J.A.S.B.*, Vol. LIV, p.122) quite incorrectly as: 'the Sayyids Ibrahim and Yaqub by the help of the troopers escaped from prison, and joined Ghazi Chak at Kamraj'. The name of the officer-in-charge is incorrectly given as جاردو Jardu instead of جارود Jarud in the text-edition.
65. The numbers are very differently given. One MS has سی هزار سوار. The lith. ed. has سی هزار کس . In the other MS and Firishtah lith. ed. it is سی سوار ; and this is followed in the text-edition. I am inclined to think that three thousand was the correct number.
66. The name is خانم جی in one MS and خانم in the other MS and in the lith. eds. of the Tabaqat and Firishtah. It will be seen from page 718 and note 5 that in the account of the events which happened immediately after Mirza Haidar's death, his widow was called Khanam in the Tabaqat, but the sister's name was not mentioned; but Firishtah lith. ed. called the widow Khanmi and the sister Khanji. I have, therefore, called the sister Khanamji following the MS. which gives her that name. It is Khanji خانجی in the text-edition.
67. The name in the text-edition is بکلی Bakli. Rodgers (*J.A.S.B.*, Vol. LIV, p. 123) has Pagli.
68. The name looks like صبرعلی in one MS and جرعلی in the other, and میرعلی in the lith. ed. The name is Sabr Ali in earlier passages.
69. Firishtah lith. ed. has سعید خان but later on he calls him سید خان .
70. Firishtah also has Banhal, but Rodgers has Banihal. There is a *parganah* called Banihal to the S.E. of Srinagar (see *Ain-i-Akbari,* Jarratt, vol. II, p. 369).
71. The MSS. and the lith. ed. have درکوه لون کوت. Firishtah lith. ed. has درکوه نون. I cannot find anything about کوه لون کوت or کوه لون. Rodgers (*J.A.S.B.*, vol. LIV, p. 123) has 'at the salt range'; but I do not know his authority for saying so. Of course it may be the Salt Range, which runs parallel to the Jhelum near Pind Dadan Khan.
72. Rodgers (*J.A.S.B.,* vol. LIV, p. 123) calls her Bibi Raba.
73. The name is Kohrad Makri in one MSS; but two lines further down it is Lohar Dankri and is Kohar Dankri and Lohar Dankri in the other and in the lith. ed. In Firishtah it is Kohar Makri. I have accepted Lohar Makri.
74. The name is خالد کر Khaldar and خالد کره Khaldkarah in the MS, and جاله کر Jalakar in the lith. ed. In the lith. ed. of Firishtah it is Khalidgarh, but Rodgers has Khagarh.
75. The MSS have طایفه دو مان , and the lith. ed. of Firishtah has what also looks like طایفه دو ماه. The lith. ed. of the Tabaqat has دونان . I do not know what

the طایفه دومان would mean. دون of course means base, vulgar, etc., and طایفه دونان may mean a group of the common people. Rodgers (*J.A.S.B.*, vol. LIV, p. 123) translates طایفه دومان یکجاشد as 'joining themselves together'.

76. See note 1 above. After لوهر دانکری words like ولندهیو and ولسه بهوه occur in the MSS. The lith. ed. has ولدسهو. Firishtah lith. ed. has no corresponding words. I have adopted the reading of the lith ed. The text-edition has ولنه بهیو.
77. The name is خیرو and جبره in the MSS, and جهرو in the lith. ed. Firishtah lith. ed. has هرو or it may be مرو ; and Rodger (*J.A.S.B.*, vol. LIV, p. 123) has Merv. I cannot decide between these various readings, but I certainly do not consider that Merv is the correct reading. In the text-edition it is جیرو.
78. The name is سمناک in the MSS., and the lith. ed. has سماک but Rodgers has Simale.
79. Rodgers (*J.A.S.B.*, vol. LIV, p. 123) translates درمزار موسی زینا as 'in the village of Musa Zina'.

Mirza Haidar Dughlat in *Muntakhab-ut-tawarikh*

While Kamran had left Humayun in the Church and returned to Lahore (in breach of his agreement that he would leave the whole of his army at Agra in the service of the King, took the whole of it with him with the exception of two thousand men whom he left under the command of Sikandar). Mirza Haidar the Mughal Dughlat, Kashmiri remained at Agra and was kindly treated.

All the Sultans and amirs of the Chaghatai tribe assembled for conference in Lahore. Hypocrisy was still the order of the day, and Muhammad Sultan and his sons fled from Lahore to Mullan while Mirza Hindal and Mirza Yadgar Nasir thought it advisable to proceed to Bhakkar and Tatla. Mirza Kamran prayed that this conference might speedily be dissolved so that he might go to Kabul. After long consultation Humayun sent Mirza Haidar with a large party who had accepted service in Kashmir to that district. It was agreed that Khwaja Kalan Beg should follow Mirza Haidar and that Humayun himself also should proceed thither after the conquest of Kashmir.

When Mirza Haidar arrived at Naushahra which is a well known place, he entered that country with the concurrence of certain Kashmiris and conquered it and on 22nd of Rajab 937/1530, he gained possession of that country.

(Badauni Abdur Qadir, *Muntakhab-ut-tawarikh*, text 353-4, 355-6, Eng. tr. 463, 465, Badauni, vol. I, tr. G.S.A. Ranking (Idrai Adabiyat-i Dehli), Delhi, 1973)

Mirza Haidar Dughlat as depicted by Abul Qasim Farishta

This year Muhammad Humayun padshah ascended the throne after the death of Firdaus Makani Zahiruddin Muhammad Babar. Since one year of Muhammad Shah's reign had already passed, Malik Kachi Chak who had gone to Wilayat of Kuhistan returned after collecting a large number of people from there and came to Kahrar where he had to fight a war against Malik Abdal Makari. He was defeated, retreated and fled to Bhir. At that time Kamran Mirza had extended his sway over entire Punjab. Shaikh Ali Beg and Muhammad Khan Mughal went to the Mughal ruler Kamran without permission of Abdal Makari and after the conquest of Kashmir requested him that if he turns his attention towards the region, there is every possibility of its easy conquest and occupation. Kamran Mirza appointed an army under the leadership of Mahram Beg. As soon as the Mughal army, accompanied by the rebel Kashmiri nobles reached Kashmir, the inhabitants of the place, the Kashmiris took fright and leaving their entire belongings rushed to Kuhistan to seek shelter. The Mughal army pillaged the city and put it to flames. These Kashmiris who had come from Kuhistan to fight against the Mughals were killed. Initially Abdal Makari suspected that Malik Kachi Chak was a Mughal ally. No sooner than he realized the truth he opened negotiations with Malik Kachi Chak. The unity of these two strengthened the power of Kashmiris and boosted their morale. Such was the terrible retaliation that the Mughals were put to flight and driven back to their own land. Since Malik Kachi Chak had noticed the pride and treachery of Malik Abdal, he did not find it agreeable to stay there and proceeded to Bhir. In the previous year in 939, Shah Said Shah Sultan Kashghar had sent his son Sikandar Khan along with Mirza Haidar Kashghari with 12,000 men to proceed via Tibet and Dar to Kashmir. Due to the pressure of their powerful and majestic authority they vacated Kashmir and without giving any fight took shelter in Kuhistan. The Kashgharis entered Kashmir and razed to the ground the high and beautiful structures of buildings which belonged to magnificent palaces of earlier rulers. The city was burnt. The treasures buried under the ground were detected and the entire army acquired immense riches and luggage. Wherever the Kashmiris had concealed themselves, they looked for them and imprisoned them. For three months, this situation continued. Malik Kachi Chak, Malik Abdal Makari and other well known Sardars sought shelter in Chakdarah and finding it insecure and feeling unsafe there they rushed towards Khawar, Barahdar and panick stricken to mountains. Finally they decided to put up a stiff resistance against the Mughals. Iskandar Khan, Mirza Haidar Kashghari faced them and a battle ensued. Sardars like Malik Ali, Mir Hasan, Shaikh Mir Ali and Mir Kamal were killed. The Kashmiris at one time were so demoralized that they thought of giving up but Malik Kachi Chak and Abdal Makari enthused their countrymen and persuaded and exhorted them to fight. So many persons died on both the sides that their exact numbers are difficult to assess. The battle continued from dawn to dusk. After nightfall when the retribution was completed both the parties went to their respective places. Some kind of truce was agreed upon. After the peace was patched up, the Kashgharis sent silk, woollen and rarities to Muhammad Shah to establish matrimonial relations. Muhammad Shah also wrote an agreement along with Abdal Makari and Kaji Chak and sent it alongwith costly presents to the Kashgharis. It was decided that the daughter of Muhammad Shah will be betrothed to Sikandar Khan. All the Kashmiri prisoners of war were to be released. Kashgharis consented and returned to Kashghar. The devastations and worries of Kashmiris came to an end and there was an atmosphere of peace and prosperity. This year (1533) two comets appeared in Kashmir and a severe famine broke out. Many people died of starvation, the survivors preferred to migrate to far-off places. All that destruction and sufferings of the period of war seemed to dwindle before the acute shortage of food and excessive devastations which prolonged for ten months. Since the time of fluorescence of dry fruits and fruits had come, there was some prosperity.

At this juncture there arose some misunderstanding and dissension between Malik Kachi Chak and Malik Abdal Makari. Malik Kachi came out of the town and settled in Zeinpura and Malik Abdal Makari was given the Wizarat of the Shah. The rulers, hakims and the ummal did whatever they liked with the subject population and none came to their rescue or redressal. After a short time Muhammad Shah was seized with fever. He gave away all wealth he had to the poor and down-trodden. Having lingered on for a while in this state he died in 1535 and the period of his reign was fifty years.

THE DESCRIPTION OF THE REIGN OF SULTAN SHAMSUDDIN BIN MUHAMAD SHAH

Apparently Sultan Shamsuddin ascended the throne after the death of his father. In unanimity with the wazirs, he decided to divide his Wilayat among his amirs. The people of Kashmir were very happy by his enthronement. In a short span of time Malik Kachi and Abdal Makari both confronted each other and their mutual dissension ended in a peace. Malik Abdal went to Gujraj Kamraj which was his jagir and Shah Malik Kachi Chak went to Srinagar. Soon Malik Abdal adopted rebellious ways and created furore in the wilayat Gujraj. But the trouble was easily nipped in the bud. No other information could be found in this context.[1]

THE THIRD ACCESSION OF NAZUK SHAH ON THE THRONE OF KASHMIR

After his father, Nazuk Shah sat on the throne. Hardly five or six months[2] had elapsed when Mirza Haidar Turk got possession of the place. During the reign of Mirza Haidar, the *khutba* was read and coins were struck in name of Nasiruddin Muhammad Humayun Padshah.

DESCRIPTION OF DOMINATION (TASSALLUT) OF MIRZA HAIDAR TURK ON THE MAMLAKAT OF KASHMIR

In the year 948 (AD 1541) Humayun was defeated by Sher Shah Afghan Sur and came to Lahore. Malik Abdal Makari, Zangi Chak and some of the nobles and grandees of Kashmir sent a petition through the good offices of Mirza Haidar Turk exhorting the Emperor to occupy Kashmir. His Majesty thereafter despatched Mirza Haidar and himself decided to follow him a little later. When Mirza Haidar reached Bhir Malik Abdal Makari and Zangi Chak joined him. At that time, the soldiers accompanying Mirza Haidar were not more than three or four thousand soldiers. When they reached Rajaouri, Malik Kachi Chak virtually ruler but the governor of Kashmir came with three or four thousand cavalry and fifty thousand infantry to the Kurtul pass where they arranged for besieging the fort (Murchalha). Mirza Haidar left that road and proceeded towards Abhaj. Out of pride Malik Kazi Chak did not protect that road and Mirza Haidar crossed through the mountains and went to the open atmosphere in Kashmir. Suddenly he occupied the city of Srinagar. Malik Abdal Makari and Zangi Chak strengthened their hold and took over the charge. A few *parganahs* were given in jagirs to Mirza Haidar. Since the life of Abdal Makri had reached to its brim he died suddenly, after having made his children secure under the patronage of Mirza Haidar. Since Malik Kaji Chak realized his inability 'to make head against Mirza Haider', he thought it prudent to go to Sher Shah Afghan Sur to Hindustan and brought 5,000 cavalry under Husain Khan Shirwani and Adil Khan their sardars along with two elephants from Sur ruler to help him. Mirza Haidar Turk joined hands with Zangi Chak. Both the armies stood in battle array and met in a war at Dunadiyar (Dhunnuj) and Kava Gava. Mirza Haidar won the war and nobles of Sher Shah Suri and Malik Kaji were defeated. Malik Kaji Chak stayed back in Bahramgalla. Mullah Muhammad Yusuf the Khatib of the Jami Mosque of Srinagar brought out and composed a new chronogram 'fathi Mukarrar'. In 950 (1543), Mirza Haidar changed his capital to Andarkat (Indrakut or Andarkul) and stayed there. Since he was growing somewhat suspicious of Zangi Chak, the latter fled to seek shelter with Malik Kaji Chak. Both of them united and in 951 marched towards Srinagar with a view to destroy the power of Mirza Haidar Bahram Chak, son of Zangi Chak reached Srinagar. Mirza Haidar appointed Bandagan Kuka and Khwaja Kashmiri to eliminate them. He could not resist and face them and fled hotly pursued by Mirza Haidar's forces. Seeing his condition, Malik Kaji and Zangi Chak thought it safer and better to run away and took shelter in Bahramgalla. Mirza Haidar Turk left Bandagan Kuka and others in Srinagar and himself marched towards Tibet. He managed to conquer and occupy one of the largest forts Luso (Lhasa) and certain other forts. In 952 (1545) Malik Kaji Chak and his son died of tapi larza (the paroxim of fever ague-fit). Mirza Haidar Turk spent this year in complete comfort and peace. In 953 (1546) Zangi Chak tried sword with the people of Mirza Haidar and lost his life. Ghazi Khan brought the heads of Zangi Chak and his son before Mirza Haidar. In 954 arrived an envoy from Kashghar. Mirza Haidar Turk along with a group of his nobles personally came to receive the envoys at Lar. Khwaja Oja, son of Masud Chak, who had continued the fight for seven years in the Wilayat of Kamran (Gujraj) and dominated the political scene and overpower all initiated the talk of peace and agreement with Jan Mirak who summoned him. When Oja Bahram came to his assembly he took out his sword from his stockings and struck him in the belly. He was wounded and fled in that condition to the forest hotly pursued by Jan Mirak Mirza. Ultimately the latter managed to catch hold of him and beheaded him. He brought the head before Mirza Haidar hoping that Mirza Haidar Turk will be delighted. Idi Zina saw the head and became agitated in a fit of anger reprimanded the culprit by saying that after peace or agreement of any kind the killing was not justified. Mirza Haidar Turk said that he was completely ignorant of these happenings. After this, Mirza Haidar turned towards Kishtwar. Bandagan Kuka, Muhammad Makari Mirza Muhammad and Yahya Zaina were sent in avant-garde. Mirza himself halted at Mauza Jahapur near Kishtwar. The advance guard completed three days journey within one day, reached Dahlut and encamped on the opposite bank of the river. The river plowed between the two forces and none did cross the water though there was a hot and continuous exchange of arrows and musketry. Next day, some stragglers from Mirza Haidar's camp lost their road and wished to join the advance guard at Kishtwar, but upon their reaching Dahar, violent gales of wind gushed and the dust-storm completely darkened the day. The people of Dahar collected round them. Bandagan Kuka who was a good Sardar along with 5 persons were killed in the battle and the remaining detachment managed to join Mirza Haidar with great distress. In 955 (1548) Mirza Haidar started to conquer Tibet, wrested Rajaouri from the hands of Kashmiris and gave it to Muhammad Nazeer and Nasir Ali. Pakli was assigned to Mulla Abdullah and Little Tibet was placed under the charge of Mulla Qasim. The Big Tibet was also conquered where Mulla Hasan was appointed.

In 956 (1549) Mirza Haidar marched against Deebal. Adam Ghakkar came and met Mirza with the petition that the misdemeanor of Dowlat Chak, nephew of Malik Kaji Chak be forgiven. Mirza accepted it. Mirza Haidar Turk and Adam Ghakkar sat in the Khargah (pavilion) and summoned Dowlat Chak who was offended because a befitting welcome and due respect was not shown to him. Dowlat Chak expressed anger and got up at once to leave. He carried with him the elephant also which he had brought as *peshkash*. People wanted to pursue him but Mirza Haidar Turk prevented them. After some time Mirza Haidar himself returned to Kashmir.

Dowlat Chak along with Ghazi Khan, Atchy Chak and Bahram Chak went to Haibat Khan Niyazi who had been defeated by Sher Shah and had thereafter taken shelter in Rajaouri. Salim Shah who had been pursuing the Niyazis reached Madwan from Naushahra. Haibat Khan Niyazi sent Saiyid Khan Niyazi one of his confidants to Salim Shah Afghan for reconciliation. The mother and son of Haibat Khan Niyazi were also brought to Salim Shah Afghan Sur[3] who thereafter returned and halted at Sialkot. The above mentioned Kashmiri partisans wanted to take Haibat Khan to Kashmir having brought him up to Baramoollah and to depose Mirza Haidar. Haibat Khan Niyazi not only rejected the proposal but sent a Brahmin to Mirza Haidar Turk to open talks for peace and to inform him about the developments. Mirza Haidar had conveyed a number of messages through that Brahmin. Haibat Khan Niyazi thereafter moved to Hir which is a dependency of Jammu. Kashmiris deserted him and went to Salim Shah Afghan Sur. Ghazi Khan Chak came to Mirza Haidar.

In 957 (1550) Mirza Haidar was contented, happy and at peace. He sent Khwaja Shams Mughal as an envoy to Salim Shah, with an excessively large amount of saffron. In 958 (1551) Khwaja Shams Mughal came from Salim Shah loaded with rarities and expensive gifts of fine muslin and horses and accompanied by Elchi Yasin an envoy from the Atyhans. Mirza Haidar thereafter sent the fine shawls and saffron and gave leave to Afghan envoy. Mirza Qara Bahadur[4] was appointed as governor of Bheerbal. From amongst the Kashmiris Idi Lama, Nazuk Shah, Husain Makari and Khwaja Haji were sent along with him. Mirza Qara Bahadur and Kashmiris came out of Andarkat and settled at Baramoollah.[5] They created dissensions and disturbances over the issue that the Mughals did not attach much importance and did not value them. When the Mughals conveyed this to Mirza Haidar, he did not believe it and commented that the Mughals are no less experts in trouble shooting and artifice than the Kashmiris. Husain Makari sent his brother Ali Makari to Mirza Haidar Turk to forewarn him against the uprising of the Kashmiris and to recall the army. Mirza Haidar refused to see reason and could not be restrained. On the contrary, he despised their strength and wondered as to how the Kashmiris could think of a riot and how and why the army could be recalled. On 27th Ramzan a great fire broke out in Andarkat. Many houses were burnt. Mirza Qara Bahadur, his companions and others requested that since their houses have been destroyed they should be allowed to return to build them up and then proceed to the Bheerbal expedition later next year. Mirza did not agree and the Kashmiris reluctantly marched towards Bheerbal. Abdi Zaina and all other Kashmiris hatched a conspiracy and separating themselves from the Mughals reached the outskirts of Bheerbal. They took Husain Makari and Ali Makari also with them to save them from the impending massacre to befall upon the Mughals. At dawn the battle with the people of Bheerbal started. Mughals were enclosed in the mountains. Saiyed Mirza rushed to the fort of Bheerbal and put eighty renowned Mughals to sword. Muhammad Nazir and Mirza Qara Bahadur were taken prisoners.

Remaining persons went to Bahramgalla via Bhuj. Mirza Haidar was very sad over this news. He ordered that the silver degs be broken and the coins that were currently in circulation within Kashmir be struck. He considered Jahangir Makari a reliable person and gave him the jagir of

Hasan Makari. Many handicraftsmen were provided with *kharj* and horses turned them into soldiers. Incessantly the news reached that Mulla Abdullah, having heard about the turnout of Kashmiris was marching towards the court. As soon as he reached Baramoollah, Kashmiris collected round him and killed him. Khwaja Qasim was put to death in little Tibet. Muhammad Nazir was imprisoned in Rajauri. All the Kashmiris joined hands and came from Bahramgalla to Hanbirpur. Mirza Haidar was forced to wage a war against them and willy-nilly came out of Andarkat with one thousand people. The entire (*Jamiat*) accompanying Mirza Haidar consisted of one thousand persons (*kas*) only. The Mughals like Abdur Rahman, Shahzada Khan, Mirak Mirza, Makna Mughal, Jar Ali and others amounted to seven hundred persons only. They journeyed with Mirza Haidar Turk and settled down at Shahabuddinpur. Daulat Chak, Ghazi Khan Chak and other Sirdars in unison with Abdi Zaina came to Bhambirpur and coming out from there assembled at Mauza Khanpur. Mirza Haidar Turk halted in the ground of Khalidgarh which is near Srinagar. Fath Chak, whose father Khwaja Bahram had been killed at the hands of the Mughals wanted to take revenge and come with three thousand persons to Andarkat. All the buildings (where Mirza Haidar lived) which were in Bagh-i Safa were burnt. When this news reached Mirza Haidar, he said 'I have not brought this building from Kashghar. It may be constructed again with the favour of God.' Jar Ali avenged this act of devastation by putting to fire all the buildings in Soyapur. Nevertheless, Haidar Daulat did not like this also. The soldiers went on rampage burning all the buildings of Abdi Zaina and Nanruz Chak in Srinagar. Mirza Haidar Turk came and stayed at Khanpur. In that Mauza, there was one tree of (willow) which was so large and shady that two hundred horsemen could stand under its shadow. Whenever one branch of this moved, the entire tree showed seemed to move. At last, Kashmiris moved from Khanpur and reached Mauza Adnapur which was at a distance of less than two *kurohs*. Mirza Haidar decided that a night-attack should be undertaken against them. Mirza Abdur Rahman nominated and appointed his younger brother (who was noble and righteous) in his stead as his successor and instructed the people to acknowledge him and himself departed to invade at night. As luck would have it, there appeared dark clouds. When they reached near the camp of Khwaja Haji who was the source of dissension and turmoil and held the post of Mirza's Wakil, they could see nothing due to intense darkness. Shah Nazar the *qurchi* of Mirza Haidar said that when he shot an arrow, the voice of Mirza Haidar was heard by him saying that 'you committed a hideous act' (*qabaqat karchi*) and realized that in the darkness when visibility was dismal the arrow had suddenly struck Mirza. It is also described that a butcher had shot an arrow on his thigh. Another version went that Kamal Kuka had killed him with a sword.

On the person of Mirza, however, there was no wound except one by an arrow shot. When in the morning, it became widespread among the armymen that certain Mughal lay slain and Haji Muhammad reached there he found that it was Mirza Haidar Turk. He (Haji Muhammad) lifted his (Mirza Haidar's) head from the ground. There were no signs of life left in him. Mirza merely opened his eyes and died immediately. The Mughals rushed towards Andarkat. Kashmiris saw the dead body of Mirza and buried him. Thereafter they went in pursuit of Mughals. The Mughals fortified themselves in Andarkat and continued to fight for three days. On the fourth day, Muhammad Rumi placed the copper coins in the Zarbozan (pulahaimasi dar zarbozan mi andakht). Wherever they shot it, the people died. Finally the wife of Mirza Haidar Turk and Khanji, his sister told the Mughals, 'since Mirza Haidar is no more amongst us, it is better to come to terms with the Kashmiris'. The Mughals accepted the suggestion and sent Amir Khan Muamma to the Kashmiris for initiating talks for peace. Kashmiris agreed with the proposal and sent a letter of agreement and commitment that they will not harm the Mughals or hold ill-will towards the Mughals. The span of Mirza Haidar's reign was ten years.

DISTINCTION OF SOVEREIGNTY BESTOWED UPON NAZUK SHAH—A THIRD TIME

When the gates of fort were opened, Kashmiris entered the Tushuk Khana of Mirza Haidar Turk and plundered all the valuables and precious rarities. The family of Mirza Haidar was brought to Srinagar and settled in the *haveli* of Hasan Manuza. The Wilayat of Kashmir was divided among the Kashmiri nobles. Thus Pargana Devsar was given to Daulat Chak, Pargana Dehli to Ghazi Khan Chak, Pargana Gajraj to Yusaf Chak and Bahram Chak. One lakh Kharwar shawl was given to Khwaja Haji Wakil. The Kashmiri nobles particularly Abdi Zaina became very powerful and raised Nazuk Shah to the throne though he himself continued to behave like de facto ruler. In 954 Shahkar Chak, son of Kaji Chak, being without a jagir and Ghazi Khan who called himself as son of Kaji Chak and held extensive jagirs wanted to go out of Kashmir. The details of the events are as follows: Undoubtedly, Shahkar Chak was the son of Kaji Chak. Although Ghazi Khan was known as the son of Malik Kaji Chak yet he was in fact not his son. Malik Kaji Chak had married the wife of his brother Hasan Chak after latter's death. It was two or three months after that betrothal that Ghazi Khan was born. Due to this reason, Shahkar Chak wanted to go out of Kashmir to Abdi Zaina. When this news spread far and wide, Daulat Chak, Ghazi Khan Chak, Ismail Hanat and Harjir were sent with hundred persons to bring Shahkar Chak forcibly if necessary. Shahkar Chak did not come at their request and went straight to Abdi Zaina. Some kind of peace was patched up and Pargana Kothar, Khawar and Maduro was bestowed upon Shahkar Chak as jagir. The dust of dissensions was removed. At this juncture, four groups in Kashmir were considered to be most trustworthy, first Abdi Zaina with his followers; second Hasan Makari, son of Malik Abdul Makari with his group; Kapoors like Bahram Chak, Yusuf Chak and others, fourth Kasiyan like Kaji Chak, Daulat Chak and Ghazi Khan Chak. Yahya Zaina gave his own daughter in marriage to Husam Khan, son of Malik Kaji Chak, the daughter of Daulat Chak was married to Muhammad Makari, son of Malik Abdul Makari; the sister of Yusuf Chak, son of Zangi Chak Kotwari was betrothed to Ghazi Khan Chak. These matrimonial alliances became source of strength and power and they scattered in different directions. Ghazi Khan Chak went to Gajraj, Daulat Chak to Sorpore and Makariyan to Bakul. Abdi Zaina sat in Srinagar completely depressed and engrossed with the idea of how to destroy these groups. Since it was the weather of brinjals, Abdi Zaina wanted that these two should be cooked together as they form a nice dish. He invited Bahram Chak, Saiyid Ibrahim and Saiyid Yaqub, while Yusuf Chak did not come, the other two arrived and were thrown into prison. When Yusuf Chak learnt about it, he marched with 3,000 cavalry and 700 infantry and met Daulat Chak by way of Gajraj. When Abdi Zaina found that Kashmiris were behaving like cowards he released the Mughals like Mirza Qara Bahadur, Mirza Abdur Rahman, Mirza Jan Mirak, Muhammad Nazir and Jar Ali from prison, showed clemency and gave horses, saropa and money to each one of them and halted at Jagpur. In the meantime, Saiyid Yaqub and Saiyid Ibrahim along with Charud who was their caretaker went to Gajraj and met Daulat Chak. Bahram Chak could not run away. Next day Ghazi Khan Chak came to Srinagar with 30,000 horsemen. Abdi Zaina sent the Mughals to fight against them. He destroyed the bridges and the Mughals remained stranded. In the meanwhile, Daulat Chak also came. Having met with them at Srinagar, they stayed at Idgah. The battle continued till Baba Khalil came to Abdi Zaina with the proposal of peace and said: 'you reposed trust in the Mughals but ignored and looked down upon Kashmiris—this was not proper'. After such comments, peace was established between him and the Kashmiris. He despatched the Mughals with their wives and children. Khanji, the sister of Mirza Haidar Turk went to Kabul via Pakli. The family of Mirza Jar Ali and other Mughals were put to death. Khanam, the wife of Mirza Haidar reached Kashghar. Following these events, the news reached that Haibat Khan, Said Khan, Shahbaz Khan Afghan who belonged to the *quam* of Niyazi were coming to conquer Kashmir. They reached the *parganah* of Panihal and entered the hill of Nun. Abdi Zaina Husam Makari, Bahram Chak, Daulat Chak and Yusuf Chak tried swords with Niyazis. In the pitched war and after terrible encounters, Haibat Khan Niyazi struck Ali Chak by his sword. Finally Haibat Khan, Saiyid Sipahbad Khan Niyazi were killed in that war. Kashmiris returned victorious to Srinagar. Their heads were sent through certain Yaqub to Salim Shah Afghan. After this, there arose mutual enmity amongst the Kashmiris. Abdi Zaina in unison with Fath Chak and Lohar Makri, Yusuf Chak, Bahram Chak and Ibrahim Chak came to Khakdet and stayed there. Daulat Chak, Ghazi Chak, Husam Makari, Saiyid Ibrahim and the group of Duman joined hands together halted at Idgah. When two months passed, Yusuf Chak, Fath Chak, Ibrahim Chak separated from Abdi Zaina and came to Daulat Chak. When Daulat Chak rode along with his followers to invade Abdi Zaina, the latter could not face the pressure and without even putting up a fight, escaped to Merv. He wanted to ride another horse but the hoofs of the horse kicked his chest. He went in hiding at Mauza Samak, and died. His mortal remains were taken to Srinagar and buried in Mauza Musa Zaina. The nobles rose in revolt and Nazuk Shah who held the sovereignty only in name was deprived of it and they thought of declaring independence. After this, Mirza Haider Turk held the rulership, a third time for ten months.[6]

(Abul Qasim Farishta, *Tarikh-i Farishta*, Persian text,
vol. II, Nawal Kishore, ed.)

NOTES

1. Tarikh-i Kashmir records that Ibrahim who had wrested the power from his father and fled after his defeat in the battle of Sullah in 932 returned and was unanimously accepted as the king. Briggs adds that Abdal Makri marched against the capital and his rival accompanied by the king defeated him in the battle near the hills and drove him to Gujraj. Ibrahim died in 1540, Briggs says, that Abdal and Zangi Chak assumed the reins of Government and immediately assigned the revenues of some districts solely for the payment of the army.
2. Briggs says twenty-five persons were killed and that Pakli was assinged to Dawood Ali (Briggs 285).

3. Briggs writes that the mother and son of Haibat Khan Niyazi were brought as part fulfilment of conditions of peace and as hostage for Haibat's good behaviour into the royal camp after which he fell back on Bhimbur, in the district of Sialkot (Briggs 288).
4. Briggs says Haibat Khan moved to Subzeea in the district of Jammoo, Ghazi Khan Chak went direct to the capital and abandoning his associates joined Mirza Haidar while the rest, quitting Kashmir retired to the court of Salim Shah.
5. Briggs gives the name as Kiran Bahadur.
6. Two pages of the text have been omitted by Briggs.

Mirza Haidar Dughlat in *Tarikh-i-Kashmir*

In the year 938 Mirza Kamran Chaghatai turned towards Kashmir with 30,000 horsemen and personally moved and halted at Naushahra. He sent his nobles Mahran Beg and Shaikh Ali Beg to Kashmir. The nobles were circumspect and took care to come in such a way that people in Kashmir did not know about their march. When the Kashmiris learnt about it, they called Malik Kaji Chak who was then outside Kashmir and the (forces) stood at Mauza Atarwachan. When the battle started, Kamran's forces were defeated and retreated. In the year 939 the ruler of Kashghar Said Khan came with a large force to conquer Kashmir and stayed at Tibet. He deputed his son Sikandar Khan under the leadership of Mirza Haidar with 14,000 brave soldiers and 27,000 additonal horses. The Kashghar armies entered the Balda by way of Dar and the inhabitants of the town were so terrified and impressed by the awe inspiring forces of Kashghar that they migrated and took shelter in various hills and mountains. The fearless Turks either put to death or captured many people from rural and tribal areas. They plundered and devastated the land. When the winter season came to an end and spring season set in the nobles of Kashmir assembled. The battle started at Babul. Mulk Ali, Husain Malik Shaikh Ali from amongst the Kashmiris came forward and overpowered Mirza Haidar's avant-garde. As soon as the Kashghar soldiers found that the Kashmiris had succeeded, Ali Beg rushed with a thousand soldiers and Mirza Haidar himself arrived with two thousand soldiers to provide support to Sharaf Mirza. At that time no reinforcements were reaching Kashmiris to assist Ali Mulk. Consequently, they were defeated and one thousand six hundred soldiers of Kashmir were killed in the war. The remaining ones took to flight. Despite this initial debacle, the Kashmiris reassembled and put up a stiff resistance. Wherever there were Kashgharis, they were not given respite by the Kashmiris. Kashghar army finally patched up a peace as they had not yet seen such a terrifying warfare. Although the peasants had done their level best to ensure good crop, nothing could help as a severe famine and broken out. Kashghar armies left the place; the Kashmir amirs untidily settled Malik Kaji Chak at Zinapur and Makaris and Malik Zangi

Chak were left in the city. The entire power was now entrusted to Malik Kaji Chak. Due to being the son-in-law, the sultanate fell to Sultan Ismail Ibni Sultan Muhammad Shah. A few years passed in this manner. In 944 Malik Kaji Chak won over many famous nobles to his side and started fighting against the Makaris. As Malik Zangi Chak had gone to seek the hand of the daughter of Rai of Jammu and no other such a wise, experienced and far-sighted man was there, the army was badly defeated and driven towards Kuhistan, where they remained throughout the winter. It was only in the beginning of spring that they moved from Jammu with Malik Zangi Chak. They halted at Gariya Gesu. In that Mauza arrived several perons like Daulat Khan Chak, Malik Ranby Chak, Malik Nauruz Chak, Saiyid Ibrahim, Malik Muhammad Chak and Malik Muhammad Nahi who joined his banner and Makaris remained in Kashmir for three years. During his reign, Malik Kaji Chak had followed one commendable particular attitude that the rebels were never accorded capital punishment. Instead, they were thrown into prison. After sometime, they were released, their mistakes and crimes were forgiven and they were assigned large jagirs. This was the reason why several of his descendants attained the grandeur of holding the high pedestal of rulership. Ultimately, Malik Abdal Makri and Malik Zangi Chak wanted to take revenge. In 947 Mirza Haidar Kashghari who was a servant (*mulazim*) of Humayun in India was invited by them to Kashmir. In those day Humayun had fallen on bad days and being disgusted with wretched Sher Khan who was his *chakar* (attendant) had gone on an excursion to Iran. At that time, Mirza Haidar was in a state of misfortune after being fortunate. Malik Abdal Chak and Malik Zangi Chak brought him to Kashmir, removed Nazuk Shah and elevated Mirza Haidar to ascendancy. Malik Kaji Chak had seen the signs of greatness and confidence over the forehead of Mirza, he, therefore, went to Sher Khan and gave his niece (the sister of Ismail Shah, son of Sultan Muhammad Shah) in marriage to Sher Khan. Sher Khan, Adil Khan and Husain Khan Shirwani and a group of others came with two thousand people to help Malik Kaji Chak. Haidar Dughlat was also unaware of the death of Malik Abdal Makri and arrival of Malik Kaji Chak. He left his wife and children at Andarkul and moved along with Malik Zangi Chak, Malik Abdi Zaina and Malik Husain Makari to face the enemy. In the war which ensued between Malik Kaji Chak and his army, he showed valour and fought bravely. But the victory is bestowed upon the winner by heavenly aid and Malik Kaji Chak was, therefore, defeated and departed to Hindustan. Mirza Haidar's victory was commemorated by a chronogram of Maulana Jamaluddin Muhammad Yusuf Kashmiri with the words 'fath-i mukarrar' (second victory) since the first victory was attained in the campaign fought against Sikandar Khan. Gradually, the environs of Kashmir from Tibet, Pakli and other regions were brought under his sway and Malik Abdi Zaina was appointed as the Sipahsalar. The *khutba* was, however, read and coins were struck in the name of Nazuk Shah following the custom prevalent among the nobles of Kashmir. Abul Fazl says that after the conquest of Kabul, which occurred (according to the chronogram of Mulla Navedi *Kabul ra girift*, i.e. Kabul was wrested) in 954 Mirza Haidar read the *Khutba* in the name of Humayun.

Mirza Haidar had taken pains to introduce good administration in the Wilayat of Kashmir during his stay of a decade there. Varied kinds of handicrafts and different type of artisans and experts were invited by him from all corners and the magnificence and beauty of the place was enhanced considerably which, thereafter, became a customary feature. The development of music was also a regular and most desired occupation for him. Many instruments new and old were used. He was a great patron of men of learning and excellence and extended all kinds of favours to this group. For him the favourite hobby was to ensure the multifarious progress of art and culture.

However, gradually Mirza Haidar grew to be an orthodox rather bigoted (*gamzan-i maslaki taasub gardida*) man. Shaikh Daniyal, son of Shaikh Shamsuddin Arafi, who had fled to Tibet due to fear of Mirza was recalled and put to death. Another person who was a disciple of that Shaikh was also cut to pieces. Qazi Mir Ali was exiled and his house was plundered. Mullah Haji Khatib was condemned for his Shia views and killed. Due to a large number of Kashgharis who had rallied round him, he no longer respected the agreements and pacts settled with people of Kashmir. He coveted the countries of Zangi Chak who happened to be a good Sardar. Malik Zangi Chak was so worried that he rushed to India. The armies started harassing and looting the poor and downtrodden and the subjects brought the petition before the dignitaries of Kashmir. Malik Abdi Zaina, Husain Makri, Khwaja Haji now started hatching a conspiracy to teach a lesson to Mirza Haidar. It was planned to lure the Kashgharis into the hilly areas. In 958 Malik Abdi Zaina acted treacherously and told Mirza Haidar that the territories in the environs of Kashmir have not yet been occupied and everywhere the armies should be deputed to conquer the place. Mirza Haidar appointed his own cousin Qara Bahadur along with certain *bahadurs* from Kashghar. Malik Abdi Zaina and Husain Makri and Khwaja Haji persuaded that Mirza should himself accompany his army. Malik Abdi Zaina sent his son Shamsuddin with the army in order to separate Mirza from his army and leave him isolated. Thus a group was sent towards Tibet, another towards Rajaouri. When they were satisfied that there were no soldiers left with Mirza Haidar, Qara Bahadur and his friends went and stayed at Aun near (Khanpur). Ghazi Khan and Malik Daulat Chak also joined them. When Qara Bahadur reached Muhammad Kuttak, Kashmiris came out of their army in open enmity and at night killed one group and made another prisoner. The troops which had been sent under the leadership of Mulla Qasim and Mulla Baqi for occupation of Tibet met the same fate as Mulla Qasim was beheaded and Mulla Baqi sought safety in flight. The group which had been sent under Mulla Abdullah was defeated and returned to Kashmir and on the way back he was killed. The renowned officers and *bahadurs* who had gone to Kishtwar under Kuka were also butchered and one thousand five hundred of his men were killed in that journey.

An enraged Mirza Haidar had marched towards Aunpur to take revenge from the Kashmiris through a night-attack and had left his treasures and family at Andarkul, the news of his departure was conveyed to the Kashmiris, they had become alert. When Mirza went alone to find out about the plans of the Kashmiris near their army, Kamal Duni a butcher was busy keeping watch over the area. He found a horseman standing in the dark. Although he had enquired from the Mirza about his whereabouts (shouting who are you and where are you going to ?), Mirza could not understand as he was not well versed in Kashmiri and, therefore, did not answer. He neither replied in Persian nor in Kashmiri. The butcher took him for a spy and shot an arrow. The wound caused from the arrow was so deep and grievous that Mirza's life was cut short. It was in 959 that the sad incident occurred. Notwithstanding their grudge against Mirza, the people of Kashmiris treated Qara Bahadur Mirza, his sons and family and followers with respect. They sent them along with their entire belongings to their country. Mirza Haidar was a maternal cousin of Humayun Padshah. After Mirza Haidar's sad demise, Malik Abdi Zaina became the ruler.

From folio 79 onwards this Ms has the account of Qara Bahadur's appointment for the conquest of Kashmir. The details of his exploits, thereafter, are given in detail.

(Narain Kaul Kashmiri, *Tarikh-i Kashmir*, Maulana Azad Library, Aligarh, Ms. University No.71, *Farsiya Akhbar*, ff.70-5)

Mirza Haidar Dughlat in *Tarikh-i-Salatin*

185. In 938, Mirza Kamran the brother of Humayun came to Naushahra and himself stayed there and sent Mahram Beg and Shaikh Ali with a group of 30,000 cavalry. As Kashmir was then divided and there were dissensions among the tribe of Chak in Kashmir, none could venture to face the enemy. He could enter the town without facing opposition. They settled themselves in a house and sent the news to Kamran. The Chak army assembled in the Mauza Athwajirm and a consultative assembly was held. Mahram Beg thereupon decided to leave the place and reached Mauza Mazbur and stood in the battle array. Though the Chak army came to *Kuh-i Sulaiman* to wage war and there was exchange of incendiary warfare and fire, Mahram Beg could no longer continue the war and finally patched up peace and returned. After his departure, there came the news that Sultan Said Khan of Kashghar had started to conquer Kashmir. Having himself stayed at Tibet, he had despatched his son Sikandar Khan along with his nephew Haidar Dughlat with 40,000 cavalry. They marched via pargana Lar and stayed at Naushahra. The inhabitants of the town finding themselves in a miserably precarious situation due to their arrival sought safety in flight.

187. The Chak amirs heard about the arrival of enemy in 939 but due to excessive cold freezing winds and snowfall they could not face the Kashgharis who won the victory. The inhabitants of the place were in a state of distress completely depressed by a sense of humiliation, and struck by restlessness and anxiety. With the onset of spring season, the Chak amirs took up courage and in the battle which followed, they showed utmost bravery and forced the enemy to retreat. Towards the end of spring, the Kashgharis finally departed and reached Tibet via Lar. Due to disturbances, war and the destructions caused by the army, the cultivated country was devastated and agricultural lands were laid waste. There occurred a famine. The scarcity of food in the town led the people to utmost physical weakness and emotional stress.

188. In 944 Sultan Muhammad Shah died and his son Shamsuddin ascended the throne and entrusted the affairs of state to Malik Kaji Chak

who happened to be renowned for bravery in his times. Since he had been keen to exterminate the Indian and Kashghar army, had shown gallantry in the task and proved his mettle and held a house at Kajiwara near hills on the frontier road to India, he did not care a bit for Sultan Shamsuddin and himself attended to every big and small affair. For one year, the Sultan remained in power and spent his time in utter misery and in the grip of insecurity. Finally he died in 945 and was succeeded that very year by his son Sultan Ismail. Since he was married to the daughter of Kaji Chak, he too allowed the latter to continue in the office. As before, Kaji Chak did not give up his evil ways, consequently problems were aggravated and dissensions arose among the dignitaries. They easily divided the *parganas* and villages among themselves. Thus Makaris, Chaks Dangaris, Chawuryan and Malkan who were in those days holding power and control over the affairs of state started fighting among themselves. A severe battle ensued in the Muhallah Alauddin Pura. Anarchy prevailed for sometime.

189. An unhappy Sultan Ismail died. His son Ibrahim was enthroned. He opened enmity with Abdal Makari, Zangi Chak and others who were all followers of Shism. These dissenters, therefore, sent their sons to Humayun to seek military assistance and to persuade him to send a qushun (detachment) for the conquest of Kashmir. In those days, Humayun was himself in difficulty. Having been defeated by Sher Khan, he went to Iran by way of Thatta and Bhakkar. Humayun was so depressed that he did not pay attention to such ambitious proposals. Mirza Haidar Dughlat, who was at that time present on his own expressed a desire, sought the permission and departed from Lahore with a small army. In 948 he managed to enter the town from Cheraudar and *fath mukarrar* was its chronogram. He had arrived earlier with the help of Kashghar ruler and had returned and had come a second time. Now Kaji Chak who did not find himself fully prepared for the task, started for India from Hirapur. Abdal Makari died, Kaji Chak went to Sher Khan who showered favours upon him and bestowed upon him the title of Khan-i-Khanan and accompanied him to assist him. By that time, Haidar Dughlat had managed to conquer the place. Such was the amicable and nice attitude of Mirza Haidar towards every one that all the people were devoted to him and gladly obeyed and acknowledged his supremacy. He settled himself in Andarkul when Kazi Chak reached Hirapur, Mirza Haidar came with his people to face the Kashmiris.

190. The battle ended in the victory of Mirza Haidar. Kaji Chak then turned towards Hind defeated and dejected. He died while on his way near Thatta. Mirza Haidar became the ruler and Khutba was read and

coins were struck in the name of Nazuk Shah. Idi Zaina was appointed as Sipahsalar. Haidar Dughlat himself concentrated upon patronising men of art learning and excellence. He was particularly interested in the development of music. Haidar Dughlat was very rigid in religious views. He put to death son of Mir Shams and his disciple. The Khanqah of Jodi Bal was burnt down. During his regime Mirza Haidar conquered Kashmir and Tibet. Idi Zaina Naji Chak and Khwaja Haji Bandi became his most active and devoted supporters. He had developed some enmity and dislike for the followers of the Shia sect and harmed them. Due to this (sectarian bigotry) there arose dissensions. In 958, Idi Zaina and others started opposing him and hatched a conspiracy. In this task they included Husain Makari and Haji Bandi. 191. According to an agreement they advised Mirza that in view of the establishment of good administration, it was necessary to invade Kuhistan. Mirza sent his nephew Qara Bahadur with Kashghar people towards Kuhistan. In the meantime, Idi Zaina and Naji Chak turned back and separating from him came to the fort of Aunpur. Mirza Haidar soon realized that it was a plot and himself started immediately to checkmate them and besieged them. After some time he got up alone and entered the fort of Aunpur. A man enquired about him, since Mirza did not know Kashmiri language well, the watchman mistook him for a spy and shot and arrow on his head. Mirza died in one stroke. In the morning when the news spread, Qazi Chak and Daulat Chak, the sons of Kaji Chak, wanted that they should go to Andarkat and plunder, humiliate and destroy the family of Mirza but Nazuk Shah prevented them. They were, with great efforts sent to Kashghar. In 959, Mirza Haidar was killed after a reign of ten years. After his assassination Nazuk Shah established himself as ruler but the conditon of Sultanate considerably deteriorated.

(Haidar Malik Jadaura, *Tarikh-i-Salatin* or *Majmuat tawarikh*, Ms. Maulana Azad Library, Sulaiman collection No. 657/35)

فہرست

بیان اقوام ارلات و دوغلات در اویماق مغول

قوم ارلات

از عمدہ اویماقہائے قیات است امرائے این قوم معزز و مکرم بودہ اند وجہ تسمیہ و بر آمدن این قوم معلوم نشدہ اما قومے شریف است و در میان مغولان بشرافت مشہور و وصلت و قرابت امرائے این قوم با اقوام بوزنجری واقعشدہ ہموارہ مُعزز و مکرم بودہ اند و امیر موید ارلات از قوم ارلات بود و شیرین بیگ آغا خواہر صاحبقران امیر تیمور گورکان در عقد او بود و در حملہ قرشی در حرب امیر موسیٰ تاجوت والیاس خواجہ خان چغتائی و حرب امیر حسین بہ بیعت برکاب صاحبقران بودہ مردانگی نمود و صاحبقران نیز باوے بہ نہایت محبت زندگانی میکرد و امیرزادہ علی و امیرزادہ عمر ابنائے او بودند و خترش سونج قتلق آغا بعقد شاہزادہ عمر شیخ میرزا ابن صاحبقران بود و این ہر سہ برادر و خواہر از بطن شیرین آغا خواہر صاحبقران بودند و جہان ملک دختر امیرزادہ علی ارلات بعقد امیرزادہ خلیل سلطان ابن شاہزادہ میران شاہ ابن صاحبقران بود بعضے نام او جہان سلطان مینویسند و ہمین صحیح مے نماید و دیگر از امرائے این قوم امیر سیر شاہ و امیر ترمش و امیر ارکن و امری تبلانجی و پیر حاجی پسر امیر تبلانجی از قوم ارلات و رامرائے عاجقرانی بودند و پیر حاجی در موضع اختاد بکتو روا قعہ مغولستان برکاب شاہزادہ عمر شیخ میرزا بودہ شہید شد و سیدی احمد ابن علی شکی ارلات بود و امیر محمد ارلات در حرب اوزبک کشتہ شد و دولت خواجہ ارلات محمد بیگ ارلات از امرائے ابوالقاسم بابر بادشاہ بودند و در زمان او قوم ارلات در کنار مرغاب یورت واشتند امیر یادگار شاہ ارلات معزز این قوم بود و میرزا رکن الدین علاءُ الدولہ دختر اور ابعقد آوردہ بود و قتیکہ بفرمان بابر بادشاہ میل در چشم جہان بین او کشیدند میرزا علاءُ الدولہ را آسیبے نرسیدہ بمکر و تذویر خود را نابینا مے نمود چون شاہ بابر بعراق رفت علاءُ الدولہ خود را از ہرات بیرون آورد و بہ فاریاب کہ یورت ارلاتیان بود رسید و او یماق ارلات بمدد او برخاست امیر سلطان محمود

ابن یادگار ارلات بر کاب او متوجه بلخ گردید و درانجا با امیر درویش محاربہ روانداده لشکر میرزا علاؤ الدولہ گریخت وامیر محمود بوفور شجاعت قدم مردانگی افشرده تاجان در بدن داشت کوشید وآخر بکمال دلیری مقتول شده پیر محمد ابن امیر یادگار شاہ ارلات بود و یادگار شاہ بعہد خاقان سعید شاہرخ سلطان مرتبہ وافر داشت و در سنہ احدی واربعین وثمانایہ درگذشت امیر زین العابدین براورزادہ یادگار شاہ بود و پیر محمد وزین العابدین از امرائے سلطان حسین میرزا بایقرا بودند و بحکم وے بلخ را از امیر علی مغول گرفتند وامیر درویش علی ارلات نیز از امرائے سلطان بود و امیر ابو القاسم ارلات امیرے معظم بود و در سنہ عشر وتسعمایہ کہ شاہزادگان گورگان را با اوزبک در کنار آب مرغاب حربے صعب واقعشد و امیر ابو القاسم کشتہ شد و محمد قاسم میرزا ارلات پسر امیر ابو القاسم بود و او نبیرہ خواہر خورد شاہ ابو القاسم بابر بود و آن بیگم دختر سلطان حسین میرزا ور عقد وی بود قومے معظم و شریف است و امرائے این قوم بسیار گذشتہ اند اما برذکر ہمین قدر اکتفا رفت ۔

اویماق دوغلات

دوغلات نیز از عمدہ اقوام قیات است اما وجہ تسمیہ او معلوم نشد بہر کیف در شرافت نسب و حسب مشہور است و قرابت وصلت امرائے این قوم با سلاطین عظام واقعشدہ از عمدہ امرائے این قوم امیر داؤد دوغلات بود در زمانہ صاجقران امیر تیمور گورکان برلاس از معظم امرا بود و قتلغ تروکان آغا خواہر اکبر صاجقران امیر تیمور گورکان در عقد او بود و در محاربہ امرائے یسوری و خوانین چغتائی وغیرہ در رکاب صاحبقران بود و در ہر معرکہ داد شجاعت و مردانگی داد و ذکرا و در احوال صاحبقران مندرج است و او در سلک امرائے معظم صاحبقرانی منسلک بود و امیر قمر الدین دوغلات از کبار امرائے این قوم بود و در مغولستان بکثرت ایل والوس اشتہار داشت و در عہد خضر خواجہ خان چغتائی امیرے مثل او بود و او در سنہ تسع وستین وسبعمایہ با لشکر خود در ماوراء النہر آمد و چند مرتبہ صاحبقران برا و لشکر کشید و امیر قمر الدین

درشجاعت ومردانگی یکتا بود در حرب وضرب لشکر برلاس داد شجاعت داده وقتے از محاربہ صاحبقران
روگردانیدہ میرفت وامرائے صاحبقران در تعاقب او میرفتند ازانمیان اوج قرابہادر تنہا با میر قمر
الدین رسید وقمرالدین تیرے براسپ اوزدکہ از پائے درافتادواوج قرا سپر برسر کشیدہ پیادہ در پے
او میرفت وامیر قمرالدین بگردیدہ بوے گفت کہ من مردانگی ترا دوست دارم ونیخواہم کہ از دست من
گزندے بتو رسد بازگرو کہ حق نمک ادا کردی ورنہ ضربدست مرا بہ بین وتیرے در سنگ خارا زدکہ
یکدست دران نشست اوج قرا متحیر شدہ باز گردید وزبان بہ تحسین آفرین اوکشاد امیر قمرالدین
مدت العمر بتاخت وتاراج ممالک صاحبقران مشغول بود وصاحبقران نیز لشکر بحرب او میفرستاد امیر
جہان شاہ پسر او بود در مغولستان بہ سنگین تاش یورت داشت ودر سنہ ثمان وعشرین وثمانمایہ کہ شاہزادہ
الغ بیگ ابن خاقان سعید شاہرخ سلطان متوجہ مغولستان گردید امیر جہان شاہ با اویماق خود قوم
کرایت با امرائے برلاس جنگید وکلان تران کرایت مقتول شدند وامیر بسبب کمی اعوان وانصار
منہزم شدہ وباز وریورت خود با سلطان ویس برلاس حرب کردہ منہزم شد چون افواج گورکانیہ
برلاس درمیان آمدہ بودند امیر با شیر محمد خان چغتائی بادشاہ پیوستن نتوانست چون خفر خواجہ پسر ستلمش
اغروق وامیر خدایداد اور ابفرمان شہزادہ الغ بیگ بہ سمرقند مے برد امیر جہان شاہ با او برخوردہ جنگی
صعب واقعشد وامیر جہان شاہ ظفر یافت چون کمک ایشان دررسید جہان شاہ عنان از معرکہ
برتافت دباز با امیر اسکندر شاہ وولی محمد برلاس امرائے شاہزادہ جنگیدہ ظفر یافت وازین قوم محمد حسین
میرزا دوغلات بود در سنہ تسع وتسعین وثمانمایہ واو داماد عمر شیخ میرزا ابن سلطان ابوسعید گورکان بود و
امیر سلطان محمد عرف محمد حصاری وسلطان حسین دوغلات ہردو امیر صاحب ایل والوس بودند در زمانہ
ظہیرالدین محمد بابر بادشاہ بمقابلہ سلطان احمد تبنل با تومان خود ودیگر تومانات معین شدہ بودند میر
زا حیدر دوغلات از امرائے کاشغر بود وبفرمان ہمایون شاہ گورکان در سنہ ثمان واربعین وتسعمایہ بہ
کشمیر رفتہ اور التصرف شد ودر سنہ ثمان وخمسین وتسعمایہ ہمدرانجا کشتہ شد میرزا عبدالرحمن دوغلات

برادراو بودواین هم واضح باد که دوغلات را بحذف الف بے نویسندو بہ تخفیف دال وغلت نیز مے گویند صحیح دوغلات است ودوغلات قومے شریف است۔

اویماق قنقرات

اویماق قنقرات نیز از معظم اویما قہائے مغول است واز قیات است اما از اولاد کدام کس است معلوم نشدُ اما در شرافت وعلو رتبت وے شکے نیست وقتیکہ میسو کا بہادر رحلت کرو دور مغولستان طوائف الملو کی پیدا شد قوم قنقرات نیز با اقوام سالجیوت وقیقین وتائجوت درساختہ باچنگیز خان جنگید ووقت ملازمت اونگ خان نیز باخان بزرگ جنگے نمودہ آخر ایل شدہ وزوجہ قبل خان ابن تومنہ خان از قوم قنقرات بودو قویلہ خان وبرتان بہادر وغیرہ شش پسراز ومتولد شدند واین قوم چون باچنگیز خان ایل شد کوچ نیکو داد وامیر قراچار قنقراتی ازین قوم بودوے بحکم قاآن بہ بیت امیر سویدائے بہادر بحرب قوم قودو مکریت رفتہ کشتہ شدند وامیر علی وسلیمان صوفی ونوروز ازین اویماق غنغرات بودند از معظم امرائے اوزبک بودند چون درسنہ ثلث وتسعین وسبعمایہ صاحقران را باتوقتمش خان اوزبک حربے سخت روئدادہ این امرا دررکاب خان اوزبک موجود بودہ واومردانگی داد ندواین قوم قنقرات را غنقرات نیز مے نویسند وبعد ازانکہ بادشاہان مغلیہ در دین اسلام درآمدند اکثر الفاظ مغلی بغیر بعضے حروف بعربی فارسی درآمدند ونیز درلغت مغولی ق را بہ جائے غین مے نویسندو مے گفتند چنانچہ قنقرات را غنغرات نیز میگویند وہر دو صحیح اند۔

اویماق غونکغرات

از عمدہ اقوام است واگرچہ تحقیق نشد کہ از قیات است یا درلکین اما در شرافت نسب این قوم کلامے نیست وظاہر از قیات مے نماید ازین قوم نیز امیر یوسف صوفی غونکغرات ابن نیفدائے غونکغرات بودوے حاکم خوارزم بودو صاحبقران امیر تیمور گورکان درسنہ ثلث وسبعین وسبعمایہ براو لشکر کشید امیر

یوسف ہم درآن آوان بمردو بر یورش حسین صوفی غونکغرات بمسند امارت نشست وبا صاحبقران ازورِ متابعت درآمده صلح نمودو دختر خود خان زاده سوین بیگ راکہ ازبطن شکر بیگ دختر خان اوزبک متولد شده بود درسنہ خمس وسبعین وسبعمایہ بعقد شاہزادہ جہانگیر میرزادرآوردوامیر زادہ محمد سلطان از متولد شد بیرم صوفی غونکغرات ہم برادر صوفی یوسف بودوامیر علی بیگ غونکغرات از امرائے توقتمش خان بود کہ ویرا بمخالفت صاحبقران تحریص مے نمود واین قوم راقونکغرات نیز مے نویسند بقاف وقاف وغین باہم بدل مے نمایند۔

اویماق اویرات

اویماتی شریف است واز قیات مینماید اما وجہ تسمیہ او معلوم نشد دراوائل جہانگیر چنگیز خان بوزنجری این قوم نیز با نائمان درساختہ بجنگ او برخاستند چون قاآن لشکر بہ ادریش برداین قوم اول ساختگی حرب کردند آخر مجبور شده ازراہِ عجز درآمدند وغجر چی شدند ودرزمان قویلا قاآن بوزنجری ازین قوم تنگیز نام حاکم این قوم بود وصاحب ایل والوس بسیار بود وقویلا قاآن اورابجاربہ براور خود ارتق بوقاخان نامزد کرداواز امرائے معظم آن زمان بودواز اولادِ تنگیز اویرات وزمانہ سلطان ابوسعید بہادر خان بوزنجری بادشاہ ایران وخراسان امیر علی بادشاہ اویرات خاں سلطان ابوسعید خان بودودرسنہ ست وثلثین وسبعمایہ سلطان موسیٰ خان راکہ ازاولادتراقاے ابن ہلاکو خان بود سلطنت برداشت وسلطان ابوسعید خان انتقال کرده بود وارپاخان از اولاد ارتق بوقابمسند نشستہ وامیر علی اویرات کہ عداوت موروثی با اولاد ارتق بوقاداشت درفکر او شده با اوجنگید وظفر یافت ودرسنہ ست وثلثین وسبعمایہ ورحرب محمد خان وامیر حسن ایلکانی جلایر نقل رسید وامرائے اویرات متفرق شد ندوازین قوم شیخ علی اویرات حاکم اردپل بودودرزمان صاحبقران قزل میر علی اویرات نیز از امرائے مغنر زاین قوم بودوسارق عمر اویرات کہ درتکریت حکومت مے نمود وقتیکہ سلطان احمد جلایراز حرب

تراکمہ قراقونیلو منہزم شد دے خدمتے نیکو بجائے آوردو امرائے این قوم درمغولستان بحکومت رسیدہ اند چنانچہ بعداز تیمور قاآن دراندک زمان ممالک ختاوچین از دست مغولان بدر رفت وبدست اولاداو کتائے قاآن غیراز قراقرم وقلماق جائے نماند امرائے اویرات قوی حال شدند وآن ولایت نیز از تصرف ایشان برآوردند ومدتے کوس حکومت نواختند وازین قوم شریف عمدہ نوئنیان بزرگ ارغون آقا اویرات بود کہ بواسطہ بزرگی ومنزلت ویرا آقا میگفتند ودرزمانہ او کتائے قاآن بحکومت بلاد خراسان مقرر بودو اودرسلک بتکچیان انتظام واشت ونوئینی بزرگ بودو بادشہان بسیار ازادروغ چنگیز خان دیدہ بودومدت العمر کوچ نیکوداد وحکومت خراسان بہ نہایت عظمت وشان کردہ وسی ونہ سال بحکومت خراسان پرداخت وبروفق عدل وداد وحسب مرادزندگانی کرد چون ہلاکو خان درستہ احدی وخمیسن وستمایہ دربلادایران وخراسان وعراق وعجم بفرمان منکوقاآن نصب شدارغون آقاروانہ اردوی قاآن گرویدوارغون آقا وجور ماغون وتایجو یونویان کہ برولایت ایران وعراق مامور بودند ماتحت ہلاکوخان گردیدند ہلاکو ارغون آقارابدستور خراسان مقرر داشت وعنایت بسیار بوے فرمودہ امر مہمات عراق وسیتان وآذربائجان نیز برائے اوموقوف واشت وارغون آقا ازسر استظہار بہ ضبط وربط مہمات ولایت پرداخت وکرائے ملک اویرات پسر خودودیگر اولاد خود درانجدمت ہلاکوخان مقرر نمودتا بخدمت خان بودہ بندگی نمایند وسلاطین مغلیہ واکابرواصاغر معقول رعایت وحرمت ارغون آقامے داشتند وارغون آقا بعداز حکومت سی ونہ سال ورسنہ ست وسبعین وستمایہ ہجری ازین جہان فانی کوچ کردویکے ازشعرادر تاریخ وفات او گوید بسال ششصد وہفتادوشش بذی الحجہ۔ زمانہ بیست گذشتہ نماز دیگر بود۔ کہ بادگردش گردون بروز یکشنبہ۔ نہ فرق خسرو عادل کلاہِ بخت ربود۔ واز جملہ پسران امیر ارغون آقا امیر نوروز بیگ اویرات بودواوبہ جمیع صفات حسنہ موصوف ودرعلم ودانش وشجاعت وسخاوت بے مثل ونظیر بود چون بعداز ہلاکوخان مقرر بود کہ ولی عہد حاکم صوبہ خراسان مقرر میشد لہٰذا اغازان خان بوز بخری ابن ارغون خان درخراسان

بودو امیر نوروز بیگ بملازمت او بسرے نمود وقتیکه ارغونخان بوقارا بیاسار سانید امیر نوروز بی از وتخلف جستہ بہ بلاد شرقی رفت و بر غازان خان لشکر آورده راه غلط کرد و بیورت بوقاری غوچی افتاده ازو جنگید و فتح یافت وتا حدود خرقان تسلط کرده شاهزاده گیسور انشانید و یرلیغها بنام اونوشتن گرفت چون غازان خان بر این حادثہ وقوف یافت بر دفع امیر نوروز بیگ ہمت گماشتہ ودرین معرکہ از افواج شہزاده غازان روئے بہزیمت نہادوترد شہزاده قیدو خان بمغولستان رفت وقیدو ویرا نوازش کرده فرمود تا والیان الوس جغتائی نیز باوے طریق استمداد مبذول دارند و امیر بالشکرے آراستہ متوجہ خراسان گردید و شاہزاده قتلق شاه و قتلق تمور و غازان خان بہادر را بدفع او مامور نمود و در میان ایشان حسربے سخت واقعشده و امیر منہزم شده بسوے سیستان رفت و در سنہ اربع وتسعین وستمایہ با اورنگ تیمور داماد قیدو خان صداقتے بہم سانیده وبا او برسپاه میسور اغلن تاخت و بسبب کثرت اعدا عنان از معرکہ برتافت و یرلیغ بنام اورنگ تمور نوشتن گرفت و نیشاپور را محاصره کرد اما ہمدرین اثنا اورنگ تمور نیز از و متوہم شد و قصد او نموده امیر نوروز قصد او دریافتہ از ورمیده بدر جست وسفیرے بخدمت شہزاده غازان خان فرستاده عفو تقصیر درخواست نمد و غازان خان در آن زمان اطاعت او غنیمت شمرد و یرلیغ استمالت فرستاد و امیر حاضر شده باہمدگر پیمان بستند چون بائدو خان از کیخاتو خان برگشتہ امرائے عاصی دیرا کشتند و غازان خان با امیر غازی نوروز مشورت کرده امیر گفت کہ اُمید آن است کہ بقوتِ تیغ آبدار شہریار را بر اورنگ خانی بنشانیم و اعدا را آواره دشت عدم سازیم اما شہزاده را باید کہ گرد کفر را بہ آب اسلام از دلِ پاک بشوید شاہزاده نیز میلے بدین مبین داشت بحضور حضرت شیخ صدر الدین حموی زبان بکلمہ طیبہ گویا گردانید و دل از ظلمت کفر صاف فرمود و مغولان بسیار ہمدران روز باوی موافقت نمودند و دین بیضائے محمدی را اختیار کردند و شہزاده بسلطان محمود غازان خان ملقب شده و بہ بایدو خان پیام داد کہ امرائے عاصی رابسپار و تا بر وفق یاسائی چنگیزی بسزا رسانیم و بالشکرے گران متوجہ او گردید امیر نوروز بیگ باشش ہزار سوار بر سرتو کال

مغلائی بایدوخان رفت و براوظفر یافت و بایدوخان وغازان خان بعد نامہ وپیام بازنمود کہ ماازمکر اعداایمن نبودیم ازین وجہ بغیر اجازت راہ سفر پیمودیم اکنون اگر فارس وعراق رابما گذارند درآئین خویش جائے دار و بایدوخان امیر نوروز رار خصت نداده او بدمدمہ وافسون ویرابقابوی خود آوردہ بوعدہ گرفتہ آوردن غازان خان رخصت حاصل کردہ راہ خود گرفت وبالشکر گران غازان خان راہمراہ گرفتہ متوجہ بائیدوخان گردید اکثر امرائے عظیم القدر را از بایدو برگشتہ بقول وپیمان نوروز بیگ بہ غازان خان پیوستند و بائدوخان فرار ورزیدہ گرفتار شد وامیر نورروز بیگ اور البفر مان بادشاہ بکشت وکلیساہائے نصاری ودیر مجوس کہ درین زمان بسیار بنیاد نہادہ بودند غارت نمود وغازان خان برتخت نشستہ فرمان واد کہ جملہ مغولان از صغیر وکبیر ایمان آرند وہر کہ درین باب اہمال ورزد سرش ازتن بردارند ودرمیان سکہ کلمہ طیبہ نقش نمودند وآل تمغا وپایزہ ویرلیغہارا ازشکل مربع متدیر فرمودند خان یاسامیشی لشکر وانتظام مال وملک مفوض بہ امیر نوروز کرو پسر براق اغلن چغتائی برین حدود لشکر کشید بسبب تبادل چند بادشاہ دراندک زمان کارین مملکت پریشان بوداما امیر نوروز زرے ازاعیان تبریز بقرض گرفتہ تجہیز لشکر نمود درنواہی ہرات باسپاہ چغتائی جنگ دردادہ ظفر یافت وحل وعقدامور دیوانی وآل تمغا کہ منصبے بزرگ است مفوض بہ امیر حاجی بیگ اویرات برادر امیر نوروز بیگ گردید ہمدرین زمان خان فرمود کہ امیر بخراسان رفتہ انتظام نماید ودرراہ امرائے غدار قصداو کردند واوازمددِ بختِ بیدار خبر دار شدہ خیام راخالی گذاشت ودرکمین ایستادہ چون ایستیمو روارسلان وسوکابرلاکہ صلاح نمودہ بودند کہ امرائے اول الذکر بادشاہ رابکشتند وآخر الذکر امیر نوروز رابعدم رسانند چون سوکابعزم شبخون رسید امیر نوروز ازکمین بیرون جستہ اورا انہزام ساخت وبادشاہ رانیز باامرائے باغی جنگے واقعشدہ امرائے غدار ہزیمت یافتند ودرین داروگیر بمدت یکماہ پنج شہزادہ ازاویماق بوزبخری وسی وہفت امیر کبار بقتل رسیدند۔

(مرزامحمد عبدالقادر خاں عرف مرزااحمد آغاجان ''اویماق مغول'' امرتسر ۱۹۰۲ص ۷۷-۷۲)

ذکر مرزا حیدر دوغلات در بابرنامہ

سلطان ابوسعید میرزا اولوع اوغلی سلطان احمد میرزا غہ قویوب ابدی میرزا دین ہج اوغول فیز بولمادی سونکرا افترت تہ شیبانی خانعہ توشوب ابدی مین کابل عنہ کیلکانہ اشاہ پیکم بیلہ سمرقندتین خراسانعہ کیلب خراساندین کابل غہ کیلد یلار شیبانی خان قندہار وانا صر میرزانی قاباغاندامین لمغان غریمی قیلدیم خان میرزا وشاہ لیکم ومہر نکار خانیم بدخشان عہ بار و یلار میرزا خان نی مبارک شاہ قلعہ طعہ غہ بتلا کاندا ابا بکر کاشعری میک چاپقونی عنہ یولوقوب شاہ پیکم نکامہر خانم وجمع ایل نیسک اہل وعیالی اسیرلق قہ توشتی اول ظالم بدکردار نینک جیسی واونیاء فانی نی وداع قیلد یلار ایکیچنی فیرمنیسک والدم قتلق نکار خانم ابدی اکثر فراق لیق لار داوفرت لار دہ مننیک بیلان بیلہ ابدی لار کابل نی الغاین مش آلتی آی سونکرا تاریخ تو قوز یوزاون پرواتنکری رحمتی غہ بار و بلاء اوچونچی قیز خوب نکار خانیم ابدی محمد حسین کورکان دوغلت قہ پریب ابد بلار پرقزی براوغلی بولوب ابدی قیز نی عبید خان آلیب ابدی من بخارا اسمپر قندے انعاندا چقمای فالیب ایدی سلطان سعید خان دین عمی سید محمد میرزا سمر قندغہ منکا ایلچی لبک کا کیلکاندا انکا قوشواب باروی سلطان سعد خان الدی اوغول حیدر میرزا ابدی اناسی نی اور بک اولتور کاندین سوک کیلب منیک ملازتم داروج تورت سیل بولدی سونکرا اجازت تیللاب کاشغرغہ خان قاشیغہ بارو باز کردو باصل خود ہمہ چیز زرصائے نقرہ وارزیز بوتاریخ داوید وراماریکم تابب بولوب بخشی طریقہ پیدا قلیب تورخط تصویر واوق وپکان وربکر ہرنمہ کا کا ایلیکی چسپاندروطبع طبع نظمی ہم باردورمکا عرضہ داشتی کبلیب ایدی انشاسی سم یمان ایماس

(ظہیر الدین بابر۔ بابرنامہ لندن ۱۹۵۷ء ص ۱۱-۱۰)

ذکر مرزا حیدر دوغلات در همایون نامه

دور تو شک دیگر عمهای ما لکه خواهران حضرت فردوس مکانی باشند، شهر بانو بیگم و یادگار سلطان بیگم و عائشه سلطان بیگم دختر و محبه سلطان خانم دختر سلطان احمد خان که به الاچه خان مشهور بود ندطغای خورد پادشاه کلاں دخانش خواهر میرزا حیدر ردختر خانه پادشاه و بیگه کلان بیگم دکیچک بیگم و شاه بیگم مادرِ دشاد بیگم دختر فخر جرفان بیگم عمه پادشاه دکیچک بیگم و آپاق بیگم دختر سلطان بخت بیگم وهر لیق بیگم عمه بادشاه دلشاد بیگم نواسه سلطان حسین میرزا از جانب مادری عمه پادشاه۔ ومهر انگیز بیگم دختر مظفر میرزا نواسه سلطان حسین میرزا بسیار دوست مید اشتند ولباس مردانه می پوشیده ند وبانواع هنر ها آراسته زهگیری تراشی وچوگان بازی وتیر اندازی داکثر سازهای نواختند وگل بیگم وفوق بیگم وجان سلطان بیگم وافروز بانو بیگم وآغا بیگم وفیروزه بیگم و برلاس بیگم۔

وبیگمان دیگر هم بسیار بودند که بتفصیل نو دوشش بیگم همه

دور آن روز ها میرزا حیدر را مگر فتن کشمیر تعین نموده اند۔ درین اثنا خبر آمد که شیر خان رسید عجب اضطراری دست داد قرار ر دادند که صباح کوچ کنند۔

درین مدّت که برادران در لاهور بودند هر روز مصلحت ومشورت وکنگاش میکردند اصلاً بیک چیز قرار نمی دادند۔ آخر الامر خبر آمد که شیر خان آمد۔ دیگر بی علاج شده یک پهر روز بود که کوچ کردند وحضرت داعیه کشمیر داشتند ومیرزا حیدر کاشغر یرا فرستاده بودند اما هنوز خبر فتح کشمیر نیامد بود۔ کنگاش دادند کر اگر حضرت متوجه کشمیر شوند وکشمیر فی الحال میسر نشود وشیر خان در لاهور باشد آن زمان بسیار مشکل میشود۔

خواجه کلان بیگ در سیالکوٹ بود متوجه ملازمت حضرت شد موید بیگ همراه خواجه بود بحضرت عرضه داشت کرد۔ خواجه وعذغه ملازمت دارد مرمی اید اما ملاحظه میرزا کامران دار داگر

حضرت بسرعت بیایند ملازمت خواجہ بحضرت با حسن وجہ میسر می شود حضرت از شنید این خبر فی الحال جیبہ پوشیدہ مسلح دمکمل شدہ متوجہ خواجہ شدند و خواجہ راھمراہ گرفتہ آوردند۔

وحضرت فرمودند کہ باتفاق برداران بہ بدخشان رویم دکابل تعلق بمیرزا کامران داشتہ باشد۔ امامیرزا کامران بر فتن کابل راضی نشد دگفتند کہ کابل را حضرت فردوس مکانی در حیات خود بوالدہ من دادہ اند۔ رفتن کابل لایق نیست حضرت فرمودند کہ در باب کابل اکثر حضرتِ فردوس مکانی میفر مودند کہ کابل را من بھیچ کس نخواھم داد بلکہ فرزندان طمع کابل نکنند چرا کہ ھمہ فرزندان راخدای تعالیٰ ایمن در کابل دادہ و اکثر فتح ھا از نشتن کابل شدہ بلکہ در داقعہ نامہ فردوس مکانی ھم متشھد این معنی بسیار مذکور است چہ شد کہ من از ردی مھربانی و برادری بمیرزا انسانیت کردم۔ میرزا الحال چنین می گوید۔

(گلبدن بیگم، ہمایوں نامہ، لاہور ۱۹۶۶)

مجمل احوال مرزا حیدر دوغلات در تاریخ الفی

احوال سلطان سعید درین سال اینست کہ چون میرزا حیدر بالشکری بطرف کشمیر روان شد و کشمیریان دردورہ بیک سرراہ بر لشکر مغول گرفتند ومغولان شبخون بر کشمیریان آوردہ غالب شدند واز تنگی لار گذشتہ بصحرای کشمیر فرود آمدند و کشمیریان متفرق شدہ شہر کشمیر کہ بسری نگر مشہور است بتصرف مغولان درآمد وبیست و چہار روز مغولان در کشمیر توقف نمودند و کشمیریان در جنوب شہر کشمیر درمیان لای وکل جای مستحکم پیدا کردہ در مقام جمعیت شدند وروز بروز اطراف و جوانب لشکریان کشمیر جمع می شدند ومغولان دیگر صلاح در توقف شہر ندیدہ بصحرا بیرون آمدند وچون کشمیریان بعد واز مفولان بیشتر بودند مغولان ہر روز در جای م بودند و کشمیریان دلیر شد از میان لای وکل بیرون آمدند واز ہر جاہ کہ مغولان کوج میکردند و کشمیریان بھمان منزل فرود می آمدند و بر گرد خود خندق کنند تا انکہ مغولان

وکشمیریان بهمان یافتند وکشمیریان جان بتنگ یا ازمعرکه بیرون بردند وخودرا بکوهی که بجنگ گاه نزد یک بود رسانید خلاص شدند ومیرزا حیدر بقصد انکه چون بطرف پایان کشمیر که عیال واطفال کشمیر بآل آنجا بود روان شوند که انجماعت متفرق خوانده می شد متوجه پایان شدند وکشمیریان فرصت یافته ازکوه فرود آمدند ودرجای که کل ولای بسیار بود اطراف خودرا بخندق وشاخ بست محکم گردانیدند مغولان چون یک منزل رفتند وکل ولای بسیار بین آمد وعبور میسر نشد ناچار همانجا قرار گرفتند وروز بروز قوت کشمیریان زیاده میشد ومغولان که میل معاودت بولایت خود داشتند میرزا حیدر را بصلح راضی ساخته باکشمیریان صلح کردند وخطبه وسکه بنام سلطان سعید کرده آنچه مقدور بود پیشکش کردند وخراج قبول نمودند ودختر محمد شاه حاکم سلطان سکندر بنکاح درآورده معاودت نمودند ودرماربول که از ولایت تبت است بملازمت سلطان که هنوز بواسطه مرض دم گیری ضعیف بود رسیدند سعید خان میرزا حیدر را به ادرسنگ تعین نمود ومیرزا حیدر باره هزار سوار جریده متوجه بادرسنگ گشت وسلطان سعید خان عزیمت معاودت بدر الملک بارکند فرمود ودرراه بار دیگر مرض دم گیری بواسطه عبور بر مواضع تبت اشتداد یافت وامراعلاج منحصر درتعجیل سیر دانسته خانرا درجهار بایلغار ازتبت بیرون آوردند اما همان روز که شانزدهم ذی الحجه الف ۵٦۰ بود ۹۳۱ جون ازموضع تبت بیرون رفتند سلطان سید خان که بغایت ضعیف شده بود درگذشت وامراء که دررکاب خان بودند مرابض بطلب رشید خان پسر سلطان سعید خان فرستادند ورشید خان درسلخ ذی الحجه باردوی پدر رسید۔ گردد درمحرم اینسال رشید خان بجای پدرش سلطان سعید خان حاکم کاشغر ومغولستان گشت ودرهمین روز بوقت ملاقات بقتل سید محمد میرزا دوغلات برادر میرزا ابا بکر که نزد سعید خان نیابت معتبر بود حکم فرمود وسید محمد میرزا با فرزند ان واقوام بغیر میرزا حیدر وبرادرانش که به ادرسنگ رفته بود بدرراه بواسطه دم گیری اسپان ایشان تلف شد وازهشت روز وراه اورسنگ معاودت نمود وغنیمت بسیار درین یورش بدست لشکر مغولان درآمد واکثر ولایت تبت که برسرراه بود قبول باج وخراج نمودند وبوقت مراجعت فوت سلطان سعید

وحکومت رشید سلطان وقتل سید محمد میرزا رسید ورشید سلطان قربانی با برادرش سکندر سلطان فرستاد که حکومت تبت وآن لشکر بتو متعلق است میرزا حیدر و برادرانش رانزد خود نگاهدارد ولشکریان مغول از استماع این خبر متفرق شده بمقام اصلی خود مراجعت نمودند وبا میرزا اسکندر وحیدر سلطان زیاده بر پنجاه کس نماند وبمشقت بسیار بماریول که از ولایت تبت است وبولایت بارکند متصل است رسیدند وجمعی از لشکر مغول که فرار نموده بودند چون سر ما بغایت بسیار بود سارکند نتوانستند رفت ناچار معاودت نموده نزد سکندر سلطان ومیرزا حیدر آمدند وپانصد سوار نزد ایشان جمع شد وآن زمستان بصعوبت تمام در بیست گذرانیدند بوقت بهار رشید خان حکم فرستاد که در تبت دیگر توقف نکنند وهر جا خواهند بروند والا دفع ایشان نموده خواهد شد سکندر سلطان از میرزا حیدر جدا شده نزد برادر رفت ومیرزا با بیست وپنج کس از راه کوهستان تبت متوجه بدخشان شد وبمحنت بسیار ببدخشان نزد سلیمان میرزا که پسر خاله او بود آمد وغایت یافت ومدعی در بدخشان بوده بکابل آمد واز انجا بلاهور نزد کامران میرزا رفته بغایت اعتبار رسید۔

ذکر وقایع سنه ثمان واربعین وتسعمایة (۹۴۸) هجرت

ذکر وقایع سنه ثمان واربعین وتسعمایۃ هجرت درین سال شاه طهماسب حاکم ایران قلعه نقاص کرجستان را مسخر ساخت ودر تبریز قشلاق گرفت وغازی خان تکلو از سلطان سلیمان خواندگار روم فرار نمود بدرگاه شاه آمد واکثر ولایت شروان مجهول او متفرق گشت ودر دهم محرم این سال حضرت جنت آشیانی در کنار آب گنگ با شیر خان افغان جنگ کرد وبواسطه نفاق جمعی از امراو سستی بعض مردم دیگر فتح بیشتر شد وناچار باکره مراجعت واقع شد ومخالفان نزدیک رسیدند ودر اگره توقف میسر شده بجانب لاهور روان شدند ودر غره ربیع الاول این سال تمام سلاطین وامراء الوس چغتائی خان در لاهور جمع آمدند ودر هر سری سودای دور هر دلی تمنای پدید آید وسلطان محمد میرزا وفرزنده که

پاره صد گونه فتنه وفساد بودند از افغانان گریخته بلاهور آمد و باز از لاهور گریخته بطرف ملتان رفته و میرزا هندال و میرزا یادگار ناصر صلاح در آن دیدند که بجانب بکر و تته می باید رفت و بعد از تسخیر آن ولایت و دفع میرزا شاه حسین ارغون تسخیر گجرات در کمال اسان است و میرزا کامران درین فکر بود که زودتر این جماعه را متفرق گردانید تنها بکابل رود و حضرت جنت آشیانی مدتی در مقام آن بود که شاید برادر را باچطور متفق سازد و بدفع مخالفان پردازد چون یقین شد که اتفاق ایشان محال است خاطر مبارکش بغایت متالم شد روزی جمیع سلاطین و امرای و ارکان دولت جمع آمده قرعه مشورت درمیان انداختند آن حضرت فرمود که قبه از اتفاق هیچ امری بمشیت نمی پذیرد و جمیع مردم که حاظر بودند خط موکد بعهد و سوگند در باب اتفاق دادند و جمیع مردم حاضریران کاغذ گواهی نوشتند و شروع در مشورت شد میرزا حیدر دوغلات که بوقت سلطان سعید خان چنانکه گذشت کشمیر را بتصرف درآورد بود بعرض رسانید که فتح کشمیر در کمال سولتست و جانیست بغایت محکم بجهة اینست خاطر سپاهی کشمیر را می باید گرفت و اهل و عیال و اسباب را بآنجا فرستاد و تمام دامن کوه را از کنار سند تا کنار جون و گنگ می توان نگاه داشت افغانان کوته صلاح اند وتوپ وضربه زن بکوهستان درآوردند بغایت مشکل است میرزا کامران که درفکر کار خود بود گفت این کاری است بغایت مشکل و غنیم نزدیک رسیده است مبادا که کشمیر بدست نیاید و اهل و عیال سپاهیان بی مأمن بماند و درمعرض تلف درآید صلاح درآن می بینم که حضرت بادشاه و میرزایان جریده باشند خواه کشمیر روند و خواه بجائی دیگر و جمیع کوچ و بلند را بمن همراه سازند که بکابل رسانم و حاضر از ایشان جمع کرده خود بخدمت معاودت نمایم چون لحظ قبل از این بر اتفاق و ترک نفاق سوگند خورده بود تمام مجلس ازین سخن که محض نفاق و اراده خلاص خود و تصرف کابل و بدست آوردن اسباب بود حیران شدند و باتفاق گفتند که هرگاه اهل و عیال سپاهیان از هندوستان بیرون رفت و چندین دریا و کوه درمیان درآمد کدام سپاهی با چنین دل نگرانی در هندوستان باوجود غنیمی چنین توقف کرد میرزا کامران بخبر همان سخن که قرارداد خاطرش

بود بگفت و مجلس بآخیر رسید و هم چنین روز میگذشت و هیچ امری قرار نمی یافت تا آن شیر خان نزدیک سلطان پور رسید و حضرت جنت آشیانی میرزا حیدر و جمعی را که قبول خدمت کشمیر ند بآنطرف فرستاد و خواجه کلان بیگ/ نیز مقرر شد که متعاقب میرزا حیدر روان شود و چون میزا حیدر بنوشهر رسید و خواجه کلان بسیالکوٹ رفت شیر خان از آب سلطان پور عبور نمود و در غره رجب حضرت جنت آشیانی از اب لاهور عبور فرموده شده با یلغار باردو ملحق شد و میرزا حیدر بکشمیر در آمد و کشمیریان که با یکدیگر مخالفت داشتند جمعی آمده میرزا حیدر ملازمت کردند و بقوت ایشان کشمیر بی جنگ و نزاع بتصرف میرزا حیدر در آمد و بتاریخ بیست و دویم رجب۔

(عارف قندهاری تاریخ الفی)

ذکر مرزا حیدر دوغلات در اکبر نامه

میرزا حیدر بن محمد حسین گورگان (۔۔۔۔۔۔۔۔۔۔۔۔ حضرت گیتی ستانی فردوس مکانی بودۂ و همراه میرزا کامران بدار الخلافه آگره آمده شرفِ منزلت حضرت جهانبانی دریافته بود۔ و بنوازشهائی فراوان ممتاز گشته) میرزا کامران بیماریٔ خود را بهانه ساخته اورا بهمراهیٔ خود سعي کرد۔ میرزا حیدر بجانب میرزا کامران میل نموده در مقامِ عذر خواهي شد۔ واز بےفکري حرفِ رخصت درمیان آورد۔ حضرت جهانباني فرمودند که اگر نسبتِ خویشي منظور است از طرفین علی السّویہ است۔ و اگر ارادت و اخلاص امت ابن نسبت بما پیشتر ظاهر ساخته۔ و اگر تلاش ناموس و مردانگي است خود باید همراه ماشوي که ما بر سر غنیم میرویم۔ و آز که میرزا کامران اظهار بیماري مي نماید تو طبیب نیستي۔ و دارد شناس نه که همراه روي و آنکه میرزا لاهور را مامن تصوّر کرده خیالِ فاسد است چه از بازبس ماندن ازین یورش اگر امرے سانح شود کنج ملامت ذر هندوستان نمیتوان بانت۔ و نیز امراز دوشق بیرون

نیست۔ اگر مارا فتح است شمارا چه دو کدام آبرو که از شرمندگی سراز زمین نتوانید برداشت که مردن بران زیستن شرف دارد۔ واگر عیاذاً باللہ حال برخلافه اینست بودنِ شما در لاهور محال خواهد بود۔ وهرکس که این کنگاش بمیرزا کامران داده دماغش خبط یافته۔ باخیانت ورزیده۔ وحق راازد پوشیده از راهِ خوشامد در آمده است۔ الحاصل میرزا حیدر بدلالت بخت بیدار طریق هدایت یافت وبدولت رفاقتِ موکب عالي معزّز وممتاز گشت۔ ومیرزا کامران از وفورِ جمعیّت خود سه هزار کس را با شلیفی عبداللہ مغل همراه ساخت۔ وخود توفیقِ خدمت نیافت۔

الیشیاٹک سوسائٹی ابوالفضل۔ اکبرنامه مطبوعه کلکته

ذکر مرزا حیدر دوغلت در اکبرنامه

ودر بیست ودومِ این ماه (محرم) درقصبه رهتک هندال میرزا و میرزا حیدر دولتِ حضورِ اقدس دریافتند۔ ودر بیست وسوم ماه حضرتِ جهانبانی درهمین منزل نزولِ اقبال فرمودند۔ اهلِ قلعه دروازهٔ شهر را بر روی آنحضرت بستند۔ وابوابِ شقاوت برخود کشودند۔ وآنحضرت بدولت وسعادت متوجه شده در اندک زمانے اهلِ قلعه را تنبیه فرمودند۔ درهفدهم صفر موکبِ والا بسهرند رسید ودر بیستم این ماه میر فقر علي در اثنای راه محملِ حیات بربست۔ وچون موکبِ عالي درحوالیٔ لاهور قریب سرای دولتخان رسید میرزا کامران باستقبال آمده ملازمت کرد۔ وآنحضرت درباغِ خواجه دوست منشي (که دلکشاترین منازل لاهور بود) بدولت فرود آمدند۔ ومیرزا هندال درراه خواجه غازي (که دران ایام دیوانِ میرزا کامران بود) منزل گرفت۔ ومتعاقبِ آن میرزا هندي از سنبل رسید۔ درخانهٔ امیر ولی بیگ نشست۔ ودیو دولتمند سعادت منش شمس الدّین محمّد (که برکنار دریا دست داده بود) آمد۔ وبنوز شهای خسروانه سربلندي یافت ودرغرهٔ ربیع الاول (۹۴۷) نهصد وچهل وهفت تمامي برادرانِ گرامي واُمرا وسایر ملازمان جمع آمدند باوجودِ چندین اسباب آگاهی وتنبیهاتِ آسمانی این عزیزان آگاه نمیشد زد۔ وکمرِ صدق برمیان همت نمي بستند۔ ودر هرچندگاه درملازمتِ حضرت

جمع آمده کنگلش میکردند. و بر اتفاق و یک جهتي عهد و پیمان مي بستند. و اکابر و معارف را برین گواه مي گرفتند. و اکثر اوقات خواجه خاوند محمود برادرِ خواجه عبدالحق و میر ابوالبقا داخل کنگاش می بودند. تا نکه روزے جمیع میرزایان و اعیانِ دولت و اکابر جمع شده بر اتفاق و یکجهتي تذکره نوشتند. وتمام اهالي راعیان گواهئ خود وا بران سجلِ سعادت ثبت نمودند.

وچون این محضرِ وثوق باختتام رسید شروع در کنگاش کردند. آنحضرت درهر باب نصایح بلند وکلماتِ ارجمند فرمودند. و بر زبانِ گوهر بیان گذشت که وخامتِ عاقبت طائفة (که از جادهٔ قویم اتفاق عدول کرده اند) بر همگنان روشن است. علی الخصوص درین نزدیکي چون سلطان حسین میرزا در خراسان کوسِ رحلت زده بجده پهرِ کامگار اقبالمند گذاشت باچنان دولتے مستقل وساماني موفور از بے اتفاقی برادران ملک خراسان (که چندین سال بمیامنِ معدلت مرکز امنیت بود) در اندک فرصتے موردِ چندین حوادث گشته بشاهي بیگ انتقال یافت. و از جمیع فرزندان بغیر بدیع الزّمان میرزا (که بروم رفت) اثرے نماند. و همه فرزندانِ میرزا بالسنه وافواهِ خواص وعوام مطعون وملوم شدند. وحضرت گیتي ستاني فردوس مکاني هندوستانے بدین وسعت رابچه مشقّت گرفته اند. اگر از بے اتّفاقي شمایان از حیطهٔ تصرّف برآمده بدست چنین نا کهان درآید دانایان شمارا چه گویند. اکنون درین باب سر بجیبِ تفکّر نیک فرو باید برد. و از گریبانِ غیرت بیرون باید آورد. تا درمیانِ خلایق سربلندي حاصل آید. وموجبِ گرد آوریِ رضائی ایزدي گردد. هریک از اربابِ عهد و پیمان واصحابِ موائیق وایمان چنین عهد قریب را فراموش کرده بمقتضای هوا وهوسِ خود حرف سر اگشت. میرزا کامران گفت آنچه بخاطرِ من میرود آنست که پادشاه و همه میرزایان جریده روزے چند درجبال بسر برند. واهل وعیالِ تمام مردم را من برداشته بکابل ببرم. وبمامنے رسیده باز ملحق کردم. ومیرزا هندال یادگار ناصر میرزا گفتند که بالفعل جنگِ ما با افغانان صورت نمي بندد. مناسب آنست که بحدود بکر رفته آن ولایت را بانتظام آید تخلیص ابن ملک باحسنِ وجوه میسّر خواهد شد. میرزا حیدر گفت

مناسب آنست که تمام میرزایان از کره سهرند تا کوه سارنگ دامنهارا مستحکم ساخته بنشینند۔ ومن متعهّدم که باندک تقویتے در۔ دو ماه کشمیررا مستخلص سازم۔ وچون خبر گرفتن کشمیر رسد هر کس متعلّقانِ خودرا بکشمیر فرستد که ما منے محفوظتر ازان نیست چهار ماه مي باید که شیر خان برسد۔ وباگر در نهاوضرب زنها که اعتضادِ محاربهٔ اوست بکوهستان نمیتوانه رسد۔ ودر اندک فرصتے لشکر افغان ویران خواهد شد۔ چون ربانِ اینها بادل موافق بود سخن ناتمام شده مجلس تمام شد۔ وهر چندگاه سخن درمیان مي آمد وآنحضرت نصائح ارجمند میفرمودند (که شاید میرزا کامران راچراغ خرد روشن شود۔ واز تیره رائي برگشته درمقام صفا آید) میرزا از سخن خود بر۔ وهمگي او آنکه هر یکے بظر وئے ویران شوند۔ وخود بکابل رفته گوشهٔ عشرت راغنیمت شمارد۔ وپیوسته در اندیشهای نادرست فرورفته بود۔ سخنانِ اقبال بخش هوش افزا اورا بیدار نمی ساخت۔ بظاهر دم از موافقت سپرد۔ ومیگفت بفلان ساعت مسعود مي برادیم واز یکدلي وبکرنگي پیکار مخالف کمر همّت می بندم واز راهِ باطن اساس مخالفت را استوارتر می ساخت۔ تا آنکه از خیرگي وتبره رائي قاضي عبدالله صدرِ خودرا پنهاني پیش شیر خان فرستاد که رابطهٔ وداد استحکام دهد۔ وپیمانِ محبّت باز بندد۔ وکام خود را از مدد دشمن جوید۔ ودر مضمون مکتوب چنان نوشت که اگر پنجاب بدستورِ سابق بر من مقرّر دارند در اندک زمانے کارهای شایسته بتقدیم رسانم۔

ذکر مرزا حیدر دوغلات در اکبرنامه

اواخر جمادی الاُخری حضرت جهانباني ومیرزایان از آب لاهور (که پایاب بود) عبور فرموده کوچ بکوچ بکنارِ آب چناب رسیدند۔ حضرت جهانباني راچون داعیهٔ کشمیر تصمیم یافته بود جمعے راهمراه میرزا حیدر ساخته میرزا را پیشتر از خود بصوبِ کشمیر فرستادند۔ چه دران هنگام (که میرزا کامران بجنگ سام میرزا بقندهار (شافت میرزا حیدر را از جانب خود بحکومت لاهور گذاشته بود۔ خواجه حاجي وابدال باکري وزنگی چک وجمعے از اُمرای کشمیر مخالفت والیٔ آنجانموده بحدود لاهور آمده

بودند که بآشنائی میرزا حیدر لشکر سے از میرزا کامران گرفتہ ولایت کشمیر رادر تصرّف خود درآند۔ وہر چند میرزا حیدر سعي ثمود نقشِ ابن آرزو صورت نہ بست۔ ودروقتیکہ میرزا ہندال خطبہ بنام خود ساختہ فتنہ انگیز شد ومیرزا کامران از حدود لاہور بدارالخلانہ آگرہ توجّہ نمود میرزا حیدر بگوشش تمام از دارالخلافہ لشکرے بباشلیقی باباجوجک (کہ از عُمدہای میرزا کامران بود) ترتیب دادہ فرستاد۔ کہ ببدرقتہ اُمرای کشمیر (کہ نام ایشان ذکر یافت) رفتہ ولایت کشمیر رادر تصرّف آرند باباجوجک در رفتن مشاہلہ نمود۔ تا آنکہ قصّۃ پُرغصّۃ گذرِ چوسہ (کہ چشم زخمِ دولتِ ابدپیوند بود) برزبانِ عام افتاد۔ مشارالیہ۔ فسخ عزیمت نمود۔ واُمرای کشمیر درحدودِ نوشہرو راجوري درشعاب جبال بسر بردہ منتظرِ امرے میبودند۔ وازایشان پیوستہ نوشتہابمیرزا حیدرمي آمد مشتمل برمُرغباتِ تسخیرِ کشمیر۔ ومیرزا آن خطوط بموقفِ عرضِ حضرت جہانباني میرسانید۔ وخاطر اقدس راروز بروز بسیر ملک دلکشای کشمیر شوق مي افزود۔ درینولا بموجبِ آن رخصت دارند کہ اولاً میرزا باجمع بنوشہر رود۔ اگر اُمرای کشمیر (کہ ہموارہ ترغیبِ رفتنِ کشمیر میکردند) آمدہ بیتند سکندر توپچي بامردمِ خود (کہ جاگیر دارِ نزدیکِ آنحدود داست) آمدہ ملحق شود۔ وچون بعقبہ رسید امیر خواجہ کلان بیگ (کہ از اُمرای کلانِ حضرتِ گیتي ستاني فردوس مکاني بود۔ ومجمل احوالِ اراایراد یافتہ) خودرا بکمک رساند۔ وچون خبر رسیدنِ خواجہ کلان بیگ بمسامعِ علّیہ رسد حضرت جہانبانی خود بدولت واقبال متوجّہ آنصوب گردند۔ آن حضرت درکنارِ دریای چناب بردند کہ میرزا کامران وعسکري میرزا باخواجہ عبدالحق وخواجہ خاوند محمود متوجّہ کابل شدند۔ ومحمّد سلطان میرزا واُلغ بیگ میرزا وشاہ میرزا از حدودِ مُلتان صیتِ تفرقہ شنیدہ برلب دریای سند بمیرزا کامران ملحق شدد۔ ودرغرّہٴ رجب (۹۴۷) نہصد وچہل وہفت حضرت جہانبانی را (کہ عزمِ رفتنِ کشمیر مصمم برد) میرزا ہندال ویادگار ناصر میرزا وقاسم حسین سلطان ابرام نمودہ بجانب سند بردند۔ خواجہ کلان بیگ (کہ ہمراہی حضرت جہانباني جنّت آشیاني قرار داد بود) از سیالکوٹ رفتہ بمیرزا کامران ہمراہ۔ شد وسکندر توپچی خودرا بکوہ بسارنگ کشید ودر

رجب (۹۲۷) نہصد وچہل وہفت (که حضرت جهانباني بمع میرزایان متوجّه حدود سند شدند۔

ذکرِ مجملے از احوال میرزا حیدر

وصورتِ حال میرزا حیدر آنکه چون تبیدِ حضرت جهانبانی بافته متوجّهِ کشمیر شد چنانچه سمت گذارش یافت) چون شهره در آمد اُمرای مذکور (که احضی آنها بیشتر گشت) مخلصانه آمده دیدند۔ وراه وروشِ در آمدن کشمیر و گرفتنِ آن را مجددا خاطر نشان نمودند۔ میرزا تکیه بر نصرت ایزدي و دولتِ پادشاهي نموده برطيّ عقباتِ کشمیر قدم پیش نهاد۔ درین اثنا تفرقه در معسکرِ پادشاهي (چنانچه مذکور شد راه یافت۔ خواجه کلان بیگ بمیل خود یا بسعي میرزا کامران آن عزم را فسخ نموده بمیرزا کامران ملحق شد۔ ومظفّر توپچي خود را بکره سارنگ کشید۔ غیر از چندے از ملازمانِ قدیم میرزا حیدر و جمعے دیگر (که حضرتِ جهانباني بکمک نامزد فرموده بودند) همراه نشدند۔ اما چون در کشمیر اختلاف واختلالِ عظیم بود و هرج ومرجِ بیحد به پشت گرمیٔ مرغباتِ کشمیریان در بیست ودومِ رجب (۹۴۷) نهصد وچهل وهفت از عقبهٔ پنوچ در آمد۔ وبے جنگ وجدل تسخیرِ کشمیر نمود۔ چه دران ایام مدّتے گذشته بود که کشمیر از حاکم مستقل خالي بود۔ واُمرا اں ملک را بتغلّب در تصرّف خود داشتند۔ وبر یکی از مدّعیانِ حکومت آن دیار اسمِ ریاست اطلاق کرده خود ملک رانی میکردند۔ درین زمان نازک شاه نام شخص باسم بے مسمای حکومت اختصاص واشتهار داشت۔ وبا این حالت هرگاه درمیان یکدیگر اتفاق و تدبیر وعقل ورای نباشد هر آینه کارِ ملک باین سرحد کشد۔ موسم چله دی بود۔ وباران باشتدادمي بارید۔ کلچي چک چون رقم استقلال از جبهه احوالِ میرزا حیدر خواند بمقتضای فریب وخداع (که کشمیري ازان گزیر ندارند) از کشمیر بر آمده پیشِ شیر خان رفت چه مقصود از آوردنِ میرزا حیدر کامروائي خود بود۔ چون آن میسر نشد بلکه نقشِ دیگر نشستن گرفت دست ازین باز داشته در اندیشهٔ دیگر شد۔ وطرحِ دیگر خیال گرد۔ وخواهر اسمعیل ولد محمد شاه را بشیر خان داد وباین وسیله خود را مقبول ساخته عادل خان وحسین خان سروانی وجمع دیگر را تا مقدارِ دو هزار کس گرفته بکشمیر آمد۔ درین اثناء

ابدال ماکري (که استظهارِ او بود) بعلّت استسقا درگذشت - ومیرزا حیدر اہل وعیالِ خود را در اندر کول (که استحکام تمام دارد) گذاشته متحصّن شد - اہلِ کشمیر همه جدا شدند - وپیشِ میرزا مردم کم ماندند - وتا سه ماه در شعابِ جبال بسر میبرد تا آنکه در روز دوشنبه بیستم ربیع الثاني (۹۴۸) نهصد وچهل وهشت جنگ دست داد - وبتائید یزداني فتح کرد - وهرچند مخالفان (چه از افغانانِ کمکي وچه از کشمیریانِ بے حقیقت) زیاده از پنج هزار سوار بودند چون کارِ ایشان بر بیوفائي مبتني بود کارے از پیش نرفته شکست یافتند - وجمع کثیر از مخالفان - بقتل رسیدند - وگردھے دستگیر شدند - وکشمیر باستقلال در تصرف میرزا در آمد وخطیب کشمیر مولانا جمال الدین محمد یوسف لفظ فتح مکرر تاریخ این فتح یافته بود وتکرار این فتح اگرچه در همین رفتنِ میرزا نیز صورت دارد اما آنچه میرزا خود اشاراتے در تاریخ مي نماید آنست که یکبار میرزا فرستاده معید خان حاکم کاشغر از راهِ دره در بکشمیر آمد - ودر چهارم شعبان (۹۳۹) نهصد وسی ونه - در تصرف در آورده - بود ودر سلخ شوالِ سالِ مذکور با اُم ای کشمیر ومحمد شاه (که اسم حکومت بنام او بود) صلح گونه کرده دختر محمد شاه را برای اسکندر سلطان پسر خود گرفته از راہے (که آمده بود) مراجعت کرد - چون درین نوبت فتح غیبي دست داد وملک کشمیر متسخر شد ملّت ده سال در انتظامِ آن ولایت سعي بلیغ نمود - وآن عرصه دلپذیر را (که حکمِ خرابه داشت) لباسِ شهري پوشانید - واتمامِ محترفه - وارباب صناعات را از هرجا طلب داشته در مقام رونق ورواجِ آن ملک شد - علی الخصوص موسیقي را بازار گرم گشت - وانواع - ساز درمیان آورد - مجملا صورت ظاهر آن مملکت (که نشأة دنیائي اوست) معني پیدا کرد - اما بواسطه تعصّبهای خنک بینمکِ میرزا (که منشای آن نارسائي با دعوي سیدگي ست) متاع معنیِ کشمیر (که عالم یکرنگي ودیداریست) کساد یافت - وتا امروز بوی تعصّب از کشمیریان مي آید که صحبت را تاثیر عظیم است - میمّا اطوار - فرمانروایان که قوي اشد میباعد - امید که به یمن آثارِ حقیقت وحقانیت حضرت شاهنشاهي صورت ومعنیِ کشمیر اتحاد پذیرد - ومتاعِ حق پرستي وخداشناسي بے شایبه تکلف وتعصب رواج گیرد - واز سهوهای عظیم (که میرزا را

روی دادو میمنت نداشت) آن بود که باوجود فتح چنین خطبه وسکه بنام نازک شاه بدستورِ اُمرای کشمیر ساخت ـ بایستی بحق نمک حضرت جهانباني بجای آورده وجوه دراهم ودنانیر ورووسِ منابر رابنامِ قدسیٔ حضرت جهانباني مشرف میاخت ـ همانا که بازمانه مدارائے میکرد ـ نه بے اخلاصي رارواج میداد ـ ولهذادران ایام (که فتح کابل شد) خطبه رابنامِ مقدسِ حضرت جهانباني ساحته سربلند شد ـ ودرتاریخ (۹۵۸) نهصد وپنجاه وهشت هجري درشبخوئے (که کشمیریان آورده بودند) مسافرملک نیستی شد ـ

ومجملے ازین سانحه آنکه میرزاازآئینِ عدالت (که نگاهبانِ دولت است) عدول نموده بمقتضای هواوهوسِ خودزیست کردن گرفت ـ وهشیاري وبردباري (که دوبازدی بختیاریست) از دست داد ـ مکروغدرِ کشمیریان (که بتدبیر وهوشمندي میرزاازپای درآمده بود) بازبرباشد ـ وابن گروه خراب باطن نفاق سرشت راه خداع درلباس دوستي کارِ دشمني ساختن گرفتند ـ وعمده ابن کار آن بود که لشکرِ میرزارابحیلها ازوجداگردند ومردم کارآمدنی اورامتفرق ساختند ـ طایفة رابجانب تبّت وبرخے رابجانب پکلي وچندے رابطرفِ راجوري فرستادند ـ وعیدي ریناوحسین ماکری و ابدال ماکري خواجه حاجي بقال کشمیري را (که مرگرده مهمات میرزابود) اُز راه برده بخود متفق ساختند ـ وجمع کثیررابخوه همداستان کرده برسرمیرزاروان شدند ـ غازي خان وملک دولت چک نیز آمده ملحق گشتند وقریب خانپور (که میانِ هیره پوروسري نگرکه اصلِ شهرِکشمیروحاکم نشین است) برسر میرزاشبخون آوردند ـ میرزانزدیک خانه خواجه حاجي رفته بودتاقرابهادررا (که دربند بود) خلاص سازدناگاه بدست کمال دولي حیات راسپري کرد ـ وبعضے میگویند که تیرے ازملازمان اوناداننسته رسید ـ

وازوقائعے (که درین سال ۹۶۸ سمت ظهوریافت) فرستادن میرزاقرابهادرخان است (که برادرزاده میرزاحیدرکورگان بود) بتسخیر کشمیرچون (درآئین معدلت گستري وقانونِ

کشور گشائیٔ امرے ست لازم کہ ہرگاہ (والیٔ مملکتے وحاکم ناحیتے بعیش وعشرت خود مشغول گردد۔ وبکامروائیٔ نفس وہواوقتِ گرامي مصروف سازد۔ وبرعیّت پروري وغمخواری ستم رسیدگان وبراند اختنِ جورپیشگان نپردازد) خدیوزمان (را (کہ ایزدتوانا قدرت تصرّف دادہ کارفرمای جہان وجہانیان گردانیدداست) لازم است کہ بجہت سپاسداری ایزدي دراستیصالِ آن مسلّط متغلّب کوشیدہ ساکنانِ آن مرزوبوم رابدادمنشانِ خردپرورسپارد۔ وآنرادیباچۂ عباداتِ گزیدہ تصوّرنماید) بنابرین مقدّمہ حق اساس درین سالِ فرخندہ (چون شوروشعبِ کشمیریان شورانگریز آشوب پیشہ وبیدادیٔ شاری خان حاکم کشمیر بمسمع اقبال رسید) حکم معلّی شرفِ نفاذ یافت کہ بسرکودگی میرزا قرابہادرخویش میرزاحیدر (کہ عارف آنحدوداست) لشکرے آراستہ متوجہ تسخیر کشمیر گرددوجمعے کثیر بکمک اونامزدشدند۔ درین ایام غازي پسر کاحی چک فرمان روای کشمیر بود کہ بعداز پدرریاست کشمیر باورسید۔ وتحقیق آنست کہ پسرحسن چک برادر کاچي چک است چون پیمانۂ عمرحسن چک پُرشد کاچي چک (ازطُغیان آزوفرط ہواوہوس یا ازجہتِ انتظام دنیا) زنِ حاملۃ اورابعقدِ خوددر آورد۔ وبعداز دوسہ ماہ ازانعقاد غازي خان متولّدشد۔

القصّہ قرابہادر چون کاردان وکارطلب نبود پس از مکثِ طویل متوجّہ خدمت شدودر شدّت گرما براجوري رسید ونصرت خان وفتح برادرزادہ دولت چک ولوہروانکري وبَجي رینا برادرِ عیدی رینا ویوسف چک پسرِ مکي چک وخواجہ حاجي آمدہ ملحق شدندوچون حالِ این لشکررا منتظم ندیدند نصرت خان وفتح چک ولوہروانکري بصوبِ کشمیر گریختند وسہ ماہ بجہت آمدنِ کمک درموضع لالی کھوکر نزدیک بہنبھر توقّف افتاد۔ وچون سرانِ این لشکر کہ نہ عملہ بودند دیرتر رسیدند۔ درامدن بکشمیر ازین قسم نیست کہ باین آہستگي وگران پائیٔ میسرشود۔ چہ مسالک آن ملک ازاں قبیل است کہ (اگرچند روز پیشتر ازآمدنِ بیگانہ والیٔ آنجاواقف شدہ تنگیہلی راہ بگیرد) اگرچہ لشکرے ازہزاران رستم آراستہ باشدگرفتن آن مشکل بلکہ محال خواہد بود۔ غازی خان (کہ آمدنِ لشکرشنید۔ وچند ماہ

برین گذشت) آنچنان طرق ومضائق راا ستحکام داد که مزیدے دران متصور نباشد۔ و پیادہای خود راازگریوہای مستحکم پیشتر فرستاد۔ ومیرزا قرا بہادر درنزدیک راجوري بعداز مقابلہ ومحاربۂ چندروزہ شکست برگشت۔ تنہا استیلا واستحکام کشمیریان این کارنکرد۔ موسم تپ لرزہ وآثار باران ونارسیدن کمک عمدہ اسباب این شکست شد۔ ودرین روزجنگِ غریب درپیوست۔ ازیک طرف بندوقچیان واز دیگرطرف تیراندازان دستبرد مي نمودند۔ ومردم پادشاہي اگرچہ کم بودند امّا بجنود تائید آسماني بیشي کردہ دادِ مردانگي دادند۔ کوچک بہادر نام رستم دلے ازین جانب تردّدہای نمایان (کہ کارنامہ دلاوري تواند بود) بتقدیم رسانید۔

ذکر مرزا محمد حیدر دوغلات در ہفت اقلیم

دو پسر جانب نختین سالتز میرزا نام داشت ودیگر محمد حیدر میرزا کہ والدہ اش عمہ یونس خان بودہ سالتز میرزا بحکم کبرسن وحسن خلق وشجاعت بجای پدر تکیہ زدہ کاشغر ویانکی حصار را برادر خود محمد حیدر میرزا دادوی بعداز چند وقت واہمہ کردہ نزد دوست محمد خان کہ ھمشیرہ اش درعقدوی بود رفت وسالتز میرزا من حیث الاستقہ الال درامر حکومت دخل فرمودہ پس ازآن کہ ہفت سال بعدل وداد ودولت واقبال بگذرانید درسال ھشصد وشصت ونہ رخت بعالم بقا کشید واز دو پسر ماند یکی ابا بکر میرزا ودیگری عمر میرزا چون پسران وی بحکم قلت سال شایستہ حکومت نبودند ھرآینہ اعیان مملکت کس بطلب محمد حیدر فرستادہ بدار یکش برداشتند درخلال این احوال دوست محمد خان بیارکند آمدہ بازماندگان سالتز میرزا رامحاصرہ نمود واھل قلعہ بقدم منازعت پیش آمد ومدت محاصرہ بتعویق انجامید وآخر صلح بدان منوال مقرر گشت کہ زوجہ سالتن میرزا بعقد وی درآوردند تا برگشتہ بموغلستان

رو دو بس از انعقاد این سلطنت میرزا ابا بکر را همراه گرفته مراجعت نمود و ولایت کاشغر بالتمام بمحمد حیدر میرزا که مرد همواره کم آزار عافیت طلب بود بیست و چهار سال حکومت نمود و چون میرزا ابا بکر بحد بلوغ رسید دوست محمد خان همشیره خود را بوی نکاح بست و در صدد تربیت او گشت و میرزا ابا بکر بعد از چند وقت از اطوار ناهنجار دوست محمد خان آزرده گشته نزد عم خود محمد حید میرزا بکاشغر آمد و چون در حد ذات کریم و راد و شجاع و صاحب اراده بود همیشه با جوانان مردانه صحبت میداشت و همواره لوای ولایت گیری می افراشت تا بخدیعت یارکند را متصرف گردیده شخصی نزد عم خود محمد حیدر مرزا فرستاده اظهار اطاعت و انقیاد نمود و بتدریج قریب سه هزار سوار کارزار که در خدمت میرزا حیدر بیقدر و کم بها بودند بروی جمع آمده اراده نمود که ختن را از میرزایان که والی آن ولایت بودند انتزاع نماید و میرزایان دو برادر بودند که منقود از امثال و اقران میز یستند و از زمان امیر خداداد ولایت بدیشان مقرر بود یکی قول نظر میرزا و دیگری خان نظر میرزا نام داشت و خان نظر میرزا را حربه بوده از آهن برمثال عصابی که هیچ کس آنرا بدو دست برنتوانست داشت و او آنرا بجای نیزه و تیغ کارفرمودی۔

القصه میرزا ابا بکر برخصت عم خود محمد حیدر میرزا مقاتله و محاربه ایشانرا پیش نهاد همت ساخت و میرزایان او را نیز استقبال نموده آن سال معامله بصلح انجامید و کرت ثانی بمکر و خدیعت میرزایانرا بقتل آورده ختن را متصرف گردید و پس از این قضیه امرای محمد حیدر میرزا و همه کرده بعرض سانیدند که عنقریب در امر حکومت مستقل شده لوای مخالفت مرتفع خواهد گردانید پیش از آنکه زاغ این فتنه در دماغ او آشیانه نساخته چاره این کار باید نمود و دست استقلال او را از دامن مامول کوتاه باید ساخت۔

و چون این سخن بمیرزا ابا بکر رسید عرضه داشتی مشتمل بر خلوص عقیدت و انقیاد و در قلم آورده نزد والده خود که بعد از فوت دوست محمد خان در نکاح محمد حیدر میرزا در آمده بود فرستاد و والده اش عرض نمود که میرزا ابا بکر بواسطه عداوت امرا تو هم کرده بخدمت نمی آید و الا در اعتقاد و اخلاص او قصوری

نیست چه همیشه یکی از ملازمان تو حکومت یارکند میکرده اند الحال اگر فرزند تو بدین خدمت مامور باشد چه فساد تولد خواهد نمود یقین جایی که دیگران را دامن سوز داو را دل خواهد سوخت و چندان او نیرنک وافسون فرو خواند که محمد حیدر میرزا از سادکی خود قبول نموده نقش جمله تقصیرات او را آب عفو فروشست و بتدریج کار بجایی انجامید که اکثر امرای معتبر خود را بنابر رضای میرزا ابا بکر و اغوای والده اش غدر خواسته رخصت داد۔

چون مردم محمد میرزا متفرق گردیدند میرزا ابا بکر برزین ملک ستانی نشسته اطراف کاشغر و یانکی حصار را تاخت و تاراج نموده چون مکر راین جرات از وی بحصول پیوست میرزا ابا بکر را سهل انگاشته با پانزده هزار کس به محمد حیدر میرزا ملحق گردید و میرزا ابا بکر با همان سه هزار کس ایشان را استقبال کرده بعد از اندک گرو فری شکست بر یونس خان و محمد حیدر افتاده تا کاشغر عنان باز نکشیدند و محمد حیدر میرزا کاشغر را محکم ساخته و یونس خان بمغولستان رفت و سال دیگر با شصت هزار سوار جهت دفع میرزا ابا بکر بکاشغر آمده باتفاق محمد حیدر میرزا که نود هزار سوار و پیاده در ظل رایتش جمعشده بودند رفته یارکند را محاصره نموده و میرزا ابا بکر روزی با پنجهزار کس بر آمده جنک در پیوست و بحسب اتفاق بر آن لشکر گران مستولی گردید نوعی ایشان را منهزم ساخت که مغولان یونس ملتفت ناشده راه فرار پیش گرفتند و محمد حیدر میرزا قطع تعلق از حکومتکرده بهمراه یونس خان بجانب اقسو روان گردید و در خدمت خان می بود تا بعد از فوت وی فوت گردید و جمله ملک موروثی بی موانعی بمیرزا ابا بکر مقرر گشت و بتدریج اختر دولتش صعود نموده مصدر اعظم فتوحات گردید و کارهای شگرف از وی بحصول پیوست چه ابتدا لشگر بجانب فرستاده تا سرحد کشمیر بتصرف در آورد و پس از آن کسان بجانب بلور تعیین نموده رایت استقلال برافراخت و ایضا مزارخات بدخشانرا تابع منقاد ساخته۔

(امین احمد رازی ہفت اقلیم)

احوال مرزا حیدر دوغلات در "طبقات اکبری"

ذکر سلطان شمس الدین سلطان محمد بعداز پدر برسریر سلطنت تمکن جسته باتفاق وزرا تمام ولایت رابرامرا تقسیم نمود ومردم کشمیر از جلوس او خوشحال شدند دراندک فرصت میان ملک کاجی وابدال تراع بهم رسیده ملک کاجی رابقصد جنگ ابدال بجانب کوه سوبرو وابدال نیز باستعداد تمام درمقابل آمد وآخر بصلح قرار یافته ابدال درکمراج که جاگیراو بود رفت وسلطان وملک کاجی بسری نگر مراجعت نمودند باز بعد چندگاه ابدال سراز اطاعت تافته درمقام فساد شده درکمراج خلل انداخت این مرتبه سرفتنه بآسانی تسکین یافت از احوال سلطان شمس الدین وتاریخ کشمیر زیاده برین یافت نشد وایام حکومت او معین نگشت بعداز وپسرش نازک شاه بحکومت نشست پنج شش ماهی نگذشته بود میرزا حیدر استیلا یافته صاحب تصرف گشت درایام حکومت اوخطبه وسکه بنام نامی حضرت جنت آشیانی محمد همایون بادشاه بود ذکر حکومت مرزا حیدر درسنه ثمان واربعین وتسعمائه دروقتی که جنت آشیانی از شیرخان شکست یافته بلاهور آمده بودند ابدال ماکرے وزنگی چک وبعضی ازاعیان مملکت کشمیر عرضداشت اختیار دولتخواهی وترغیب گرفتن کشمیر نموده بوسیله مرزا حیدر فرستادند وآنحضرت میرزا حیدر رارخصت کرده قرار فتن خود نیز دادند وچون میرزا حیدر نیز رسید ابدال ماکری وریکی چک آمده ملحق شدند همراه مرزا حیدر زیاده برچهارصد سوار بنود وچون براجوری رسید کاجی چک که حاکم کشمیر بود باسه هزار پنجاه هزار پیاده کوتل کرسل رآمده محکم ساخت مرزا حیدر ترک این راه واده براه بنج روان شد وکاجی ازروی کمال غرور محافظت آن راه تمود میرزا حیدر راز کوه گذشته بفهاے۔ کشمیر درآمده بناگاه سری نگر رامتصرف شد وابدال ماکری وریکی چک استقلال یافته مهمات از پیش خود گرفتند وپرگنه چند بجاگیر میرزا نامزد نمودند اتفاقاً درهمان اثنا ابدال ماکری راعمر بسرآمده وپسران خود رابه حیدر سفارش نموده درگذشت وبعداز درآمدن میرزا حیدر بکشمیر کاجی چک پیش شیرخان افغان بهندوستان رفته

پنجهزار سوار که حسین شروانی و عادل خان سردار آنها بودند با دو فیل با کومک آوردو میرزا حیدر باتفاق ریکی چک متوجه جنگ اوشدند فریقین مابین موضع وته بارو موضع کاره صفها بیاراستند و نسیم فتح بر پرچم علم مرزا حیدر ورزیده امرای شیر خان کاجی چک هزیمت یافتند کاجی چک در بیرم کله قرار گرفت وملا محمد یوسف جامع تاریخ فتح مکرریافته بودو در سنه خمسین وتسعمائه مرزا حیدر در قلعه اندرکوٹ اقامت نمودو بجهت بدگمان شدن مرزا حیدر در باب ریکی چک اوگریخته تر دکاجی چک رفت وهردو اتفاق نمودو در سنه احدی وخمسین وتسعمائه بقصد استیصال مرزا حیدر روی بسری نگر نهادندو بهرام چک پسر ریکی چک خودرا بسری نگر رسانید مرزا حیدر بندگان کوکه وخواجه حاجی کشمیری را بدفع دی نامزد کردواوتاب نیاورده بگریخت وچون لشکر مرزا تعاقب نمودند کاجی چک وریکی چک فرار راغنیمت دانسته وزبیرم کله قرار گرفتند ومرزا حیدر بندگان کوکه در سرے نگر گذاشته متوجه تسخیر تبت شده از قلاع بزرگ قلعه کوسوار را با چند قلعه دیگر فتح کردو در سنه اثنی وخمسین وتسعمائه کاجی چک وپسر او به تپ ولرزه بمردند مرزا حیدر اینسال را بالفراغت گذرانیدند ودر سنه ثلث وخمسین وتسعمائه ریکی چک بامرای مرزا حیدر جنگ کردو کشته شدو سرش باسر پسرش غازیخان پیش مرزا آوردند ودر سنه اربع وخمسین وتسعمایه ایلچی از کاشغر رسیده مرزا حیدر باستقبال ایلچی درلار آمد وانجه بهرام ولد مسعود چک که مدت هفت سال درکمراج جنگهای خوب کرده برهمه غالب بود باخان میرک مرزا سخنان صلح درمیان آورده عهد وشرط قرارداد خان میرک مرزا بعهد وسوگند اورا طلبید وقتی که انچه بهرام در مجلس او آمد وے خنجرے از موزه کشیده بر شکم وی زد واو همچنان زخم خورده گریخت ودر جنگل درآمد خان میرک مرزا متعاقب او شتافته اورا گرفت وسراورا جدا کرده نزد مرزا حیدر درلار آورد بگمان اینکه مرزا حیدر خوشحال خواهد شد عیدے زنیا بعد از حاضر ساختن از دیدن سراو در قهر شدو بغضب برخاست وگفت بعد از شرط وعهد کشتن یکی لائق بنا شد مرزا حیدر گفت من ازینواقعه خبر ندارم بعدازان مرزا حیدر از راه لار متوجه کشتوار شد بندگان کوکه ومحمد ماکری وملکیه مغول ومیرزا محمد یحی وعبدے رنیا راهراول لشکر ساخته خود

درموضع دوجهابرنزدیک کشتوارقرارگرفت وجماعت هراول سه روزه دریک روزقطع نموده بموضع دوست که درین جانب آب ماریاست رسیدندولشکرکشتوارازآنجانب آب بود جنگ تیروتفنک درمیان آمدهیچ یک ازآب عبورنتواستند کردروزدیگرلشکرمرزاحیدررازراه راست انحراف ورزیده خواستند که درکشتوار درایند چون بموضع داررسیدند باوتند برخاست وتاریک شدمردم لارهجوم نموده برسرایشان آمدند بندگان کوکه سرداربود باکس بسیارقتل رسید وازانجا که روان شدند دراره محمد باکری وپرسش بابست وپنجکس خوب کشته شده بقیه السیف بهزارمحنت بمرزاحیدرملحق شدندمرزاحیدرازانجا برآمده درسنه خمس وخمسین وتسعمائة متوجه تبت گشت وراجورےرازدست کشمیریان برآوردومجمد نظرو میرعلی واوه پکلی راابملا عبدالله وتبت خورورابملا قاسم مقررنموده وتبت کلان رافتح نموده محسن نامی راںحکومت آنجاتعین کرودورسنه ستة وخمسین وتسعمائة مرزاحیدرمتوجه قلعه دبیل گردیدلکهرآمده مرزارا دیدودرخواست گناه دولت چک براورزاده کاجی جک نمودمرزاحیدرآدم درخرگاه نشسته بوددولت جک راآنجابطلبیدندودولت چک قهرکرده ارمجلس برخاست وفیلی راکه جهت پیشکش آورده بودهمراه گرفت روان شدمردم خواستند که اوراتعاقب کنندمرزاحیدرمانع آمدوبعدازچندگاه مرزابکشمیر مراجعت کرده دولت چک وغازیخان وحسین چک وبهرام چک نزدهیبت خان نیازیکه ازپیش اسلام خان هزیمت خورده درراجوری آمده بوده آمدندواسلام خان بتعاقب نیازیان درموضع بدوار ولایت نوشهررسیده بودسیدخان عبدالملک نام راکه ازمعتبران اوبودنزدهمیت خان فرستادوسیدخان مقدمات صلح درمیان آورده ماورو پسرهیبت خانرانزداسلام خان آورداا سلامخان بگشته ورموضع بن از نواحی سیالکوٹ آمده قرارگرفت وکشمیریان مذکورهیبت خان رادروابله آورده خواستند که اورابکشمیر بروه مرزاحیدررااز سیان برادرمذهیبت خان انمغی رابخودنتوانست قراروو برهمنی که نزدمرزاحیدر فرستاده مقدمات صلح درمیان آوردمرزاحیدرخرجی وافربدست آن برهمن فرستادوهیبت خان ازانجا بموضع برکه ازتوابع ولایت جموست آمدوکشمیریان ازوجداشده نزداسلام خان آمدندوغازیخان

پیش مرزا حیدر رفت و در سنه سبع و خمسین و تسعمائه مرزا حیدر خاطر از اطراف جمع کرده خواجه شمس مغول را با زعفران بسیار برسالت پیش اسلامخان فرستاد و در سنه ثمان و خمسین تسعمایه خواجه شمسی از پیش اسلام خان باسباب و قماش بسیار مراجعت کرده یاسین افغان ار پیش اسلام خان همراه خواجه شمسی آمد مرزا حیدر شال و زعفران بسیار با ایلچی اسلام خان داوه رخصت نمود و قرابهادر مرزا بحکومت بهرسل تعین نموده از کشمیریان عبدے رینا و نازک شاه و حسین ماکری و خواجه حاجی را همراه او کرد و قرابهادر و کشمیر یان از اندر کوٹ بر آمده در باره موله اقامت کرده در مقام فتنه شدند و بعلت اینکه مغولان ایشانرا اور نظر نمی آرند مغولان این مضمون را بعرض مرزا حیدر رسانیدند مرزا حیدر این سخن باور نکروه گفت که مغولان در فتنه قرار برین داوند که لشکر را باز طلبیده مرزا حیدر ہیچ آگاه نشده گفت که کشمیریان چه حسد داشته باشند که بشما عذر اندیشند لشکر واپس بطلبیده دور بست و هفتم رمضان در اندر کوٹ آتش عظیم پیدا شده اکثر خانهارا سوخت و قرابهادر و سائر مردم پیغام کردوند که چون خانهاء ما سوخته اگر حکم شود بیائیم و خانها راست کنیم و در سال آینده متوجه بهربل گردیم مرزا حیدر اصلا باین راضی نشده خواه ناخواه این لشکر متوجه بهربل گشت عیدی رینا و سائر کشمری یان اتفاق کردوند چون شب شد از مغولان جدا شده برکنار بهرمل بر آمدند و حسین ماکری و علی ماکری را از مغولان جدا ساخته همراه خود گرفتند تا با مغولان کشته نشوند چون صبح شد میان مغول و مردم بهرمل جنگ شد و مغولان در کوسها بند شدند و سید مرزا گریخته در دمل رفت و قریب هشتاد مغولان نامدار بقتل رسیدند و محمد نظر و امراء دستگیر شدند بقیة السیف از راه پنج در بیرم کله آمدند مرزا حیدر از استماع این خبر بغایت مخرون گشت و فرمود تا ویگهای نقره شکسته بهنسی که الحال در کشمیر رائج است سکه زدند و جهانگیر ماکری را معتبر گردانید و جاگیر حسن ماکری را باو واد و اکثر اهل حرفت راسپ و خرجی داده سپاهی ساخت متعاقب این خبر رسید که ملا عبدالله از استماع خروج کشمیریان متوجه ملازمت بود چون نزدیک باره موله رسید کشمیریان هجوم کرده اورا کشتند و خواجه قاسم در تبت خورد کشته شد و محمد نظر در راجوری گرفتار گشت و کشمیریان جمعیت کرده از بیرم کله در هیره

پورامدند مرزا حیدر بقصد نا چار بجنگ ایشان از اندر کوٹ بر آمد همگی جمعیت مرزا هزار کس بود واز مغولان مثل عبدالرحمٰن وشاه زاده دبنگ خان سرک مرزا ومر کمکته وصبر علی ودیگران که همه قریب هنقصد کس بودند همراه مرزا حیدر در شهاب الدین پورا اقامت نمودند ودولت چک وغازیخان ودیگر سرداران نامدار باتفاق عبدی رینا جمعیت نموده درسپره بور آمدند وازانجا بر آمده در موضع جانپور جمیع گشتند ومرزا حیدر درمیان خالد گڈه که متصل سری نگر است نزول نمود فتح جک که پدرا واز دست مغولان بقتل رسیده بود بقصد انتقام پدر خود اجه بهرام باسه هزار کس دراندر کوٹ درآمده عمارات مرزا حیدر را که درباغ صفا بود بسوخت مرزا حیدر چون خبر شنید گفت این عمارات راز کاشعر بیاوروه بودیم بازبعنایت الٰهی میتوان ساخت صبر علی عمارات سلطان زین العابدین را که درسوپو بود بعوض عمارت مرزا حیدر سوخت مرزارا این عمل خوش نیا مدو عمارات عبدی رینا ونور روز چک درسری نگر نیز بسوخت ومرزا حیدر ور موضع مانپور آمده اقامت نمود ودرین موضع درخت خبازی است که درسایه آن دویست سوار تواند ایستاد وبتجر به رسیده که هرگاه یک شاخ اورا حرکت دهند تمام درخت درجنبش مشاهده مولف تاریخ نظام الدین احمد درمرتبه مانی که رایات عالیات حضرت خلیفه الٰهی بسیر کشمیر رفت درملازمت بود وآن درخت راو دیده وامتحان کرده القصه کشمیریان از خانپور حرکت کرده درموضع ارب پور آمدند وفاصله زیاده از دو کرده نماند ومیرزا حیدر قرارداد که شبانخون برسر اعداد بردور مرزا عبدالرحمٰن برادر خود را که بصفت صلاح وتقوی آراسته بود بولی عهدے وصیت کرده از مردم بیعت بنام او گرفت وباتفاق سوار شده بقصد شبخون بر آمدند از قضا دران شب ابر بسیار پیدا شده چون نزدیک نجیمه خواجه حاجی که ماده فساد ووکیل مرزا بود رسیدند از تاریکی هیچ نمی نمود شاه نظر قورچے میگوید درین وقت تیر انداختم واواز میرزا حیدر بگوش من رسید که گفت قباحت کردی دانستم که تیر من به مرزا رسید ونیز بمنقولست قصابی برران او تیر سه وروایت دیگر آلسنّت که کمال دوبی اورا بشمشیر کشت امابر قالب او غیر از زخم تیر وبتر چزی دیگر بنود مجملا چون صبح شد درلشکر کشمیریان مشهور شد که مغلی کشته

افتاده است چون خواجه حاجی پسر اور سید دید که مرزا حیدر راست سر او راز زمین برداشت رمقی بیش نمانده بود چشمها باز کرده جان بجهان آفرین سپرد و مغولان باندر کوٹ گریختند و کشمیریان بتعاقب ایشان رفته نعش مرزا حیدر را برداشته در وبد و مزار برده دفن کردند و خلائق از مردن مرزا حیدر تاسف بسیار خوردند مغولان در اندر کوٹ در آمده تحصن جستند و تا سه روز جنگ شد و روز چهارم محمد رومی پلهای سی را در ضربه زن انداخته افگند بهر که میر سید میم د آخر خانم زن مرزا حیدر و خواهر اد بمغولان گفتند که چون مرزا حیدر را ز میان رفته صلح بکشمیر یان بهتر ست مغولان این سخن را قبول کرده امیر خان معمار را جهت صلح تر د کشمیریان فرستادند کشمیریان بصلح راضی شده خط بعهد و سوگند نوشته دادند که با مغولان در مقام آزار بنا شند حکومت مرزا حیدر ده سال بود ذکر نازک شاه چون دروازهای قلعه واشد کشمیریان در توشک خانه مرزا حیدر در آمده نفائس امتعه بردند و اهل و عیال مرزا حیدر را ادر سری نگر آورده در حویلی حسن متوجاوادند ولایت کشمیر را در میان خود تقسیم نموده۔

(نظام الدین احمد۔ طبقات اکبری مطبوعہ نولکشور)

تذکرۂ مرزا حیدر دوغلات در منتخب التواریخ

شیر خان بعد از فتح باز گشته به بنگاله رفت و بدفعات بشکل مختلف جنگ کرد و جهانگیر قلی بیگ را با جمعیت او علف تیغ ساخت و دوران دیار خطبه خوانده خود را شیر شاه خطاب کرد و سال دیگر با جمعیت تمام و لشکر انبوه بقصد تسخیر آگره عازم گشت کامران میرزا قبل از واقعه جوسه بعد از استماع غلبه شیر خان و مخالفت میرزا هندال با پادشاه از قندهار بلاهور مراجعت نموده و از انجا در سنه ست و اربعین وتسعمایة (۹۴۶) باگره رسیده بود و میرزا هندال خود پیش از

رسیدن میرزا کامران دهلی را که میرفخرعلی و میرزا یادگار ناصر دران حصاری شده بودند
در ایام غیبت پادشاه در محاصره داشته و کاری نساخته با میرزا کامران ملاقات نمود
و میر فخر علی نیز آمده دید اما میرزا یادگار ناصرمرزا قلعه بدر نیامدآخر میرزا هندال
از میرزا کامران جداشده بالوررفت وخاطر بادشاه ازشنیدن این اخبار بیشترغبار ملال
گرفته بود تاآن قضیه شکست حادث شدو پادشاه چون بعد از شکست چوسا ایلغار
نموده باچند سوار معدود در آگره ناگاه در سراپرده میرزا کامران رسیدندو میرزاراخبر نبود
هردو برادر بکدیگررادر یافته آب چشم گردیدند بعدازان هندال میرزاومحمد سلطان میرزاوفرزندان او
که مدتی مخالفت ورزیده بودند آمده بوسایل ملازمت نمودند وگناهان ایشان عفوشد وبمشورت
نشستند وبظاهرسخن میرزا کامران این بود که چون لشکر پنجاب تازه زوراست بادشاه مرارخصت
فرمایند تابدفع ورفع شیر خان کوشیده انتقام ازوی کشم وخود بفراغت دربای تخت باآسایش وعیش
مشغول باشند چون پادشاه این معنی راقبول نفرمودند میرزارا داعیه رفتن پنجاب پیدرآمدوتوقعات بی
اندازه می نمود که رنگ تکلیف مالایطاق داشت وباوجودآن پادشاه جمع ملتمسات اوراجابت فرمودند
غیرازمراجعت وخواجه کلان بیگ درمراجعت میرزا کامران بجانب پنجاب سعی می نمودواین گفت
وگوبه شش ماه کشیدودار گیر برهیچ امری قرارنگرفت درین اثنا میرزا کامران بامراض متضاده صعب
بیمارگشت وچون متخص شد که ماده مرض زهریست که از دست حوادث ایام درکام جان اوریخته اند
بگفته های بدگویان برپادشاه بدگمان شدو چندان پنداشت که مگر پادشاه اورازهرداده باشند وهمچنان
بیمار بلاهورمتوجه گردند وبخلاف قرارداد سابق که تمام لشکرخود درخدمت بادشاه باگره گذارد وتتمه را
همراه خود بردوغیرازدوهزارکس که بسرداری سکندرگذاشت ومیرزاحیدرمغول دوغلات کشمیری نیز
درآگره ماندورعانت تمام یافت وشیرخاں ازمراین نفاقها دلیرگشته درآخرسال مذکوربکنارگنگ آمده
جمعی راهمراه پسرخودقطب خاں نامزدساخته وازآب گنگ گذرانیده برسرکالپی واتاوه فرستادوقاسم

اسکندر سلطان در نواحی کالپی جنگ کرده پسر شیر خان را با جماعة کثیر بقتل رسانیدند وسرها را باگره فرستادند و پادشاه با جمعیت فراوان که بیک لک سواری کشید بدفع شیر خان متوجه شد واز آب قنوج گذشته تا مدت یک ماه در برابر غنیم نشتند ولشکر شیر خان مجموع از پنج هزار سوار زیاده نبود درا ینچنین محل محمد ملطان میرزا وفرزندان او دیگر بار از پادشاه فرار نمودند وکومکیان میرزا کامران نیز بلاهور گریخته رفتند ومغلان سپاه پادشاه باطرا فتفرق گشتند و بشکال ورسیده و چون محل نزول لشکر پادشاهی درزمین نشیب بود خواستند که ازآن جا کوچ کرده در جای بلند فرود آیند در همین اثنا شیر خان افواج را ترتیب داده بحاربه آمد واین معرکه دهم ماه محرم روز عاشوره سنه سبع واربعین وتسعمایة (۹۴۷) روی نمود وخرابئ ملک دلی تاریخ یافتند واکثری از سپاهیان مغول ترتیب جنگ ناکرده روی بهزیمت نهادند وجمعی قلیلی که بجنگ پیوستند مردانه دادکوشش دادند اما چون کار از دست رفته بود فایده نکرد و پادشاه عنان تاب شده خواستند که بربلندی بایستند این معنی خودمردم را بهانه گریز شد وشکست قوی افتاد چنانچه پادشاه در دریای گنگ نیز از اسپ جدا شده بودند و بمدد شمس الدین محمد غزنوی که در آخر اتکه حضرت خلافت پناهی شده بود در هندوستان بخطاب اعظم خانی سرفراز گشت واز آب بیرون آمده باگره مراجعت نمودند چون لشکر غنیم بتعاقب می آمد ازانجا نتوانستند قرار گرفت وبسرعت راه پنجاب گرفته طی نمودند ودر غره ربیع الاول این سال جمیع سلاطین وامرای چغتیه در لاهور جمع آمده بکنگاش نشستند وهنوز هم نفاق بحال بود ومحمد سلطان وفرزندانش از لاهور بجانب ملتان فرار نمودند ومیرزا هندال ومیرزا یادکار ناصر صلاح در رفتن بجانب بهکر وتته میدیدند ومیرزا کامران از خدا میخواست که این جمع زودتر متفرق شوق تا او بکابل رود و بعد از کنگاش بسیار پادشاه میرزا حیدر را باجمعی کثیر که قبول خدیعت کشمیر کرده بودند بانطرف فرستاده مقرر کردند که خواجهکلاں بیگ متعاقب میرزا حیدر روان شود تا بعد از تسخیر کشمیر پادشاه نیز بانطرف متوجه شوند وچون میرزا حیدر بنوشهره که جائیست مشهور رسیده باتفاق بعضی کشمیریان دران ولایت درآمد وفتح نمود بتدریج بیست ودوم

رجب سال مذکور آن ولایت را متصرف شد و خواجه کلان بیگ تا به سیالکوٹ رخته بود که خبر بپادشاه رسید که شیر خان از آب سلطان پور عبور نموده بشی کروهی لاهور آمد و پادشاه در غره ماه رجب سال مذکور از آب لاهور گذشتند و میرزا کامران بعد از نقض سوگندهای غلیظ شدید برهمراهی بادشاه تا نواحی بهیره بنابر مصلحتی موافقت کرد و خواجه کلان بیگ از سیالکوٹ ایلغار کرده باردوی پادشاه ملحق گشت و میرزا کامران در نواحی بهیره با میرزا عسکری پادشاه جدا شده باتفاق خواجه کلان بیگ بجانب کابل و پادشاه بطرف سند متوجه شدند و میرزا هندال و یادگار ناصر میرزا نیز چند منزل در خدمت بوده جدا گشتند و بعد از روزی چند به نصیحت امیر ابوالبقا باز آمدند و در کنار دریای سند در اردوی پادشاه قحطی عظیم چنان افتاد که یک سیر غلهٔ جواری گاهی بیک اشرفی هم پیدا نمی شد و اکثر لشکر ازین ممر جمعی معدود و گذر بجانب جسلیمر و ولایت مارواراافتاد آنجا قصایای غریب عجیب روی نمود و بعد از مشقت ومحنت بسیار لایت مارواراافتاد آنجا قضایا غریب عجیب روی نمود و بعد از مشقت ومحنت بسیار که کار چرخ همیشه برین قرار بوده است خود را به عراق رسانیدند و کومک ار شاه طهماسپ آورده قندهار وکابل را متصرف شده و جمعیت تمام بهم سانیده باردیگر هندوستان را فتح نمودند۔

(عبدالقادر بدایونی۔ منتخب التواریخ به تصحیح مولوی احمد علی صاحب کلکته ۱۸۶۸)

ذکر مرزا حیدر دوغلات در "گلشن ابراهیمی" (تاریخ فرشته)

ودرین سال فردوس مکانی ظهیر الدین محمد بابر بادشاه از عالم فانی انتقال نموده جنت آشیانی نصیر الدین محمد همایون پادشاه بر سریر شاهی تمکن فرمود و چون یکسال از شاهی محمد شاه گذشت ملک کاجی چک که بولایت کوهستان رفته بود جمعیت انبوه ازان ولایت بهم سانده در نواحی لهرار آمد و ملک ابدال ماکری استقبال نموده جنگ کرد ملک کاجی گریخته به بهیره آمد و ازانکه درین ایام کامران میرزا

بولایت پنجاب تسلط تمام واشت شیخ علی بیگ ومحمد خان مغل که بعداز فتح کشمیر برخصت ابدال ماکری مراجعت کرده بودند بخدمت کامران میرزا آمده بعرض رسانیدند که چون مایان برتمام ولایت کشمیر اطلاع یافته ایم اگراندک توجه فرمایند بدست آوردن آن ولایت درکمال آسانی ست کامران میرزا محرم بیگ راسردار لشکر ساخته باتفاق آن امرا که از کشمیر آمده بودند برسر کشمیر تعین نمود وچون افواج مغل به کشمیریان تمام اسباب واموال خودرا از هراس درخانها گذاشته جانب کوهستان گریختند وافواج مغل رفته شهررا تاراج کردند وآتش درزوند وبعضی کشمیریان که از کوهستان بجنگ مغل آمده بودند بقتل رسیدند وابدال ماکری اول باین عقیده بود که ملک کاجی چک به لشکر مغل همراه است چون یقین اوشد که داخل مغول نیست اظهار اتحاد ودیگانگی نموده اورابا پسران وبراوران طلبیده عهد وسوگند درمیان آوردواین معنی باعث قوت کشمیریان شده دل برجنگ نهادند وباتفاق جنگ عظیم بامغولان کردند ومغولان طاقت نیاورده بملک خویش رفتند وبعد چندگاه ملک کاجی چک بواسطه مکر وغدر وغروریکه از ملک ابدال معاینه کرده بود ببودن آنجاراضی نشده به بهیر رفت ودرین سال گذشته که سنه تسع وثلثین وتسعمائة باشد شاه سعید شاه سلطان کاشغر پسر خود شاهزاده سکندر خان ابهمراهی میرزا حیدر کاشغری بادوازده هزارکس ازراه تبت ولار بسر کشمیر فرستاد وکشمیریان ازآوازه وصلابت ومهابت ایشان کشمیررا خالی کرده بی جنگ باطراف گریختند وپناه به کوهستان بروند کاشغریان بولایت کشمیرد ورآمده عمارات عالیه که ازشاهان سابق بودوبخاک برابر ساختند وشهررا آتش زوند وخزاین ودفاین که درزیرزمین مدفون بود همه را بتفحص برآورده تمام لشکررا پر از مال داسباب کردند وهرجا که اهل کشمیر پنهان شده بودند خبریافته برسرایشان میرفتند وایشان رابه قتل میر سانیدند واسیر میساختند وتاسه ماه این صحبت درکار بودو ملک کاجی چک وملک ابدال فرود آمدند بجنگ مغولان قرارداده روان شدند اسکندرخان ومیرزا حیدر کاشغری نیز بالشکرانبوه دربرابرایشان آمدند وجنگی عظیم روید اواز سرواران کشمیر مثل ملک علی ومیر حسن وشیخ میر علی ومیر کمال کشته شدند واز

کاشغریان نیز مردم خوب بقتل آمدند وکشمیریان خواستند که پشت معرکه دهند اما ملک کاجی چک وابدال ماکری پای جلادت محکم داشته کشمیریان دیگر را بجنگ ترغیب وتحریص نموده واوجلات ومردانگی واوندواز طریقین چندان مردم مقتول گشتند که از خیر شمار بیرون بود چند قالب بی سر برخاسته بحرکت آمدند ووجه آن سابقاً مذکورشد ار بام تا شام جنگ قایم بوده چون شب درآمد طرفین از غنیم خود حساب گرفته هر یک بجای خود رفتند وهر دو طائفه از جنگ برآمده به مصالحه راضی شدند پس کاشغریاں صوف وسقرلاط وسایر نفائیس نزد شاه محمد شاه فرستاده نسبت خویشی قرار دادند ومحمد شاه نیز باتفاق آمده ابدال ماکری وملک کاجی چک صلح نامه نوشته باغرایب کشمیر بجانب کاشغریان فرستاده قرار یافت که دختر محمد شاه درعقد ازدواج شاهزاده سکندرخان درآمد وبندیان کشمیر که دردست مغلان بودند رها کنند القصه کاشغریان باین صلح راضی شده متوجه کاشغر گشتند وپریشانی که درکشمیر پیدا شده بود باامن ورفاهیت مبدل شد درین سال دوستاره ذات الاذناب یعنی دم دار طلوع نموده بود وقحط عظیم درین ایام پیدا شد چنانکه اکثر خلایق به بلای گرسنگی هلاک گشتند وبقیه که مانده بودند جلای وطن اختیار نموده بجاهای دور رفتند وحکایت دلجو که قتل عام کرده بود از دلهای مردم فراموش گشته در جب این حادثه آسان مینمود واین محنت تا ده ماه امتداد یافته انقطاع یافته وچون وقت میوه نیز رسید فی الجمله رفاهیت رونمود ودر ینوقت میان ملک کاجی چک وملک ابدال ماکری رنجش درمیان آمد ورینصورت ملک کاجی چک ازشهر برآمده درزین پور قرار گرفت وملک ابدال ماکری بوزارت شاه قیام نمود وحکام وعمال برسمی که برعایا میخواستند میکردند وهیچکس بدادنمیرسید بعد چندگاه محمد شاه تب محرق بهم سانیده هر قدر زر یکه داشت بتماجان بخشید وبهمان بیماری از عالم گذشت مدت شاهی او پنجاه سال بود۔

ذکر سلطنت سلطان شمس الدین بن محمد شاه

ظاهرا سلطان شمس الدین بعد از پدر بر تخت شاهی تمکن جسته باتفاق وزراء تمام ولایت را برامرا تقسیم

نمود و مردم کشمیر از جلوس او خوش حالیها کردند و در اندک مدت ملک کاجی چک و ابدال ماکری را باہم نزاعی بهمرسیده ملک کاجی شاہر القبصد استیصال ملک ابدال ماکری بجانب کوسوار بر دو ملک ابدال ماکری نیز باستعداد تمام در مقابل آمد آخر بصلح قرار یافته ملک ابدال ماکری در کمراج که جاگیر او بود رفت و شاه و ملک کاجی چک بسری نگر مراجعت نمودند و باز بعد چندگاه ملک ابدال ماکری سر از اطاعت تافته در مقام فساد شد و در ولایت کمراج خلل انداخت اما این مرتبه نیز فتنه بآسانی تسکین یافت الغرض از احوال این شاه در تاریخ کشمیر زیاده براین یافت نشده ایام شاہی او مشخص نگروید۔

ذکر کشتن نازک شاه کرت ثانی بشاہی کشمیر

بعد از پدر پسرش نازک شاه بر مسند شاہی نشست اما ہنوز پنجشش ماہی نگذشته بود که میرزا حیدر ترک استلا یافته متصوف گشت و در ایام حکومت میرزا حیدر رخطبه و سکه بنام نامی جنت آشیانی نصیرالدین محمد همایون پادشاه بود۔

ذکر تسلط میرزا حیدر ترک بر مملکت کشمیر

در سنه ثمان و اربعین و تسعمائه بوقتی که جنت آشیانی نصیرالدین محمد همایون بادشاه از شیر شاه افغان سور شکست یافته بلاہور آمد بود ملک ابدال ماکری و زنگی چک و بعضی اعیان مملکت کشمیر عریضه مبنی بر ترغیب گرفتن کشمیر نوشته بوسیله میرزا ماحیدر ترک فرستادند وانحضرت میرزا حیدر ترک را رخصت آنصوب کرده قرار رفتن خود نیز داد چون میرزا حیدر ترک به بهیر رسید ملک ابدال ماکری و زنگی چک آمده ملحق شدند و همراه میرزا حیدر ترک زیاده برسه چهار ہزار سوار نبود اما چون به راجوری رسید ملک

کاجی جک که حاکم کشمیر بود باسه چهار هزار سوار و پنجاه هزار پیاده کهتل کرتل را آمده بمورچلها محکم ساخت میرزا حیدر ترک این راه را ترک داده براہج روان شد و ملک کاجی چک از روی غرور محافظت آن راه نمود و میرزا حیدر ترک از کوه گذشته بفضای کشمیر در آمد و بناگاه شهر سری نگر را متصرف شد و ملک ابدال ماکری و زنگی چک استقلال یافته مهمات از پیش خود گرفتند و پرگنه چند بجاگیر میرزا نامزد فرمودند اتفاقاً در همان اثناء ملک ابدال ماکری را عمر بسر آمد لیکن پسران خود را بمیرزا حیدر ترک سفارش نموده در گذشت بعد از در آمدن میرزا حیدر ترک به کشمیر ملک کاجی جک پیش شیر شاه افغان سور بهندوستان رفته پنج هزار سوار که حسین شروانی و عادل خان سردار آنها بود مع دو فیل بکومک آورد میرزا حیدر ترک باتفاق زنگی چک متوجه دفع او شد و فریقین مابین موضع دنه دیار و موضع کاوه صفها آراستند و نسیم فتح بر پرچم علم میرزا حیدر بیگ ترک ورزیده امرای شیر شاه افغان سور و ملک کاجی جک هزیمت یافتند و ملک کاجی چک در بهرام کله قرار گرفت و ملا محمد یوسف خطیب مسجد جامع سری نگر تاریخ فتح مکرر یافته و در سنه خمسین تسعمائه میرزا حیدر ترک در قلعه اندرکوٹ اقامت نمود و از آنکه در باب زنگی چک بدگمان شد از وگریخته نزد ملک کاجی جک رفت و هر دو اتفاق نموده در سنه احدی و خمسین و تسعمایه قصد استیصال میرزا حیدر ترک رو بسری نگر نهادند و بهرام چک پسر زنگی چک خود را بسری نگر رسانید و میرزا حیدر ترک بندگان کوکه و خواجه حاجی کشمیر را بدفعه وی تعین کرد و او تاب نیاورده بگریخت و چون لشکر میرزا تعاقب نمودند ملک کاجی چک و زنگی چک نیز فرار را غنیمت دانسته دور بهرام کله قرار گرفتند و میرزا حیدر ترک بندگان کوکه و جمعی دیگر را در سری نگر گذاشته متوجه تسخیر تبت شد و از قلاع بزرگ قلعه توسورا با چند قلعه دیگر فتح کرد و در سنه اثنی و خمسین و تسعمایه ملک کاجی چک و پسرش محمد چک از مرض تب لرزه بمردند میرزا حیدر ترک این سال را بالفراغت گذرانیده در سنه ثلث و خمسین و تسعمایة

ملک کاجی چک و پسرش محمد چک از مرض تب لرزه بمردند و میرزا حیدر ترک این سال را بالفراغت گذر
انیده در سنه ثلث و خمسین و تسعمایة زنگی چک با مردم میرزا حیدر جنگ کرده کشته گشت و سرش رانا

سر یسرش غازیخان پیش میرزا آورد و در سنه ربع وخمسین وتسعمایه ایلچی از جانب کاشغر رسید ند میر زاحیدر ترک با جمعی خود باستقبال ایلچی درلار آمد وخواجه اوجه پسر مسعود چک که مدت هفت سال درولایت کامراج جنگهای خوب کرده بر همه غالب بود باجان میرک سخنان صلح آمیز درمیان آورده عهد وشرط قرار دادند ومیرک میرزا بعد سوگند اورا طلبید وقتیکه اوجه بهرام در مجلس اودر آمد خنجر از موزه کشید برشکم اوزد واو همچنان زخم خورده گریخت ودر جنگل در آمد وجان میرک میرزا بتعاقب اوشتافته اورا گرفت وسرش از تن جدا کرده نزد میرزا حیدر درلار آورد بگمان اینکه میرزا حیدر ترک محفوظ خواهد شد لیکن عیدے زینا بعد از دیدن سر او در قهر شده بغضب برخاست وگفت بعد از شرط وعهد کشتن یکی رالایق نباشد میرزا حیدر ترک گفت من از این واقعه خبر ندارم بعد ازین میرزا حیدر ترک متوجه کستوار شد بندگان کوکه محمد ماکری ومیرزا محمد ویحی زینا را هراول ساخته خود در موضع جهانپور نزدیک کشتوار قرار گرفت وجماعت هراول سه روزه راه دریکروز قطع نمود و بموضع دهلوت که در آنجانب اب مارهست رسیدند چون لشکر کستر ار انجانب آب بود جنگ تیر وتفنگ درمیان آمده هیچیک از آب عبور نتوانستند کرد روز دیگر لشکریان میرزا حیدر راز راه راست انحراف ورزیده خواستند که بکشتوار آیند چون بموضع وهار رسیدند بادتند وگرد آلود برخاست وروز تاریک شد مردم دهار هجوم نموده برسر ایشان آمدند بندگان کوکه که سردار عمده بود با پنجکس خوب کشته وبقته اسیف با هزار محنت بمیرزا حیدر ترک ملحق شدند ومیرزا حیدر ترک از انجا برآمده در سنه خمس وخمسین وتسعماته متوجه تبت گشت وراجوری راز دست کشمیریان برآورده بمحمد نظیر وناصر علی داد وپکلی را بملا عبدالله وتبت خورد را بملا قاسم مقرر نمود وتبت کلانرا فتح نموده ملاحسن نام را بحکومت آنجا تعین کرد ودر سنه ست وخمسین وستعماته میرزا حیدر ترک متوجه قلعه دنیل گرو آدم کهکر آمده میرزا را دید ودرخواست گناه دولت چک برادرزاده ملک کاجی چک نموده میرزا قبول کرد ومیرزا حیدر ترک وآدم کهکر در خرگاه نشسته دولت چک را آنجا طلبید ند غالباً چنانچه مرضی او بود اعزاز واکرام بجانیاوردند بنابران دولت چک قهر کروه برخاست فیلی راکه

بجہتپیشکش آورده بود همراه گرفته روان شد مردم خواستند که او را تعاقب کنند میرزا حیدر ترک مانع آمد بعد از چندگاه میرزا حیدر ترک به کشمیر مراجعت کرد و دولت چک را با غازیخان او جی چک و بهرام چک نزد هیبت خان نیازی که از پیش سلیم شاه افغان سور هزیمت خورده براجوری آمده بود رفتند و سلیم شاه چون بتعاقب نیازیان بموضع مدوار از ولایت نوشهره رسید هیبت خان نیازی سید خان نیازی را که از معتبران او بود نزد سلیم شاه افغان سور فرستاد و سید خان نیازی مقدمات صلح درمیان آورده مادر و پسر هیبت خان نیازی را نزد سلیم شاه افغان سور آورد سلیم شاه افغان سور برگشته در موضع بن از نواحی سیالکوٹ آمده قرار گرفت و کشمیریان مذکور هیبت خان نیازی را در باره موله آورده خواستند که او را کشمیر برده میرزا حیدر ترک را از میان بردارند و چون هیبتخان نیازی این معنی را بخود قرار نتوانست داد برهمنی را نزد میرزا حیدر ترک فرستاده مقدمات صلح درمیان آورد میرزا چون حرفی وافر بدست آن برهمن فرستاد هیبت خان نیازی از انجا در موضع همیر که از توابع ولایت جموست آمد و کشمیریان از وجدا شده نزد سلیم شاه افغان سور رفتند و غازیخان چک پیش میرزا حیدر ترک رفت و در سنه سبع و خمسین و تسعمائة میرزا حیدر ترک خاطر از اطراف جمع کرده خواجه شمس مغل را با زعفران بسیار برسالت پیش سلیم شاه افغان سور فرستاد و در سنه ثمان و خمسین و تسعمایة خواجه شمس مغل از پیش سلیم شاه افغان سور با سباب و قماش بسیار و ایلچی یٰسین نام افغان بکشمیر مراجعت کرد میرزا حیدر ترک شال و زعفران بسیار با یلچی سلیم شاه افغان داده رخصت نموده میرزا قرابهادر را بحکومت بهرپل تعین نمود و از کشمیریان عیدے زینا و نازک شاه و حسین ماکری و خواجه حاجی را همراه او کرد و میرزا قرابهادر و کشمیریان از اندرکوٹ برآمده در باره موله اقامت کرده در مقام فتنه شدند بعلت اینکه مغلان ایشانرا در نظر نمی آوردند و مغلان این مضمون را بعرض میرزا حیدر ترک رسانیدند میرزا حیدر ترک این سخن را باور نکرده گفت مغلان در فساد و فتنه کم از کشمیریان نیستند حسین باکری برادر خود علی باکری را نزد میرزا حیدر ترک فرستاده تا از غدر کشمیریان او را آگاه کند و برین دارد که لشکر را باز طلبد میرزا حیدر ترک هیچ آگاه نشده

گفت کشمیریان چه طاقت داشته باشند که بشما غدر اندیشند ولشکر را واپس بطلبد ودر بیست وهفتم
رمضان درآندرکوٹ آتشی عظیم پیدا شده اکثر خانها سوخت میرزا قرابهادر وسائر مردم پیغام کردند که
چون خانهای ما سوخت اگر حکم شود بیائم وخانهاراست سوخت میرزا قرابهادر وسائر مردم پیغام کردند
که چون خانهای ما سوخت اگر حکم شود بیائیم وخانهاراست کنیم تا درسال آینده متوجه بهرپل گردیم
میرزا حیدر ترک اصلا بااین راضی نشده خواهی نخواه این لشکر متوجه بهرپل گشت وعیدی زنیا وسایر
کشمیریان اتفاق کرده چون شب شد از مغلان جدا شده برکتل بهرپل برآمدند وحسین ماکری وعلی
ماکری را از معتمدان جدا ساخته همراه خود گرفتند تا با مغلان کشته نشوند چون صبح شد وبامردم بهرپل
جنگ شده مغلان درکوهابند شدند وسید میرزا گریخته درقلعه بهرپل رفته وقریب هشتاو مغل نامدار بقتل
رسیدند ومحمد نظیر ومیرزا قرابهادر دستگیر گشتند وبقته السیف از راه بج به بهرام کله درآمدند میرزا حیدر
ترک از استماع اینخبر بغایت محزون گشت وفرمود تا دیکهای نقره شکسته وبقته السیف از راه نهج به بهرام
که درآمدند میرزا حیدر ترک از استماع نیخبر بغایت مخرون گشت وفرمود تاو یکهای نقره شکسته زریکه
الحال درکشمیر رائج ست سکه زدند وجهانگیر ماکری را معتبر گردانیده جاگیر حسن ماکری باو داد واکثر اهل
حرفت را اسپ وخرجی داده سپاهی ساخت ومتعاقب این خبر رسید که ملاعبدالله از استماع خروج
کشمیریان متوجه ملازمت بود چون نزدیک باره موله رسید کشمیریان هجوم کرده اوا کشتند وخواجه قاسم
درتبت خورد کشته شد ومحمد نظیر درراجوری گرفتار گشت وکشمیریان جمعیت نموده از بهرام که دربنبهره پورا
آمدند میرزا حیدر ناچار بقصد جنگ ایشان از اندرکوٹ برآمده همگی جمعیت میرزا هزار کس بود واز
مغلان مثل عبدالرحمٰن وشاهزاده وخان میرک میرزا ومکنه مغل وجرعلی ودیگران که همه هفتصد کس
بودند همراه میرزا حیدر ترک درشهاب الدین پورا اقامت نمودند ودولت چک وغازیخان چک ودیگر
سرداران بامداد باتفاق عیدی زینا جمعیت نموده بنبهر پور آمدند واز انجا برآمده درموضع خانپور جمع
گشتند ومیرزا حیدر ترک درمیدان حالدگڈه که متصل سری نگرست نزول نمود وفتح چک که پدرا

واز دست مغلان بقتل رسیده بود بقصد انتقام پدر خود خواجه بهرام باسه هزار کس در اندرکوٹ درآمده عمارات میرزا حیدر را که در باغ صفا بود بسوخت و میرزا حیدر ترک را چون این خبر رسید گفت این عمارت از کاشغر نیاورده ام باز بعنایت الٰہی میتوان ساخت وجر علی عمارات شاه زین العابدین که درسویه پور بود بعوض عمارات میرزا حیدر ترک بسوخت اما میرزا را این عمل خوش نیامد ولشکریان عمارات عیدی زینا ونوروز چک که درسری نگر بود سوختند و میرزا حیدر ترک در موضع خانپور آمده اقامت نمود و درین موضع درخت بیداست که درسایه آن دویست سوار توانند ایستاد معهذ ابتجر به رسیده که هرگاه یکشاخ او حرکت دهند تمام درخت بحرکت وجنبش درمی آید القصه کشمیریان از خانپور حرکت نموده در موضع ادنیٰ پور آمدند وفاصله زیاده از دو کروه نماند میرزا حیدر ترک قرارداد که شبخون برایشان برد پس میرزا عبدالرحمٰن برادر خورد خود را که بصفت صلاح وتقوی آراسته بود بولی عهدی وصیت کرده از مردم بیعت بنام او گرفت وباتفاق سوار شده بقصد شبخون برآمد قضارا دران شب ابری سیاه پیدا شد که چون نزدیک بخیمه خواجه حاجی که ماده فساد ووکیل میرزا بود رسیدند از تاریکی هیچ نمی نمود وشاه نظر قورچی میرزا حیدر ترک میگوید که دریں وقت چون تیری می انداختم آواز میرزا حیدر ترک بگوش من رسید که گفت قباحت کردی دانستم که دران تاریکی ناگهانی تیری به میرزا رسید ونیز منقول ست که قصابی برران او تیر زد ودرروایت دیگر انست که کمال کوکه اور ابزخم شمشیر کشت امابرقالب او غیر از زخم تیر چیزی دیگر ظاهر نبود مجملاً چون صبح شد درلشکر کشمیریان مشهور شد که مغلی کشته افتاده است چون خواجه حاجی برسر اور سید دید که میرزا حیدر ترک ست پس سر او از زمین برداشت چون رمقی از وبیش نمانده بود چشمها باز کرد وجان بجان آفرین سپرد آخرش مغلان باندرکوٹ گریختند وکشمیریان نعش میرزا را دیده دفن کردند ومتعاقب مغلان شتافتند مغلان در اندرکوٹ تحصن جسته تا سه روز جنگ کردند وروز چهارم محمد رومی پولهای مسی درضرب زن می انداخت واو بهر که میر سید میمرد آخر خانمی زن میرزا حیدر ترک وخانجی خواهر او بمغلان گفتند که چون میرزا حیدر ترک از میان رفت صلح

باکشمیریان بهتر باشد مغلان این سخن قبول کرده امیر خان معمار راسجهت صلح نزد کشمیریان فرستادند کشمیریان بصلح راضی شده خط بعهد وسوگند نوشته دادند که بامغلان درمقام آزار نباشند حکومت میرزا حیدر ترک ده سال بود۔

(ابوالقاسم فرشتہ: گلشن ابراہیمی۔ مطبوعہ نولکشور)

زندگانی شگفت آور میرزا حیدر دوغلات در تاریخ کشمیر

ودر سال تهصد وسی وهفت میرزا کامران چغتائی باقریب سی هزار سوار متوجه تسخیر کشمیر کردید بذات خود درنوشهره ترول نموده موکب منصور رابسر کردگی محرم بیک ماشلیقی شیخ علی بیک کشمیر تعین نمود وسرداران مذکور درآمدن نوعی حزم واحتیاط بکار بردند که تاوصول بحوالی بلده کشمیر امرا خبردار نشدند چون برپنچال اطلاع یافتند درقلعه چره اودرجمع شده ملک کاجی چک راکه بردن کشمیر بود طلب داشته در موضع اته داچن بحرب ایستادند محرم بیگ وشیخ علی بدان جانب لوای مبارز افراشته تلاقی فریقین اتفاقی افتاد لشکر مرزا کامران شکست یافته طبل ارتحال کوفتند دور سال نهصد وسی ونه والی کاشغر سعید خان بالشکری کران بقصد تسخیر کشمیر بخش آمده درتبت رخت اقامت کشوده پسر خود سکندر خان باسر کردگی میرزا حیدر باچهارده هزار سوار جرار بیست وهفت هزار اسپ دیگر که سوائ اسپان سواری اسپان سوارے همراه داشتند یکشمیر تعین نمودد کاشغریان اول میران از راه لار داخل بلده کردیده اهل شهر ازبیم وهراس سطوت کاشغریان جلاشده بشعاب حال ومناقد وزوایا وکهوف پناه بردند واتراک بیباک اکثر مردم دهاقین راقبیل واسیر ساخته دقیقه از دقایق نهب وغارت فرونکذاشتد چون زمستان پایان رسید وآغاز بهار وآوان کل درصحرای چاه بابل امرای کشمیر جمع آمده مستعد حرب وقتال استادند ودر آن صحرا تلاقے فریقین دست داد وملک علی وحسین ربه چارده ملک شیخ علی ازامرای

کشمیر داد شجاعت و دلاورے واوه ملک علی پانصد سوار از برادران مقابله شرف مرزاے کاشغری اورا مغلوب ساخت جون کاشغریان غلبه از جانب کشمیریان دیدند علی بیک ارجانب مرانعار باهزار سوار ومیرزا حیدر از طرف جوانغار بادو هزار سوار خود را بمدد شرف میرزا رسانید و درانوقت از احرای کشمیر بعلی ملک ترسید واحرای کشمیر اهترام بافتند هزار و ششصد تن درآن معرکه ار بهادران کشمیر بقتل رسیدند و بقیه ایسف راه کریز بیش گرفتند باوجود سکسی حنین امراے کشمیر باز درهان صحرا جمع سلکر انتقام برمیان همت استوار بستند ورهرمکان که کاشعریان منزل وقار وامحا گزیدند امرای کشمیر کمین نگذاشتند وومارایشان برمی اوردند وکاشعربان صرفه کار درا قامت ومجادله ومجار به ندیده باامرای کشمیر صلح گونه کرده دراداخرار دی بهشت طبل ارتحال کوفته معاودت نمودند باوجود ضیق موسم اکرچه دهاقین بحرب وغرس استعال ورزیدند اما ازان زراعت بے حاصلی بحصادتا درآن سال قحطه عظیم بوقوع پیوست چون کاشعریان معاودت نمودند امرای کشمیر بتشید مانے صلح وصفا پرداخته وپیمانرا بایمان موکد ساخته سالک مسالک وفاق واتفاق کردیدمدسکی ملک کاچی چک درزینه پور قرار داوندرماکریان ملک وملکی زنگی چک کاهی درشهرمی گذرانیدند وکاهی درمنازلی که سپردنا سهر ومواضع درساتین داشتند بسر بامی بُردند زمام بست کشاد امور ورقبضه اقتدار واختیار ملک کاحی چک فتاد داشت ونسبت دامادی ملک کاحی چک اسم لی مسمای سلطنت سلطان اسمٰعیل ابن سلطان محمد شاه مقرر کردید وچند سال برهیمنوال کذشت وودرسال نهصد چهل وچهار ملک کاحی چک اعوان بسیار ازامرای نام دار نجود متفق ساخته بطرق جدال وقتال ماکریان پیش آمد چون ملک زنگی چک خواستکاری دختر رای جمورفته بود و دیکرکسی از مردم صاحب تجربه ماراے وروبت وعقل ودرایت بنود بهبتی تدبیرے لشکرش شکست یافت ومنهزم بجانب کوهستان به هند شتافت درزمستان درآن نواحی بسر بردور آغاز بهار باتفاق ملک زنگی چک که از جمومعاودت نموده بودوباو پیوسته رایت عزیمت به انهاض آورده درقربه کیسوترول نمود وموضع مذکور دولتخان چک وملک رنبو چک وملک لوروز چک وسید ابراهیم ملک محمد

چک وملک محمد ناجی درظل لوای نصرت جمع آمدند یا کرمانزا مستاصل ساخت وتا سه سال حکومت کشمیر بطریق استقلال وانفراد ماملک کاجی بود درایام حکومت واستیلا عادت ملک کاجی چک این بود که ارباب فتنه وفسادرا باوجود ایقاع جریمه که ماعب میل انها شده مقید ومحبوس داشت واقدام برقتل نمی نمود بعداندک روزے بشفاعت عفوار جرایم مجرمان گذشته جاگیری وافی کافی بانجماعه مقرر مینمود یمن همیں ست چندتن ارادلاداد بمرتبه بلند سلطنت وفرمانروائے فانیر کردیدند الحاصل ملک ابدال ماکری ملک زیکے چک کمرانتقام ملک کاجی چک درمیان همه استوار بسته درسال نهصد وچهل وفت میرزاحیدرکاشعررا که درهندوستان ملازم حاقان جم جاه همایون پادشاه بودو پادشاه بدنوردرحی که به مقتضائے تصارف ایام ازدست شیرخان افغان که کمینه چاکراو بود آزروه خاطر کشته متوجه سیر ایران زمن بودو درانوقت میرزا سعادت استیلام رکاب دولت حرمان نصیب کردیده ملک ابدال ماکری وملک ربکی حک ازینمعنی وقوف یافته هندوستان رفته میرزارابکشمیر آوردندوارراه چیره هاربشهر نزول نمودندوملک رادرحبطه تصرف خودآوردندواسم شاهی برنازک شاه نامی رانے نسبت دوری بحکام کشمیر داشت اطلاق کرده خودوحیدرملک میکردندوملک کاجی چک چون رقم استقلال ازجبیه احوال میرزا حیدرخواندمیس شیرخان رفت وهمشیره زاده خودخواهراسمٰعیل شاه ولدسلطان محمدشاه بشیرخان دادو شیرخان عادلخان حسین خان شیروانے وجمعی دیکرمقداردوهزارکس بکومک ملک کاجی چک تعین نمود بکشمیر آمدمیرزاحیدرهم از رهکدرآمدن ملک کاجی چک وهم ازمروفات ملک ابدال ماکری که دراعتضادواستظهاراوبودمکدرکردیده اهل وعیال خوددراوراندرکول گذاشته باتفاق ملک زنکی چک وملک عبدی زینه وملک حسین ماکری بحرکت آمده دردیهه نارتلاقی فریقین انفاق افتاد کرچه جنودکاجی چک دقیقه ازدقایق محاربت ومبارزت فوت وفروگذاشت نکردندوپائے ثبات درمیدان کارزارافشردندازآنجا که فتح نصرت آسمانیست ملک کاجی چک منهزم کردیدوعنان غریمت بجانب هندوستان معطوف داشت دودرمنزل به بارو هنه همی بصوب دیارنیستی کشید چون میرزاحیدرتائید

ملک اکبر بفتح وظفر فایز گردید خطیب کشمیر مولانا جمال الدین محمد یوسف لفظ فتح مکرر تاریخ ان فتح یافته چه فتح اول با سکندر خان کاشعری بود و فتح ثانی این است بالجمله اطراف و اکناف کشمیر را از تبت و پکلی وددوالکی مصافات دیکر بحیطه تصرف در آورد و سپه سالار بملک عیدی زینه تفویض نمود و خطبه دسکه بنام نازکشاه بدستور امرای کشمیر ساخت زبده اعاظم امرا افضل الفضلا دعلم العلما شیخ الوالفضل در اکبر نامه آورده که در آن ایام که فتح کابل شد و فتح کابل موافق بتاریخ ملانویدی که کابل را کرفت سنه نهصد و پنجاه و چهار سنت مرزا حیدر خطبه کشمیر بنام مقدس حضرت جهانبانے جنت مکانے ساخته سر بلند شد الحاصل مرزا حیدر مدت ده سال در انتظام ولایت کشمیر سعی مبلغ نمود و اقسام محترفه دار باب صباعات را از هر جا طلبداشته رشته در مقام رونق ورواج این ملک شد علی الخصوص موسیقی را باز ار گرم گشت و انواع ساز درمیان آورد اهل فضل و کمال را بسیار دوست میداشت در عایت ایں طایفه بسیار میکرد د به آخر ها کام زن مسلک تعصب گردیده شیخ دانیال ولد شیخ شمس الدین عراقی را که ار هراس میرزا به تبت گریخته بود طلبیده کشت و شبکلی رلی را که یکی از مریدانشیخ بود بود بند از بند جدا نمود هر طعمه السلس ساخت و قاضی میر علی را اخراج نموده خانه اورا تاراج داد ملا حاجی خطیب را نیز به تهمت تیشع به قتل آورد میرزا حیدر براجتماع وکثرت مردم کاشعر مستظهر کشته رشته عهود و مواثیق را که با مردم کشمیر مستحکم داشت بریده قصبین ملک زنکی چک که سردار عمده بود نمود ملک زنکی چک مستغر گشته به هندوستان گریخت و کاشغریاں به عجزه و فغان دست تطاول دراز آوردن گرفتند رعایا ار بیداد آنها بستوه آمده نظم پیش اعیان کشمیر اوردند ملک عبد رینه وحسین ما کری و خواجه حاجی مامدی پیمانرا بایمان موکده ساخت به تدبیر هدم پنان دولت وشوکت میرزا حیدر وقرار برین بافت که راه خداع پیش کرفته کاشعر بانزادر شکسی جبال سالار وفرمان و ملک سروال تیمی نمایند در سال نهصد و پنجاه و هشت ملک عبدی زینه به مرزا حیدر رکفت اطراف جبال کشمیر نواحی در حیطه ضبط نمی آید و جابجا جنود مسعود تعین بامد کرد میرزا حیدر قرابهادر برادر خود را با جمعی ار بهادران کاشعر نامزد این مهم نمود و ملک عیدی زینه حسین

ما کری دخواجه حاجی فرموده که شما هم جمعیت خود همراه و هید ملک عیدی زینه شمس الدین پسر خود همراه داد لشکر میرزا را به حیلها از جدا کرده مردم کار آمدنی اور امتفرق ساخته طائفه را بجانب تبت برخی راصوب پکلے دچندی رابطرف کشتوار وراجور فرستادند چون خاطر جمع کردید که چندان موکبی پیش میرزا حیدر نماند خود نیز مداعیه اعدام وافتای قرابهادر درفقاانے او به انتهاض آمدند دبراون نزدیک خانپور است رفته نشتند غازی خاں وملک دولت چک نتر بآنها ملحق شده اند چون قرابهادر به محمد کوٹ رسید شب ازور کشمیریان خود راار لشکراو پرون کشیده دراه معاودت کاشعریان بصوب کشمیر گسته برقله کوہی شاخ برآمده نبع خلاف از علاف تراع برآورده گروہی راقتل وبرخی رااسیر ساختند قرابهادر درزمره اشاری بود وفوجی که بسر کردگی ملا قاسم وملاباقی ضبط ملک تبت فرستاده بود ورآن لواحی ملا قاسم بقتل رسید وملاباقی راه فرار پیش کرفت وزمره که بسرداری ملاعبده الله بشهنک تعین کرده ملاعبدالله از آنجا سکته دید حال به کشمیر آمده درحین رسیدن ببارہموله بقتل رسید وجمعی که تا سلیقی کوکهه خود که ارجمله بهادران نامی بود بسمت کشتوار روانه کرده بود کوکه مزبوردران ساخته مقتول کردید وهزار وپانصد نفرار قضای اودرآن سفر کشه شدند میرزا حیدر باوجود مشاهده ومال کوکب اقبال اہل وعیال راورقلعه اندرکول کداشته بقصد انتقام امرای کشمیرلوای مبازرت بصوب قریه اون یور برافراخته مقرر نمود که پرسرامرای کشمیرشیخون آوردامرای کشمیر برین تدبیر مطلع کردیده کاربند به نقط وانتباه شدند میرزا تہاشی بقصد تفتیش احوال امراء کشمیر سوارشده درون معسکر رفت ودہیاج شاخندی.بنهان ماند قضارا ہمدران وقت قصالی کمال دونی نام بتلبح کاری اشتغال داشت دید که سواری پسرون الستاده است پرسید کستی وکجا آمدی میرزا چون زبان کشمیر خوب یادنکرفته پود جوابی جوابی دادنه فارسی بودونه کشمیرقصاب وانست که جاسوس میرزادست تبری که بکارکاوداشت ارہمان تبرزخمی انداخت که تشقیقه میرزارسیده وبہمان زخم مسافرملک نیستی گردیدانیواقعه درسال نہصد وپنجاه ونه دست واوصه عنبری که نیداخت کمان بصیرخاشا که قواندسپرس شدندبیر ہرچند که تدبیر کندمردخردلیکن نتوان شد بقضا

جارو پذیرت اہل کشمیر باوجود جراحانے کہ از مرزا داششد باقرابہادر میرزا وفرزندان ومباعالش باوب پیش آمدہ باتمام جہات واسباب وطن روانہ نمودند میرزا حیدر نسبت خالہ زادگی بہ جناب ہمایون پادشاہ داشت چون میرزا حیدر ارمبان رفت ملک عبدی زینہ کوس دولت وحکومت بلند آوازہ ساختہ دلوای کامکاری وملک رانی باوج فلک اعتبار افراختہ

قرابہادر مرزا در برادرزادہ میرزا حیدر را کہ از راہ رسم کشمیر وکشمیریان نیک مطلع بود باد وازدہ ہزار قوم مغل بصوب کشمیر آوردند بجز داستماع این خبر غازیخان سرعت سیر ار برق وباد استعارہ نمودہ خود را بہ تہہ رسانید روز دیکر از آنجا کوچ کرد بد بلوہر کوت دایرہ نمود درسمان جانلاتی فریقین دست داد غازیخان حکم نمود کہ ہرکس سر مغل بیارد یک اشرفی انعام خواہد یافت چون وعدہ انعام بہ حیان طایفہ ارقوم کہ ارذل الناس اندو بسرقہ شہرت تمام دار یدہفت ہزار سر از صبح تا ظہر بدرکاہ غازیخان آوردند وانعام را اضعاف مضاعف یافتند پیش از انکہ نوبت جنگ مبارزان صاحب ناموس وننگ می رسید بقیۃ السیف منہزم گردیدند غازیخان بفتح وفیروزی میراجعت نمود بعد ازین فتح ہا ہمگی ہمت ابر شاعت عدل درافت مصروف داشت۔

(راج نرائن کول تاریخ کشمیر مخطوطہ نمبر خ ۱۴۸ علی گڑھ یونی ورسٹی مولانا آزاد لائبریری)

ذکر مرزا حیدر دغلت در تاریخ سلاطین

درسنہ نہصد وسی وہست میرزا کامران برادر ہمایون پادشاہ بعد وفات بابر شاہ پادشاہ ہند کو سکہہ وخطبہ ہندوستان بتاز کی تعلق باو کرفتہ بود اجازت کونہ حاصل نمود و بابن نواحی آمدہ درنوشہرہ رسید وخود درانجا استقامت نمودہ محرم بیگ وشیخ علی بیگ را با جمعیت سی ہزار سوار رواہہ ساخت چون کشمیر

درقبله چکان تقسیم شده بود هیچیکی بمقابله لشکر غنیم به پرداخته بی ممانعت مخالفت داخل شهر کردیده درمکان چره آودر فروکش نمودندو برای میرزا کامران اخبار وردارسال داشتند پس لشکربان چکان در موضع اتهه واجن جمع شده درفکر مقابله غنیم بمشوره اجلاس نموُدن ومحرم بیگ بجمعیت تمام از جیره آودر کوچ نموده درموضع مزبور آمدو بجک بایستاد لشکریان چکان برکوه سلیمان برآمده بمقابله پای ثبات استوارنمودند وفیما بین فریقین آتش حرب وضرب شعله ورکردید درآخر بعد محاربه ومجادلهٔ موفور محرم بیگ تاب مقابله درخود نیافته لاچاراز دراستمال درآمد و بصلح بازکشت روانه نشد بعد رفتن اوخبر رسیدند سلطان سعید خان ازکاشغر بعزم کشمیر آمده خود درتبت ماند سکندرخان بجه خود میرزا حیدر برادرزاده خود راروانه ساخت وباجمعیت چهار هزار سواراز راه پرکنه لارونوشهره رخت اقامت کشودند ومردم شهرراز ورود آنها زحمت بسیار قرین حال کردیدوُ راه فرار پیش کرفتند بمجر داستماع این اخبار امراء چکان درسنه نهصد وسی ونه از حرصاودر لغوم مقابله غنیم هیبب شدت وبرودت زمستان از دست انها کاری صورت نگرفته کاشغریان رابکلان خود فتح سرسری ست داد بعد فراغت از طرف دشمن بصوب مراح روانه شدند باشندکان شهرایام زمستان بصعوبت وخواری وتعب وبیقراری بسر بردند چون اثار بهار بر عرصه روزکار پدیدار کردید امرائے چکان کمرهمت بسته وبازوی دلاوری کشاده درمیدان کارزار بقرار واقعی دادمردانکی داده دشمنان رازیروزبرنموده پس کشیدند وتاچند مدت مقابلهٔ جانبین برروی کاربود آخربهار وراساس استقامت کاشغریان خلل راه یافته قرین حرمان ویاس بنابرپاس آبرو بصلح تن درداده از راه لاربطرف تبت چاده پیمای دشت ادبارشدند از قرار تفرقه وهرج ومرج که دراول بهار برُوی کاربود درزراعت وکشت وکار قصور وفتور راه یافته قحط غله برصفحه روزکار نمودار کردید ومردم شهراز روی نایابی آذوقه وبزنج بزنج وبتیابی کرفتار آمدند بحدی که پدر از پسر و مادر از دختر چرخوردنی دریغ میداشت همکی اناس وبشر بکرسنکی هلاک وابتر کشتند فردقحط تاحدی که خلق از فرط بی قوتی چوشمع ملاجسم خودراسوختی برآتش وبردی بکارهافی المقصو دو سلطان محمد شاه درسنه نهصد وچهل وچهار بخواهش

خالق کردکار چاده پیماے شاہ راہ قضا کرد بدہ سلطان شمس الدین پسرش بعد فوت پدر فرق خودرا تاج وافسر پیراستہ بر تخت حکومت جلوہ کرد دید امور ملک را در قبضہ اختیار کاجی چک کہ دران اوآن از دلاوران نامور بود سپردہ چون او در دفع لشکریان ھندو کاشغر مردانگی از حد بیشتر بکار بردہ بود نیز مکان کاجی دارہ کہ سرحدی راہ بس صعب کوھستان ھندوستان است در تصرف داشت سلطان شمس الدین رابخیال نمی آوردو خوددر ہر امور کاروامیشد ہمکی یکسال یہ بی استقلالی وپریشان حالی کذرایندہ در سنہ نہصد وچہل وپنج ازین سرای سپنج رخت غریمت بعالم بقا کشید بعد وفات او در ہمان سنہ سلطان اسمٰعیل برادرش برتبہ سلطنت اختصاص یافتہ کاجی چک را کہ دخترش در عقد داشت بدستور برادر عنان اختیار بدست اوداده او مذہب شیعہ برروی کار آوردوارین روا کابران زمانہ بدستور سابق جادہ نورد منازعت ومخاصمت کردیدہ پرکنات ودہات راباز باہمدیکر تقسیم ساختند و ماکریان وچکان ودانکریان وچاوربان وملکان کہ درآن زمان از ارباب اقتدار ودر امور ملکی صاحب اختیار بودند بہ منازعت ومخاصمت پرداختہ در محلّہ علاوالدین پورہ کہ بدستور قلعہ واقع بود جنک ہای نمایاں بظہور آوردند وچند مدت بدیمنوال بکذشت بلجملہ سلطان اسمعیل چندکاہ بہ عین بی استقلابی واکراہ کذرانیدہ وفات یافت بجای او پسرش سلطان۔ ابراہیم دہم حکمرانی برناز ک افتخار گذاشتہ باابدال ماکری وزیکی چک وغیرہ کہ پروی مذہب شیعہ داشتند خصومت ونزاع بہمرسانید ازین سبب آنہاچبہ ہای خوددر خدمت ہمایون بادشاہ وائی ھندوستان بنابراستدعای فرستادن قشون بجہتہ تسخیر کشمیر روانہ ساختند درہمان ایام پادشاہ مربورارزوی علیہ شیرخان افغان ہزیمت خوردہ ارزاہ تہتہ وبہکر بطرف ایران میرفت دریں حضوص بعرض اور سایندچوں اور خود آرزدہ خاطر بود پرداخت اظہار آنہانکردہ کوشکدارنشد وبتغافل گذرایند میرزاحیدرکہ در حضور حاضر بود بخواہش خود ازلاہور رخصت کونہ حاصل کردہ بتحریک آنہا بامعدودی لشکرروی بانیجد ودآوردو در سنہ نہصد وچہل وہشت ازراہ چرہ اوردرواردشہر کردید وفتح تاریخش نوشتہ اند باعتبارانیکہ چون باعانت پادشاہ کاشغر

اول مرتبه آمده بازگشت رفته بود و حال مرتبه ثانی در اینجا رسید کاجی چک که سروسامان مقابله کی در خود ندیده از راه هیره پور رو هندوستان کردید و ابدال ماکری وفات یافت کاجی چک در نزد شیرخان ریسده از خدمت او مشمول مهربانی مخاطب بخطاب خان خانانی شده بهمراهی کومک او باز بخود معاودت نمود میرزا حیدر تا هنگام ورود اد تسلط حکمرانی یافته نوعی سلوک می کرد که همگی مردم در اطاعت او بدل و جان ساعی بودند و جای سکونت خود در اندرکوت قرار داد کاجی چک وارد هیره پور۔ کردید میرزا حیدر باتفاق مردم خود مردمان کشمیر بمقابله برآمده تا مدت فیما بابین فریقین ابواب جنگ و جدل مفتوح بود بعد جد و جهد بسیار فتح و نصرت نصیب مرزا حیدر کردیده کاجی چک راه هزیمت وستداده باز بادل سمند بجانب هندراهی شد و در منزل تهیه راه نورد بادیۂ عدم گشت مرزا حیدر بتائید خداوند اکبر به فتح و ظفر بهره یاب کردید و سکه و خطبه بنام سلطان تارک شاه جاری نموده و عیدی رینه را مرتبه سپه سالاري داد و خود در پرداخت اهل فضل و هنر ساعی بود خصوصاً ارباب موسیقی را نهایت دوست میداشت در آخر ساز تعصب کوک نموده شیخ دانیال بچه میر شمس عراقی و شکلی ریشی مرید او را از تیغ کدز اینده طعمه آتش ساخت و خانقاه جدی بل را آتش کشید و در هنگام استقلال اکثر کوهستان کرد نواح کشمیر و تبت را در حیطه تصرف در آورده عیدی رنهه و ناجی چک و خواجه حاجی باندی وغیره در اطاعت او بدل و جان ساعی و سرگرم بودند با مردم شیعه خصومت و عداوت بواقعی بکاری بر دور آخر مردم کاشغر را رواج داده با مردم کار روادار ازار کردید بصدور این فتنه و فتور در سه نهصد و پنجاه و هشت عیدی رینه وغیره جماعه ارباب زمانه قصد مخالفت او ر بخاطر آورده با حسین ماکری و حاجی باندی عهد و پیمان در میان برآورده اند آنها باندیشه انیکه فشون و آدم های کاری او متفرق سازند میرزا حیدر را۔ کفتند نابر نظم و نسق باطراف کوهستان لشکرکشی لازم است او قرابها در برادر زاده خود را با مردم کاشغری همراه داده روانه ساخت در آن اثنا عیدی زینا و ناجی چک از وروکردان شده در قلعه آدن پوره استقامت نمودند بسوح ابن روداد میرزا حیدر را دریافت کردید که اینهمه بازي است پس خود بد

انطرف روانہ کردیدہ بمجاصرہ آنہا پرداخت بعد چند روزشمی از جایی خودتنہا برخاستہ دراندروں قلعہ آون پورہ رفت قضارا قصابی اورادیدو پرسید کہ کیستے نام توچسیت چون بزبانکشمیر بخوبی ماہر بنود ارکفتاراودریافت کہ کسی از جاسوسان لسکر میرزاست وتیری از آہن دردست داشت وفی الحال برسرش کوفت وبکضرب جان دادصبح کہ ایمقدمہ اشتہار یافت غازی چک ودولت چک پسران کاجی چک خواستہ بوودند کہ دراندرکوت رفتہ بہ ننگ وناموس اودست اندازی کنید سلطان نازک شاہ مانع آمدنکداشت کہ بآنہا تصدیسعی رسد پس وابستکانش راروانہ کاشغرساخت درسنہ نہصدو پنجاہ ونہہ میرزا حیدر کشتہ شدہ دہ سال حکمران بود بعد از کشتہ شدن او دراساس حکومت سلطان نازک شاہ استحکامی نماند وسلطنت سلاطین بواقعی ابترشد

حیدر ملک جادورہ تاریخ سلاطین سلیمان گلگشن مخطوطہ نمبر ۳۵/ ۶۵۷ مولانا آزاد لائبریری مسلم یونی ورسٹی علی گڑھ ص (۱۹-۸۵)